UNDER OUR SKIN

'In this engrossing memoir of growing up in South Africa in the
1970s and 1980s, McRae not only remembers but helps us to
understand what it was like and in the process brings a man back
to life. It all adds up to a gripping re...
continuously seems to flow. Fro...
trajectory into adolescence a...
short of read...
The Tim...

'*Under Our Skin* is a remarkable account of the McRae's struggles
against not only the government, but one another ... [it] serves
both as a monument to that achievement and as a love letter,
from son to father'
Sunday Times

'McRae's sober, well-crafted memoir captures the moral nuances
as well as the horrors of the apartheid era ... *Under Our Skin* is
also a coming-of-age memoir of a more conventional stamp, full
of the sounds and smells of an African childhood. McRae
recaptures the gaucheness of his teenage years with humour and
tenderness ... deft and fascinating'
Sunday Telegraph

'McRae's exquisitely framed memoir, *Under Our Skin*, recalling a
not-so-distant era when people were dying, and being tortured,
and being conscripted to fight in defence of a twisted ideology.
Artistic expression and political expression really were a
matter of life or death ...'
Observer

UNDER OUR SKIN

A WHITE FAMILY'S JOURNEY THROUGH
SOUTH AFRICA'S DARKEST YEARS

DONALD McRAE

SIMON &
SCHUSTER

London · New York · Sydney · Toronto · New Delhi

A CBS COMPANY

First published in Great Britain by Simon & Schuster UK Ltd, 2012
This paperback edition published by Simon & Schuster UK Ltd, 2013
A CBS COMPANY

1 3 5 7 9 10 8 6 4 2

Simon & Schuster UK Ltd
1st Floor
222 Gray's Inn Road
London WC1X 8HB

www.simonandschuster.co.uk

Simon & Schuster Australia, Sydney
Simon & Schuster India, New Delhi

A CIP catalogue record for this book is available
from the British Library

PICTURE CREDITS
Courtesy of the author: 1, 3, 5, 6, 7, 8, 9, 13, 18, 19, 20, 22, 23
Getty Images: 4, 11, 12
IDAF/Noel Watson: 21

ISBN: 978-1-84983-137-6
ISBN: 978-1-84737-967-2 (ebook)

Typeset by M Rules
Printed and bound by CPI Group (UK) Ltd, Croydon, CR0 4YY

For my parents, Ian & Jess, and my sister, Heather
– and, as always, Alison

CONTENTS

Heather, Jess, Ian and Don McRae, 1966

PROLOGUE:

DIFFERENT CURRENTS

A SOFT CLICK broke the silence as the policeman hand-cuffed the doctor to the metal arm of a chair. Lieutenant Whitehead looked down at a bruised and exhausted Dr Neil Aggett. He waited a moment and, when Neil did not respond, he turned away from the chair. They had used it so often it had begun to brown with rust. Whitehead's assistant plugged the cord into the nearest socket in a corner of room 1012 at John Vorster Square, the security police headquarters in downtown Johannesburg.

Sergeant Chauke, a black policeman, handed over the white towelling hood. Neil felt its wet and suffocating heaviness as Whitehead covered his face and head. It worked as both a blindfold and a mask. Whitehead tied the hood so tightly around him that it was difficult for Neil to breathe.

The first shock, when it came, made him scream compulsively. It lit up his body in a flaring sheet of pain. As he screamed, the bag was sucked deep into his mouth. It became impossible to breathe. Neil did not know if they planned to electrocute or suffocate him to death when, suddenly, they turned off the power.

His body was still juddering as they dragged the bag off his head. Tiny drops of moisture clung to his beard.

They asked him some more questions and then covered and wet

his head again. It was worse the second time, and then the third as well, because they lengthened the period of each electrocution. He tried to stop himself from screaming, so that he might be able to breathe inside the bag, but he was helpless. The current surged through him . . .

IN THE DRY SUMMER of 1982, at the end of another year of apartheid, I could not shake the images from my head. The details had been exposed during the inquest into the death earlier that year of Neil Aggett, the only white South African ever to die in detention. Security policemen had used electricity to torture Aggett, a twenty-seven-year-old white doctor who had been detained with his girlfriend, Liz Floyd, another doctor, in November 1981.

Ian McRae, my father, would soon be known as 'Mr Electricity' in South Africa. He was on his way to becoming the chief executive of Eskom, the state-owned electricity company; but he didn't care about his title. Dad had a grander vision in mind. People in our black and white land needed to understand that electricity was colourless. It was a great, jolting force for good.

My father had begun to dream of a different South Africa, of a country saved by the healing power of electricity. Whenever he flew back to Johannesburg at night, dad always put his briefcase away near the end of his flight. In his window seat he stared into the African night. Dad picked out the distant pinpricks of light, marvelling at the way they broke up the empty sky. The gleaming city rose up as if one layer of darkness after another was being peeled from the eyes of a blind man who could finally see.

When they hovered over Johannesburg's vast galaxy of electricity, with illuminated skyscrapers shining down on the brightly-lit streets and houses, dad felt surging pride. 'Look at this,' he called out to his colleagues, encouraging them to join him at the small window so they could also see how their work helped light up the largest city in Africa.

He felt uneasy only when he looked towards Soweto, where a million black people lived. The township appeared to be covered by a blanket at night. Only a low glow here and there, coming from smouldering coal-fires, punctuated the blackness.

Dad faced more immediate trouble at home.

At war with my parents, I insisted I would never start my compulsory two years of military service. Mom and dad tried to help me. They persuaded me to see a series of psychiatrists in an effort to break the deadlock. I was young, and so I surrendered. I visited three doctors, telling each one of them that I was utterly sane. I would rather leave the country forever, or go to jail or even die, than step into the uniform of the South African Defence Force. I was ready to abandon my family and never come back.

The last doctor seemed confused in her strange, blue-walled room. She held individual sessions with my parents and my sister, Heather, to discuss me and my problem with the army. In one session the doctor recommended that I be given ECT [Electro-Convulsive Therapy]. The doctors believed they might need to shock sense into me. It was one possible treatment for a white boy who refused to serve in the South African army.

I did not believe my parents would ever allow electrodes to be pinned to the side of my head. My dad, a compassionate connoisseur of electricity, would resist the shuddering shortcut. And my mother, being so strong and kind, would not stand the idea that, to neuter me, a chunk of my brain should be burned.

My sister was less certain. 'You've got to be careful,' she warned.

Dusk settled over our home town on that long summer evening. I stared into the gathering darkness, my head reeling as I tried to understand how we had ended up so shocked and traumatised.

PART I

A SMALL
WHITE BOY

(1966–1975)

Beware of the natives. The Transvaal, South Africa, the 1960s

CHAPTER ONE

A BOY CALLED JOHN

THE OLD GREY Holden picked up speed as we went looking for a black boy. On that early Saturday morning in the South African spring of 1966 I rode upfront, next to dad, while our dog stood excitedly in the back. Her furry paws rested on dad's seat as she gazed out of his open window. Shandy's long ears, which we pinned above her head with a plastic peg whenever she buried her face in a bowl of dog food, flew behind her in the wind. She looked as if she was grinning as we headed towards the coal dumps where the mining boys had been waiting since dawn.

On weekends they tried to pick up extra work in pretty white gardens like ours at number 7 Dahlia Street in Witbank, an Afrikaans coal-mining town in the south-eastern Transvaal. I thought the black miners were lucky to become garden boys for a day, especially if they caught my dad's eye when he wound down his window and shouted out, '*Woo-hoo*, John!'

Dad, being so tall, had folded himself into the front seat as if he was a spring that had been pushed down into a box. He wore a short-sleeved checked shirt, cream shorts, long fawn-coloured socks and shiny brown shoes that had been polished so brilliantly by Maggie, our black servant, they doubled as mirrors. You could smile at yourself when you looked down at dad's shoes. Meanwhile, up top, his short-back-and-sides was kept in place by a lick of Brylcreem. It left a dark oily patch on the upholstery above his head.

I wanted to be like dad. Even if I preferred flip-flops to socks and shoes, I wore the same checked shirt and shorts. My hair was also shaped in a neat Brylcreem bop and, just like dad, I leaned back in the front seat on another gorgeous South African morning.

'Breathe in deeply,' dad murmured after reminding me that we lived in the most beautiful country in the world. 'Doesn't it make you feel good to be alive?'

I filled my little lungs with the crisp air and nodded. It felt wonderful.

'We're very lucky to live here,' dad said.

We were on the hunt for a black boy in Witbank which, in English, meant 'White Bank'. But the dirt streets around our house were named after English-sounding flowers – Amaryllis, Dahlia, Gladioli and Iris. In Dahlia Street, mom and Heather, my big sister, who was three years older than me, were at home. They were getting ready for the weekend as Maggie washed our breakfast dishes.

I loved sitting next to dad, rather than being in the back with Heather or Shandy. Dad, as usual, was in a good mood as we cruised along Watermeyer Street, the main road leading out of town. I hummed along as he impersonated a rough-voiced black man, Louis 'Satchmo' Armstrong, and sang his favourite song:

> *Hello, Dolly*
> *This is Louis, Dolly*
> *It's so nice to have you back where you belong*
> *You're looking swell, Dolly*
> *I can tell, Dolly*

I laughed every time he followed a pause at the end of a line with that punchy catchphrase of *'Dolly!'* And dad then sang it again so he could swap 'Dolly' for 'Donny' and pretend he was singing about a little South African boy rather than some swell-looking woman from America.

He was a very clever man. Everyone knew that in 1961, just before I was born, dad became the youngest-ever power station manager in South Africa. He was the big boss at Komati Power Station, in the middle of nowhere, between two Afrikaans towns called Middleburg and Bethel. But we moved to Witbank when dad was given something he called 'a promotion' at Eskom – the country's electricity supply commission.

Dad was very proud of Eskom. He always reminded us that Eskom gave us light. Eskom gave us warmth. Eskom, dad said, gave us something magical: electricity. Dad loved that word; and his company. He said we would be lost without electricity and so he often pointed out the streetlights and giant pylons. They all carried electricity from Eskom.

His new office was just a few blocks away from our house. Most weekdays, he came home for lunch. Heather would be at school but I sat with mom and dad at the dining room table. I liked it most when mom made us toasted sandwiches and sprinkled cheese and onion crisps on the sides of our plates.

Every lunchtime that week mom and dad had listened to our red radio. They were quiet and I was worried. Sensing my confusion, they tried to explain to me what had happened.

Four days earlier, on 6 September, 1966, our Prime Minister, Dr Hendrik Verwoerd, had been killed in Cape Town, a thousand miles from where we lived. He was in parliament – where they made all our country's laws. Just after two o'clock on that Tuesday afternoon a mad man with a Greek name, Dimitri Tsafendas, had walked quickly towards Dr Verwoerd. The Greek man was a messenger in the house of laws. That day he had carried his message, a large knife, inside his jacket.

The mad man used the knife to stab our prime minister four times in the chest.

Other men pulled him away and knocked the knife out of his hand. But it was too late. Dr Verwoerd was dead even before they got him to hospital.

A strange word, 'assassinated', hissed like a snake from my parents' radio. Dr Verwoerd, dad said, had been assassinated.

In the car I asked dad about the Greek man. Why was he such a bad man? Dad held the steering wheel he had covered with sheep-skin to keep it cool on hot summer days. I liked the way he turned his head to look at me sitting so small in the seat next to him. We drove free and easy in those days, without buckling up, and dad closed his window so he could talk to me.

Dad said there were all kinds of people in the world. Most of us were good; but some were bad or even mad. Dimitri Tsafendas was a dangerous man. His father was white but his mother was not Greek. She was black. I was shocked. People still thought that Dimitri was light enough to be white. But he wanted to be called a 'Coloured'. He wanted to become 'non-white'. I was puzzled. White people were happy. White people drove cars and lived in houses like ours on Dahlia Street.

Maggie lived in the maid's room at the bottom of our garden. But most natives, black and coloured and Indian people, lived in places called locations. Their houses were tiny and made out of corrugated iron. They could not catch the same trains or buses as us. They hardly went to school and, if they did, they were a long way from Robert Carruthers Primary – where Heather was in Standard One and where I would join her in four months time. They could not sit on a bench in the park or swim in a pool. I could not understand why the Greek man wanted to become a 'Coloured'.

Dimitri Tsafendas said a tapeworm in his stomach had made him kill Hendrik Verwoerd. He said it was the tapeworm of truth. The tapeworm was hungry. It made him stab our prime minister.

I was frightened. Did I have a tapeworm in my tummy? Dad shook his head and smiled. There were no tapeworms in our family.

The yellow veld around us looked dry and empty. It stretched out as far as I could see. Nothing seemed alive. Even the big black birds perched on top of the steel pylons didn't move. In the back seat, our little cocker spaniel also lay still. But I knew Shandy wasn't dead. She was just asleep.

Eventually, the coal dumps rose up like dark mountains. The silver colliery silos glinted against the blackness of the dumps. Hand-operated conveyor belts shuttled the coal from the silos to the open-backed yellow trucks which, on a Saturday morning, were silent.

We could see hundreds of natives in the hazy distance. They waited on both sides of the dirt strips lining the tarred road. As we came closer and closer some of them waved – hoping that we would stop and choose them.

An old man cupped his hands. He looked more sad than hopeful that we might pick him. 'Look at that boy,' I laughed. 'He's too old to work in our garden.'

My father knew the kind of garden boy he wanted and so, having opened his window again, he leaned over and made his familiar cry: '*Woo-hoo*, John!'

As a smiling black boy ran across the road I asked dad a question: Why were all black boys called John?

'He's not called John,' dad said. 'It's just better to call him "John" than "boy."'

The miner reached our car. 'Hello, master,' he said.

'Hello, John,' dad answered. 'You work hard, John?'

John nodded eagerly. 'Yes, master ...'

Natives always called my parents 'master' and 'madam'. 'OK,' dad said, opening the back door. The black boy slid into the Holden. 'Morning, *baasie* [little master],' he said softly to me. His white teeth shone in their pink gums.

I did not say hello to John. Instead, I stared at his black skin and noticed that the inside of his hands were much paler. Smelling the stale sweat on his body, I wrinkled my nose, and wondered if, underneath his dusty T-shirt, an even darker tapeworm moved inside him. Shandy crept around the side of the front passenger seat and lay quietly at my feet.

At home she would leap around cheerfully if she saw a white person. But black boys made Shandy whimper or bark. She raced up and down, woofing alongside our low garden wall, whenever a native walked past. Shandy knew they were different from us.

John needed a good wash. But I knew dad would never invite him to use our shower. Boys like John knew their place – just like Maggie understood she had to scrub our bathroom without ever standing beneath the shower's jets of hot water or, even worse, stretching out in our clean white bath. We could sack her on the spot if she dared be so cheeky. But Maggie was a good girl. She washed herself in a metal tub outside her room in our backyard.

Maggie was waiting for us when we got home. She greeted the boy in a funny language and did what mom told her to do. She made John a mug of tea while he walked round the garden with my parents. Mom did most of the talking, telling John where he needed to weed and trim the edges, while dad got out the hand-held lawn-mower that would cut the grass down the side and in front of our house. They listed all the other jobs he needed to do that day.

'Yes, madam,' John said to mom. 'Yes, master,' he said to dad.

I slipped away because, with Heather and the McKenzie boys who lived next door, we were hiking out to the quarry again. We loved the deep red hole of earth because it felt as if the quarry belonged just to us. Even the walk there was an adventure, from the moment we stuffed a khaki rucksack with a beaker of Oros orange squash, sandwiches, sliced biltong, naartjies, condensed milk *piekies* [sachets] and a box of our favourite biscuits: Romany Creams.

The McKenzie boys led the way as we crossed the wide patch of veld opposite our houses. The grass was up to my waist as we waded through it, like explorers. Heather and the boys chatted away while I followed silently, just glad to be included.

It usually took us an hour to reach the abandoned quarry. But we always stopped first at a large cement water reservoir, which marked our halfway point, and had a plastic cup of squash and a couple of Romany Creams each. That morning, however, we had not even made it to the reservoir when one of the McKenzie boys nearly stepped on a snake. It disappeared too quickly for them to see it properly – but we did not dare move for the next minute in case it was a rinkhals, a ring-necked spitting cobra, or a far deadlier puff adder. Eventually, turning round to look at us, the oldest boy, Mac, grinned.

'It's gone,' he said.

Heather and the boys started to walk forward carefully but I refused. 'Come on,' my sister urged. 'It's safe now.'

I shook my head. I didn't care if they walked all the way to the quarry. I knew a rinkhals could jump out when you least expected it. Dad had told us how, at Komati, he had once hit a rinkhals by mistake while driving mom's white MG. The snake was so smart it managed to flip itself up and coil around the open metal hubcap. Dad said he'd had a devil of a job getting him out. You could never take a chance with a rinkhals.

Heather and the McKenzie boys tried to coax me forward, but I wouldn't move. Ten minutes passed and the three older children became angry with me – a small serious-faced boy with slicked-back blond hair. I had not taken a single step forward.

When they could stand it no longer they gave up. Heather said we might as well go home. I nodded happily. I had ruined the day but at least I hadn't been bitten by a rinkhals or a puff adder. I munched cheerfully on another Romany Cream Heather had pressed into my hand.

When we reached our house I heard John, the mining boy, singing a lullaby in the garden. Maggie called to him from the kitchen window, and they both laughed. I wondered if they guessed I was too frightened to walk to the quarry.

Later that day I watched Maggie make John his lunch. She cut off the two thick ends of a brown loaf and smeared the hunks with peanut butter – just the way a black boy liked it. Maggie placed the bread and a green apple on a yellow enamel plate and filled a tin cup with cold water. I carried the plate out into the garden while Maggie followed me with the water she was careful not to spill. She said John would be very thirsty after working hard in the baking sun. He would have another mug of tea once he had cooled down and finished eating.

John had ripped off his shirt. His black skin shone with fresh sweat. 'Thank you, *baasie*,' he said.

I sat under the shade of an apple tree at the bottom of the garden and whistled to Shandy. She ambled over, her tail wagging, and sat down heavily beside me. Shandy licked my hand with her pink tongue, as if she could guess the kind of rough morning I'd just had.

John knew he could not lie next to me and my dog. Ten feet away from us, on the freshly mown grass, he took a large bite from his peanut butter sandwich.

He had switched on the sprinkler and, while he chewed, John watched the spray arc back and forth across the lawn. Shandy ran towards the sprinkler. She put her furry face close to the metal line of tiny holes shooting their tracers up into the clear blue sky before they curled back down to the ground. Shandy kept opening and snapping her mouth shut as she tried to bite big chunks out of the sprinkler. Her face became wet as she barked and bit the water.

I might have laughed had John not started chuckling first. For a moment I almost joined him until I remembered the difference between us. I was white. He was just a native. He was a boy and I was the *baasie*. Shandy was my dog and he was laughing at her.

'You're the stupid one,' I shouted.

John stared at me. His half-eaten peanut butter sandwich curled in his hand. I could not help myself. 'I'm telling the master,' I said as, tugging at Shandy, I pulled my shivering dog away from the sprinkler and the black boy.

John pushed aside his enamel plate and shook his head. But I knew he had done wrong.

In the cool of the kitchen I let Shandy loose. She shook herself dry while Maggie tutted as water sprayed across the floor she had just wiped. I told Maggie that John was a stupid boy. She started to hum quietly to herself, as if she had not even heard me.

'John is a stupid boy,' I said again.

Maggie looked down at me. She must have been my mother's age, in her late thirties, but she was not as smartly dressed as mom. Maggie wore red slippers, a pink checked overall and a white *doek* [scarf] on her head. Her slippers were always on her feet, whether she was working in the house or walking to the corner shop. She also had a big gap between her front teeth. Once, when I was much smaller, I had sat on the iron grid of the drain outside. I liked the way that water from the dripping tap bounced off my knee. But, after a few minutes, I'd run screaming into the kitchen because a small army of red ants had marched into my underpants and bitten hard. Maggie had stripped me and wiped every last ant off my bare bottom. And then she had dried my tears and sliced some chunks of peeled apple to keep me sweet.

'I'm going to tell the master about John,' I warned.

'His name is not John,' Maggie said quietly. 'His name is ...'

She said an African name so quickly I could not understand her.

I went back into the garden. Shandy followed me out into the heat, panting every step of the way. John was singing again. He must have known that I had not said anything to dad. The sun beat down and the boy grinned and held his black thumb aloft. I did not know what else to do, so I lifted my own thumb. It looked small and pale in the African sun.

THE DAYS SLID PAST under blue skies and in sunlit gardens. I swam in the local pool and climbed trees and walked with Heather and Shandy to the closest shop where they sold Chappies bubblegum. Sometimes, if you got lucky, the shopkeeper would run out of five cent pieces and so, instead of change, he'd slip you a couple of small squares of pink bubblegum in bright yellow wrappers covered by blue and red stripes and the head of a chipmunk.

When my sister and I opened the wrappers and popped the gum into our mouths we chewed and chewed and then blew out our cheeks so that we looked exactly like Chappie Chipmunks as we tried to make huge white bubbles in the air. And when that worked for Heather but not for me we turned back to the inside of the empty wrappers where three questions would be listed under a heading of *Did You Know?* We loved the questions almost as much as the gum.

'Did you know,' Heather read as we chewed and walked slowly back to Dahlia Street, 'that all the swans in England are owned by the Queen?'

'Yes,' I said.

'Liar,' Heather replied, not fooled for a second as she blew another bubble. It got bigger and bigger until it popped and left stringy strands of gum all over her face. She pulled them back into her mouth and began to chew all over again.

'Did you know,' she asked again, reading from her Chappies wrapper, 'that the longest case of hiccups lasted thirty-seven years?'

I couldn't believe it. Heather had once had hiccups for two days, when we were on holiday at the coast. We had taken her to the doctor in the end because holding her breath, drinking a glass of water through the side of her mouth and giving her a great big *skrik* [fright] couldn't stop her hiccupping. The doctor, somehow, cured her.

Heather had already moved on to her last question. 'Did you know,' she asked, 'that coconuts kill more people in the world than sharks?'

It didn't matter. I would always be more frightened of a shark than a coconut; and I shivered at the thought of a Great White or even a hammerhead closing in on my dangling legs in the sea. Heather said we didn't have to worry about either sharks or coconuts in Witbank.

Chappies were as delicious as they were full of incredible facts. But there were some questions they would never dare print inside a yellow Chipmunk wrapper. Heather asked me one of them. Did I know that John Lennon had said the Beatles were bigger than Jesus?

Heather loved pop music and so I had heard of The Beatles. I even knew some of their songs. But I couldn't believe that they had said they were more famous than Jesus. My parents, who took us to church every Sunday, shook their heads. At least the government did their best to protect us. John Vorster, our new prime minister who looked like a bullfrog, banned the Beatles' records. If The Beatles ever dared visit South Africa they would be locked up in jail. They would be taught not to say anything bad about Jesus.

At Sunday School, Heather and I learnt a lot about Jesus and the Bible. But it was far harder stepping out on my first day of proper school when, in January 1967, I pulled on my khaki shirt and short trousers and held my mom's hand tightly as she walked me and Heather from Dahlia Street. Heather was about to go into Standard Two, and her fourth year of school, and she swung her little brown case cheerfully as she walked just ahead of us in her gingham dress.

I was determined not to cry. But it became more difficult when little boys and girls around me burst into tears in the school hall after we were told to say goodbye to our parents and join a line for all Grade 1 pupils. I thought about peeing in my underpants but decided, instead, to leave my mom without a word. She would later tell dad how brave I had been. It suddenly seemed worth it.

Settling quickly at school, I was happy and cheerful. But then, in April 1967, just after my sixth birthday on a cool autumn evening, dad came home from work and told mom that he had some news. I heard them talking in the kitchen while I kicked a ball in the hallway outside. The plastic ball bounced against a wall but their conversation sounded important. Picking up my ball, I stood quietly at the half-opened door.

I heard dad say it would be an even bigger job for him in Johannesburg. Mom sounded pleased but, like a Chappies wrapper, she was full of questions: When would we leave? Where would we live? What would we do about school? Would we be able to buy our own house at last?

Through the crack in the doorway I watched Maggie peel potatoes at the sink. Her gaze never left her work as she stripped long curls of brown skin from potatoes turning white in her hands. But I knew she was listening as she washed the skinless potatoes in cold water. Her head, like mine, must have been spinning.

I burst into the kitchen then. I didn't want to leave Witbank. I didn't want to go to Johannesburg. The words came out in a tearful rush. Maggie smiled sadly at me. She knew how I felt.

Dad knelt down low so that he could become almost as small as me. His tie bounced gently in front of me as he rocked on his haunches.

We wouldn't have to live in Johannesburg, dad said. We were going home to Germiston.

I was confused. Witbank was home. But dad reminded me that he and mom had been born in Germiston, as I had been too. Everything had begun for our family in Germiston. My four grandparents had left Scotland after World War I and ended up in Germiston – close to Johannesburg.

I loved my grandparents, especially my dad's dad, Granddad George, but I tried to think of another excuse to stop our move. 'What about Shandy?'

Mom laughed. Shandy, of course, would live with us in Germiston.

'And Maggie?' I asked.

'We'll talk to Maggie,' dad said, 'once you've gone to bed.'

Maggie Thabang had been born in Witbank and lived her whole life in a town of black coal dumps and white Afrikaners. But she had become part of our family – even if she was not allowed to use our cups and plates, our knives and forks. Maggie slept in a brick room away from the house at the bottom of our garden.

She still belonged to us. Maggie was our girl; and I could not bear the thought of losing her.

George McRae (1898–1974), World War I soldier and grandfather

CHAPTER TWO

SOLDIER STORIES

T EN MILES FROM Johannesburg, criss-crossed by train tracks and surrounded by abandoned gold mine dumps, Germiston was not the prettiest town on earth. It looked cold and hard on a bright winter day. But our new home in the leafy suburb of Lambton was different. It was as beautiful as it was enormous – a white double-storey mansion with four tall pillars and a pale green balcony at the front. Two towering fir trees stood like sentries on either side of the house.

The glass doors from the lounge opened onto a patio and a huge garden. I already knew that in this garden, and in my head, I would score goals for South Africa in a World Cup final, as well as a dazzling try against the All Blacks, before hitting the winning runs against Australia. A creaking swing, shaded by a berry tree, offered the perfect place to dream up such moments.

Behind the swing, and purple trails of bougainvillea, an ivy-lined alley took you past the double garage and down to the cement backyard where there was a white wall against which Heather and

I could smack tennis balls as long as we liked. Dad said the ivy covering the lower wall would work as a dark green net. On the day we moved to Germiston, in July 1967, in the afternoon sunlight streaming through the overhanging fig trees, our new court looked gorgeous.

On the corner of Cachet Road, at number 24, we had only one set of neighbours. Frikkie and Leenie Oosthuizen, a middle-aged Afrikaans couple, had already popped over with rusks and *melktert* [milk tart] to say how pleased they were that they now lived next door to a couple of children. Heather and I scowled shyly.

We were more interested in a long curved banister. The polished handrail was wide enough for me to sit on as I slid down two flights of stairs to the ground floor where, beyond the lounge, there was a study, a dining room, a kitchen and a laundry for two maids to do our washing and ironing. With four bedrooms and a sewing room upstairs we had masses of space; but we knew Maggie would sleep outside, behind our imaginary tennis court.

A narrow corridor led to her room. It was opposite a dark alcove where, dad said, we would store coal and wood for the fires we'd light on winter nights. Maggie's room was small and crammed with her cases and boxes. In the middle of the muddle, Maggie and one of the black removal men had laid out four piles of bricks and, when I crept inside, they were carefully lifting up her bed. Each of the metal legs would rest on its own sets of bricks. There were eight bricks per pile which meant that, once they had settled it securely, Maggie's bed would be two feet above the ground.

Maggie had done exactly the same in her room in Witbank. She told me that she needed to be kept safe from the *Tokolosh*, an evil dwarf that could be sent to torment her by the witchdoctors. As long as she slept a long way from the floor he would not be able to reach the bed and attack her. Heather and I had once been terrified of the *Tokoloshe*; but in Witbank we had grown used to the story of the little man. We were more fascinated by climbing onto Maggie's steepling bed. It felt surprisingly steady on its makeshift stand of bricks.

I was happy that Maggie had chosen to leave her family so she could live with us in Germiston. After the black boy had gone back inside the house to unload the rest of our containers I asked Maggie if she would help Heather and me put our own beds on bricks. We would then also be perched too high for the Germiston *Tokoloshe* to take us away in our sleep. Maggie told me not to be so silly. There was only one *Tokoloshe*. He was not interested in white children.

Maggie quietly unpacked the rest of her possessions. She placed two small photo frames on the cardboard box next to her bed. The black and white photographs were of her children. I stared at the little natives. Maggie said they were being cared for by their grandmother. I told her not to look sad. She had me and Heather.

Before I left I sneaked another peek under Maggie's bed. The *Tokoloshe* was nowhere to be seen. I still raced past the coal hole, just in case he was hiding in the shadows.

Later that night, as the sun disappeared behind our high garden wall, Germiston became a scary town. After my parents had tucked me in and switched off the light in my new bedroom, I shivered under the clean sheets and heavy blankets. How would it feel to lie on a bed suspended on bricks? What if Maggie turned over in her sleep and, just like I sometimes did, rolled off the edge? She would make a loud thump on the cement floor.

I almost giggled when, suddenly, an eerie sound spread goose bumps across my arms and legs. It was like nothing I had ever heard before. I thought it belonged to a gruff *Tokoloshe*.

'*Tsa-huuuhhh! Tsa-huuuhhh!*'

It stopped, began again and then drifted away. When it started up a minute later, sounding too far away to be in striking distance, I slid out of bed and crept towards the window. I pulled back the zebra-patterned curtains mom and Maggie had already managed to hang.

A few natives, wearing balaclavas against the cold, huddled beneath a yellow neon sign outside the shop opposite our house. The shop, a Greek-owned newsagent and corner café, was shut for the night. Despite its blackened windows there was enough light from the Chiclets Chewing Gum sign to allow the crouching boys to play a game of dice. Whenever one of the natives picked up the dice he blew on his hands. Then, he'd flick the little numbered cubes onto the ground with a moan:

'*Tsa-huuuhhh! Tsa-huuuhhh!*'

'*Dad! Dad!*' I shouted. My dad took the stairs two at time with his long legs, and sat on the edge of my bed. The noise of the black boys drifted across the street.

'It's OK,' he said. 'It's just the natives. You should listen to the trains instead.'

Germiston was the largest railway junction in Africa and the reason why my dad's own grandfather had arrived here from Scotland. Great-granddad Donald had been a train driver in Aberdeen and he had found work on the steam locomotives trundling up and down the thousand miles of track stretching from Germiston to Cape Town.

His son, my granddad George, had followed him to South Africa in 1920. Having recovered from all he had seen as a soldier in World War I, George came in search of a new life. He eventually became a maintenance man at the Victoria Falls Power Company – which soon turned into Eskom. George was then joined by the young woman he had courted in Aberdeen. My granny Netta had crossed the Atlantic on her way to an unknown continent. She was met by George in Cape Town. They were so overcome, after a year apart, they immediately found a magistrate's court. Within an hour of her arrival, at the bottom of Africa, they were married.

Granny and Granddad McRae had lived in Germiston ever since. Granddad George had worked at Eskom for forty-five years – just as my own dad was now an Eskom man. Even mom had been an Eskom girl, before she married dad. It was like a big family circle. The old stories worked like a spoken lullaby. I felt soothed by the tip-toeing approach of sleep, and an understanding that we had come a long way to be together again.

GRANDDAD GEORGE had once been a trained killer. It was still hard to believe. His big craggy face was warm and twinkly and he was always getting into trouble with my stern granny. She scolded him for resting his elbows on the table, for spilling soup on his tie and for falling asleep after Sunday lunch at our house. Having eaten more than he should have done, he usually dozed on the green-cushioned swing under the berry tree. He would open a sleepy eye and wink at me before letting slip a rumbling laugh.

But if you stuck a gun in his back, Granddad George could flip you over and leave you sprawled on the ground in front of him. He was fast and lethal because, after four years as an infantryman in World War I, he knew how to fight a bayonet-wielding soldier with his bare hands.

Our granddad was the most honest man we knew; but he had told a lie that almost ended his life. He had only been sixteen when, on 5 August, 1914, he'd joined a battalion of the Gordon Highlanders in Aberdeen. Britain and France had declared war on Germany a week earlier. They knew the Germans planned to storm through Belgium and invade France.

George felt it was right to stop the Germans. And so he lied about his age and signed up to the famous old regiment of kilt-wearing Highlanders. When he and all the other new young recruits gathered together in Aberdeen they were told the war would be over by that Christmas.

But Granddad George spent four Christmases in the trenches, hunkered down against the cold, the bullets and the mustard gas. He won four medals for bravery and distinguished conduct, but lost thousands of his fellow Highlanders. Fifteen million people died in the Great War; and dad said it was a miracle Granddad George had survived. It meant we were incredibly lucky, too. Even I had figured out that without granddad there would have been no dad and no me.

Machine-gun nests, gas masks and hope kept him alive. On the Western Front, granddad always believed he would return home to Scotland and his girl, Netta. He was helped in different ways. Once, after a bad day, with dead bodies all around, George was stunned by the sight of a tiny bird perched on the parapet. The bird, which looked like a robin, lifted its beak toward the black smoke curling up in the sky. George could not understand how a creature so small and delicate could exist in such a nightmarish place. The little bird even had the courage to tweet softly.

The sounds were usually disturbing. One night, after his battalion had pushed deep into German territory, George's sleep was ruined by a ghostly groaning. Everyone else was too hurt or exhausted but George edged his way out of the trench. The terrible noise came from a blockhouse to his left. Thinking he might find a wounded Scot or Frenchman, George moved more quickly.

He peered around a corner of the blockhouse. In the moonlight, he saw a man lying in a stagnant pool of water. The man was dying. A bullet had torn a hole in his grey uniform. He was bleeding from the stomach and his leg dangled at an awkward angle. The German soldier whimpered as George covered him with his coat. He looked into my granddad's face. George knew it was better to end his agony.

It was strange to think that our granddad, the gentle and funny man we loved, had seen such sights fifty years before. Granddad George made as laugh; and it felt as if he watched over us.

Dad said that George had been the same with his own regiment. He won the DCM in 1917, after a disastrous battle when all the officers in his regiment were killed. George took command and organized a ravaged company, bolstering their morale as they kept fighting. He then led them back across the front to safety. We discovered all this only by looking at his war records, and old copies of the *Aberdeen Star* and *London Gazette* which granny kept at the bottom of a drawer.

When the whisky flowed and he was relaxed enough to tell us another story, granddad preferred to talk about people rather than any of his medals. I was entranced most by a graveyard memory.

On a foggy night in France, the Highlanders were being picked off, one by one. Sometimes an hour or more would pass between killings but the dread was constant. Individual soldiers were shot by an unseen enemy. A German sniper was embedded somewhere near their trench and, with icy accuracy, he killed one Scot after another. George had to bring him down.

He slipped out of his foxhole and crept towards the area where he thought the sniper operated. But, as the shooter was so quiet, George had to lie in the mud for a long time. He could not risk breaking cover to search for him. But he was sure the man was out there, in the spreading fog.

Small wooden crosses covered the ground. In this makeshift cemetery George had often helped bury the bodies in freshly-dug mud and secured the footing above each grave with a plank of wood. The crosses were made out of wood stripped from old ration boxes, and prayers would be said. It was better than nothing.

As he stared at the misty crosses George's breath caught in his throat. A hundred yards from where he lay, one of the crosses began to tilt. George saw the hole open up in front of him. He was chilled by the sight of a glinting metal gun rather than a ghost. The sniper took his time to rise out of the grave.

He did not need to expose more than his head and his upper body before he settled into position. George watched the sniper look up and down the Highland trench. He was searching for his next victim. But it was difficult to see in the fog and he soon slipped back down into the grave.

George was waiting for him when he next lifted the wooden cross and stuck out his rifle and his head. George aimed at the man's hand with such conviction that the German soldier let his gun fall into the muddy hole. Climbing from the grave, he raised his hands. After spending so long with a corpse he had decided he would be better off being a prisoner. George led the sniper to the camp they had set up for wounded or captured Germans.

FIFTY YEARS LATER, in the South African sunshine, Granddad George snored softly on our garden swing. After forty-five years of work at Eskom he had retired. A year earlier, in the middle of 1966, he had turned sixty-eight and passed the company's retirement age. He was lauded at his leaving party, but George did not receive a pension. Four-and-a-half decades of work amounted to nothing in the end.

My dad was one of the new young stars in the same company. But it had also been a struggle for him. When he passed the first year of his engineering degree, he decided it would not be fair to his parents to expect them to pay for another three years at university. As a maintenance man George earned a meagre salary and university fees were exorbitant. My dad delayed his degree for a few years while he earned a little money as an Eskom apprentice.

Three years later, Ian McRae became the first Eskom employee to be awarded a company bursary and he was able to return to the University of the Witwatersrand in Johannesburg. He graduated in 1954 and, having delayed their wedding so he could complete his degree, my parents married in Germiston the following year. The Eskom scholarship had been vital, but there was little generosity in their refusal to offer any long-serving workers, like old Granddad George, a pension.

George had to find another job in retirement. He became the caretaker and groundsman at Germiston High School, where both my parents had been students. Heather and I would eventually go to the same school. Our eldest cousin, Brian, who was nine years older than me, was already there. He had been fourteen in 1966 when granddad began his new role. No-one knew anything about his distinguished war record. He was simply 'Mr Mac', the cheery old caretaker happy to tackle any task asked of him.

Brian had been startled when, on granddad's first few days in his new school job, George avoided all eye-contact. Whenever they neared each other on the playground or along a corridor, George looked away. Brian thought he must have offended granddad in some way.

The truth soon emerged. George worried that Brian would feel embarrassed if everyone knew his grandfather worked as a caretaker. But Brian said he could never be ashamed of George. The old Scottish soldier looked down at his teenage grandson and nodded. And, from then on, they greeted each other cheerfully when crossing paths at school.

Mister Mac became as popular with the teachers and pupils as he was with his army of black labourers who helped him look after the school. He was his usual twinkly self, unless someone stepped across the cricket pitch which had become his most treasured achievement in old age. George was a pure-blooded Scot, until it came to his fervour for producing a wicket as fair as it was true for the very English game of cricket. No-one dared ruin his masterpiece.

George and Netta lived on Angus Street in the centre of Germiston. The houses on Angus Street were small, but George seemed the happiest man in the world. He loved the fact that his home was in such a Scottish-sounding place. Only a few years before it had been called India Street; but that colonial name had been too brown for Germiston. Echoes of Scotland were all around. Argyll and Bruce and Selkirk Streets were nearby and, a block away, there was even a George Street. It could have been named after our great old granddad.

W E HAD OUR FIRST family Christmas in Germiston in 1967. In mid-summer, our skins were darker than the light brown berries covering the ground around our garden swing. Yet Heather and I were besotted with snowy white images of Christmas. Our sunny lounge was filled with cards of snowmen and candle-lit scenes of life from a wintry European town. Rosy-cheeked children sledged down Alpine mountains while a beaming Santa skated across a frozen lake. We even had an old ceramic snowman that we stuck on top of an artificial pine tree dad brought up from the cupboard below the stairs. It was as if, being so white in an African country, we needed to imagine what might have been if my grandparents had never moved continents.

Outside, the grass had been baked yellow after a month without rain. The sky was a shimmering blue, with no sign that the missing storm clouds would bring late-afternoon respite from the heat. We didn't mind. Christmas was coming and, rather than thinking about the drought, my mind fixed on the piles of presents Father Christmas would leave beneath the plastic pine.

Christmas Eve delivered something magical first. A giant African sun changed colour from yellow and orange to red and pink as it sank behind the disused gold mines. Despite the feasting mosquitoes, leaving itchy bumps on our arms and legs, the growing darkness brought excitement as we headed west towards Johannesburg – or Egoli, the Golden City, as Maggie called it.

We were on our way, with my grandparents and cousins, to an early show at His Majesty's Theatre. It would be a special evening because Kenneth McKellar, the kilt-wearing Scottish tenor, was one of only a few overseas performers willing to risk the world's scorn by ignoring apartheid and touring South Africa. Granddad George was thrilled. There could be no better start to Christmas and Hogmanay than being surrounded by his family as a great Scot stormed the stage.

Once Kenneth McKellar appeared, George could not stop himself. Even when granny dug her bony elbow hard into his ribs George refused to lower his booming voice as he sang along. My embarrassment reached a blushing crescendo when, in tandem, the McKellar & McRae duo belted out the toe-curling 'Donald, Where's Your Troosers?' It was as if they were singing a song about me, a little South African boy who had the misfortune of being called Donald. George sang along in delight, his face crinkling with tears of laughter as he looked down at me and echoed the Scottish burr of the man skipping across stage singing:

> Let the wind blow high, let the wind blow low,
> Through the streets in my kilt I'll go,
> And all the lassies shout 'Hello,
> Donald, where's your troosers?'

George seemed happier than ever on the drive home, chortling over granny's grumbling and my near trooser-filling horror during the communal sing-song. By the time we reached our house he was in the mood for a large whisky. He was not usually much of a drinker, Granddad George, but it was Christmas Eve and the Scotch uncorked stories from deep inside him. He spoke in a thick but bubbling broth of an accent. Even when he veered away from the Highlands to Belgium and France, granddad's dark and gripping war-time tales drew us back into the past and the memory of his first war-time Christmas.

D ECEMBER 1914 marked George McRae's fifth month as a soldier. He had just turned seventeen, but he was still too young to be an official soldier with the Gordon Highlanders. Some of the officers in the 4th Battalion, to which he had been assigned in August, when he'd first lied about his age, had been suspicious of his boyish looks. He wangled a transfer from the territorial Fourths to the 6th Battalion where the commanders were too in need of fresh troops to bother with birthdates.

War, said Granddad George, seemed like an adventure at first. A few months away from home were no hardship. The Gordon boys wore their kilts proudly and wrote regularly to those they loved most in Aberdeen, believing they would be home in time for Christmas.

By late November, however, not long after George had switched to the 6th Battalion on the Western Front, it became plain that the war would not be over for another year or more. The Germans, just like the French and the British, were well stocked with machine-guns and artillery.

A harsh winter settled across Belgium by early December. The trenches which the Highlanders dug were badly made and soon flooded. They became slimy boltholes where it was hard to keep hopeful. The Highlanders formed part of a thin British and French

line which ran south for twenty-five miles from the Ypres Salient to
the La Bassée Canal.

Granddad George said the battle intensified throughout
December. Both sides suffered heavy losses and by Christmas Eve
the misery was eased only by the arrival of letters from home and
a Princess Mary Box for each surviving soldier. The silver box fea-
tured a stamped image of the head of the seventeen-year-old
Princess Mary, the daughter of King George V and Queen Mary.
George's own seventeen-year-old princess, Netta, waited for him in
Aberdeen.

It was still a treat to get a box from a princess. The contents had
been donated by the British public in answer to a nationwide
'Soldiers' Christmas Fund'; and the many smokers amongst
George's fellow Highlanders received a box crammed with twenty
cigarettes, a pipe and an ounce of tobacco. As George was too
young to smoke legally, his box contained a pencil, a small bag of
sweets and a standard greeting from Princess Mary, commending
his courage.

George guzzled down his sweets and stamped his mud-caked
boots in an effort to warm his feet. At least the shellacking they had
received night after night from the Germans had ceased. The rain
had also stopped. Some of the men said the weather might even be
a little warmer on Christmas Day, when they had been promised a
proper meal of cooked beef and plum pudding.

During the previous three weeks Granddad George's battalion
had suffered frightening losses. But he knew they had inflicted
almost as many fatalities on the Germans. Bodies, frozen rigid
beneath the snow flurries, were strewn across the 200 yards separating enemy lines. It was too dangerous, even when the firing
eased at night, to drag back the Scottish and French corpses.

On Christmas Eve a light frost had turned the ground glis-
tening white. The black sky above the trenches seemed

miraculously starlit. George did not know how long he had been slumped in his trench when a voice murmured that the Germans had been silent for the longest spell anyone could remember. What were they planning? The braver boys peeked out of the trench.

They were stunned. The Germans had decorated the parapets of their own trenches with candles. A pretty line of flickering light stretched out into the winter night. And, then, it began.

The sound of men singing filtered across the battleground. It was a haunting and beautiful sound, as Granddad George heard the chorus of 'Stille Nacht' – the German version of 'Silent Night'. Men from the 6th Battalion of the Gordon Highlanders around him soon responded by singing the same song in English, with a Scottish burr to it. The French joined in; and the Germans answered across enemy lines with a different carol. All the guns were stilled, and the night filled with singing. Soldiers shouted 'Happy Christmas!' to each other, and a strange peacefulness settled over that small section of the Ypres Salient.

Christmas came the next morning to the Western Front, just as it did to Aberdeen or Berlin, and it brought the gift of a pale blue sky. Soldiers felt the warmth on their chapped skin. They re-read the latest letters they had received from home. And, still, there was no shooting from either side.

He could not quite remember how it happened, but George heard something even more incredible as word filtered down from man to man. It was said that further along the trenches some of the Highlanders had begun to leave their foxholes and cross the muddy wasteland separating the armies. The Germans had apparently risen first and, holding their hands high to show that they carried no weapons, they had walked through No-Man's Land towards the Scottish and French lines. George was told that the Germans had shouted festive greetings across the eerie divide. Some of the

Highlanders had answered and, encouraged by the response, they had then climbed out of the trenches to meet the men they were meant to kill.

A brief truce had been agreed. Soldiers exchanged gifts after it had been decided that each side would collect their dead without being fired at on Christmas Day. George and the other bewildered men in his trench stood in the muddied field that stretched out before them. They could see German soldiers in the distance, 150 yards from where they were now positioned. They felt vulnerable until they saw that the Germans were attending to their own collections and burials. One of the grey-coated German soldiers waved at them, and they waved back.

Their task was gruesome. They lifted the bodies of men who had been dead for days, often lying face-down in ice-ringed puddles. It was grim work, and it took a few hours to bring back and bury each body they found. At the end they held a Christmas service, and prayed for the men they had just covered with wet earth. They also prayed for the people they had left behind, and they prayed for themselves and even for the men opposite who had shown such humanity.

The mood soon lightened. They could hear laughter further down the line. Men on their side of the front sounded happy and the reason soon became obvious. They were in the company of German soldiers, shaking hands and speaking to each other in a broken mix of languages. George heard that, less than a mile away, a gaggle of Highlanders and Germans had chased a hare together amid much hilarity. It seemed right that on such a peaceful day the hare should escape.

He was told that those same Scots and English and even German soldiers kicked a football around for twenty minutes. They ate their lunch in peace; and that informal Christmas truce held all day.

It could not last. At some point the next day, a ghostly seventeen-year-old version of Granddad George hunkered down again in his trench as machine-guns rattled all around him.

FIFTY-THREE YEARS LATER, in another country, on a different continent, granddad drained his glass. He had not spilled a drop of whisky on our gold-patterned carpet in the lounge. Granddad George lifted me onto his knee. It was time for bed. Father Christmas was on his way, an old man even kinder and wiser than granddad. He would come to us first, at the bottom of Africa. I did not know if he would brave the townships of Witbank to see Maggie's children but our Christmas cards told me he'd visit white boys and girls in Scotland and Germany, and just about everywhere else in the world.

After I had gone upstairs with mom, and changed into my pyjamas, I persuaded her to allow me to go down again to say goodnight to Granddad George. I found him and dad on the side veranda, overlooking the garden. They sat on a couple of comfortable chairs, drinking beer and whisky as they watched a black bat flutter and squeak in the starlit sky. I was afraid of bats, and I huddled into dad. I would be too scared to ever become a soldier.

Dad's gaze had settled on the crinkly face of his father. Granddad George had undone the top button of his short-sleeve shirt and loosened his tie. He clinked the ice in his Scotch, and smiled at the sound.

'Happy Christmas, dad,' my father said as he and granddad George touched glasses.

'Happy Christmas, son,' granddad said, before turning his watery old eyes on me. 'And a Happy Christmas to you, laddie.'

Dad kissed me goodnight and, just before I raced upstairs to join Heather and my mother, Granddad George caught me by the hand.

He looked down at my bare legs, thin and chocolate-brown beneath my shortie pyjamas.

'Och, Donald,' he said, his voice thick with laughter, 'where's yer troosers?'

A man called Dolly ... Basil D'Oliveira teaches cricket to his children, 1968

CHAPTER THREE

FORCES FAVOURITES

E VERY SATURDAY AFTERNOON, on a radio programme called *Forces Favourites*, they played the same old songs. They were songs for our boys in the army, chosen by girls who sent them stacks of love alongside ditties like The Shirelles's 'Soldier Boy' or The Bee Gees' 'Gotta Get A Message To You'. Dedications were topped off by Afrikaans slogans like '*Min dae, baie hare*' [Few days, lots of hair] and '*Vasbyt*' [Hold on].

Stretched out on the grass, next to the swimming pool at the Rand Refinery, where they refined most of the world's gold, I closed my eyes. My mother played tennis at the refinery, where my uncle Frier was the boss, and Heather and I whiled away the afternoon at the pool. Small black dots from the sun danced on the inside of my eyelids as I listened to *Forces Favourites*, while waiting for the Saturday afternoon sports programme which began at three o'clock.

It felt like we were locked inside a giant army camp as Pat Kerr, the old honey-voiced presenter, told us about soldiers called Jannie and Karel, Kevin and Gary, and how their girls back home longed to see them. They were asked to stay bright and keep smiling until they got back to Civvie Street. But at their base camps, from Voortrekkerhoogte and Potchefstroom to Upington and Walvis Bay, they needed to 'Vasbyt'.

Pat Kerr said the word again and again, her English voice taking on an Afrikaans edge as she pronounced it correctly, replacing the 'v' with a flat 'f' and lengthening the 'y' in 'byt' into the more open-ended 'bait'. Fuss-bait. *Vasbyt*. We knew that, through her, tearful girlfriends and pregnant wives were telling their soldier boys to hold on through the hard times.

Being a girl, and too young to have a boyfriend, Heather did not worry about the army. She lay on the other side of the pool and listened to LM Radio, the pop station she was hooked on. LM stood for Lourenço Marques, the capital of Mozambique, and they played the banned Beatles and the devilish Rolling Stones. Broadcast not far from the border where our bravest boys were based, LM played whatever records they liked.

I kept on listening to the songs and messages for the soldiers keeping us safe. In between Elvis crooning 'Love Me Tender' or Petula Clark yelping that we should meet her 'Downtown', Pat Kerr's sunny voice became serious whenever she played a special record for the boys on the border. It sounded as if she was having to fuss-bait herself when she read a message to Piet or Paul and told them to shoot straight and keep their heads down.

A year earlier, in 1967, it had been made compulsory for every white boy to go into the army once he finished school. A minimum of nine months of military service was essential because, on the border between South-West Africa and Angola, the communists and terrorists were gathering. They wanted to make our millions of natives attack us. We had to stop them.

That Saturday morning, before *Forces Favourites*, I had played tennis. To reach the courts at Delville, named after a World War I battleground, I'd cycled over a metal bridge which crossed the railway tracks. The right side of the bridge was signposted for Europeans Only/*Slegs Blanke* [Whites Only]. It seemed normal that, in English, we should be classified as 'Europeans' while, in Afrikaans, the colour of our skin mattered most. The other side of the bridge was reserved for Non-Europeans/*Slegs Nie-Blankes* [Non-Whites Only].

No native ever dared walk along the wrong side of the bridge. They would be locked up in jail if they did. Even if a communist told them to break the law they would say '*Aikona!* [No way!]'. My yellow bicycle had freewheeled down the empty white corridor. The high metal barrier separated me from the stream of black people who had just got off the township train and were heading for work in the white suburbs. I could only see the bobbing tops of the coloured *doeks* worn on the heads of the shortest women. But most of the black men were tall enough to peer over the dented metal wall. A few stared blankly at me flying past them on my bike. But they winked more often and said, 'Morning, master!' They did not look like they would ever attack me.

Our lives were sweet and easy. We already said that very word, 'sweet', when we wanted to show we were pleased. See you later? *Sweet*. Fancy a chocolate milkshake? *Sweet*. How was that goal? *Sweet, my china*. 'China', taken straight from Cockney rhyming slang, with china plate meaning 'mate', had become part of our schoolboy lingo. We were all sweet. We were all chinas.

We only groaned at the fact that television was banned in South Africa. The government insisted on the ban because they wanted to protect us from communism and racial mixing. Dr Albert Hertzog, the Minister of Posts and Telegraphs, said television would be introduced 'over my dead body'. Speaking on radio, he said, 'Friends of mine, recently returned from Britain, tell me that one cannot see a programme which does not show black and white living together, where they are continually propagating a mixture of the two races. We could never allow that.'

A COLOURED MAN called Dolly changed the way the world looked at us in 1968. Basil D'Oliveira, or Dolly as everyone called him, was quiet and gentle. Eight years earlier, he had left Cape Town so that he might play cricket in England. Dolly had been born two years after my father, in October 1931, and been classified as a Cape Coloured. But he played cricket like a dream; and had scored eighty centuries in the coloured leagues around Cape Town by 1956. He was still not allowed to play cricket against white players, and definitely not at Newlands, the beautiful Test match arena in Cape Town.

The sports minister, Frank Waring, warned everyone: 'If whites and non-white start competing against each other there will be such viciousness – as never seen before.'

Dolly had become so miserable he'd contacted John Arlott, the BBC cricket commentator, in the hope of finding a new life in England. In 1960, with Arlott's help, D'Oliveira began playing cricket in the Central Lancashire League. It took him four years but, eventually, he made it to county cricket after Worcestershire offered him a contract and he became a British citizen. He took the biggest step of all when, in June 1966, he was selected to play for England against the all black West Indies.

In 1967, Dolly was named as one of *Wisden*'s five Cricketers of the Year. He featured regularly in our sports pages. I had begun a scrapbook by then and I cut out pictures of great sportsmen and stuck them down onto the dark blue pages. Sport helped me to become, fleetingly, colour-blind. Alongside photographs of white

Springbok sportsmen, like Frik du Preez, the rugby player, Graeme Pollock, the cricketer, and Paul Nash, the sprinter, I pasted in images of my favourite black boxer, Cassius Clay, who was just about to become Muhammad Ali, and of Dolly.

It still seemed odd that a South African, even a coloured man, might want to become English. Dolly had taken the opposite journey to Dimitri Tsafendas, a white man who had stabbed the prime minister because he wanted to be reclassified as coloured. Basil D'Oliveira, dad explained, was far from mad. He posed a different sort of problem to the government. England were due to tour South Africa in late 1968 and the prospect of D'Oliveira returning to play against the country of his birth turned our politicians purple with anger. Piet Le Roux, the minister of the interior, said: 'We will not allow mixed teams to play our white teams over here. If this player is chosen he would not be allowed to come here. Our policy is well known here and overseas.'

We felt isolated. In May 1968 the International Olympic Committee had banned our white team – which meant South Africa was barred from competing in the Mexico City Olympic Games later that year. I asked dad why the world wanted to hurt us. His answer made my head hum.

Even though they had never met us, people around the world had decided we were unfair to our black natives. It made me mad. They knew nothing about Maggie. I could bet they had never seen a bed on bricks or even heard of the *Tokoloshe*. How could they say we were unkind to Maggie when we told her jokes and gave her food at every meal? They didn't know how much we loved Maggie, and how much she loved us.

Dad said the outside world didn't understand how we lived in South Africa. They thought things were just black and white when we actually lived in a very colourful and sporting country.

Alongside football, cricket was my favourite sport. I loved the way dad and I, in early spring, coated my bat with linseed oil. The bat's willowy face turned golden as a warm smell filled the room. At the age of seven, I could pretend to be Graeme Pollock, the world's greatest batsman, playing against England at the Wanderers in Johannesburg.

England were due to arrive in late 1968 for a four-match Test series, where, with Graeme, and his fast bowling brother, Peter Pollock, we would prove we were the best side in the world. But the adults around me and on the sports pages seemed preoccupied by one question: what would happen if England selected Basil D'Oliveira?

He had just scored 158 to set up England's victory in the final Ashes Test against Australia. It seemed as if his seat on the plane back to South Africa had been booked – whatever our government might say.

If I was surprised a week later when dad told me that England had dropped Dolly, I was also relieved. The tour was definitely on because, cleverly, England's selectors had saved us a headache by excluding him.

Dolly was 'devastated'. Dad said that meant he was very sad. I could imagine how much Dolly must have wished he could be back in Cape Town, finally playing at Newlands, while looking up at Table Mountain. But he had to remember he was Coloured. In the end he would be better off staying in England.

There was, however, a twist. Tom Cartwright, the bowler, was injured and had to withdraw from the England squad. D'Oliveira would replace him, and tour South Africa after all. He was ecstatic and proud.

But Dolly was also less surprised than most by Vorster's reaction. On Tuesday, 17 September, 1968, I came home from school to hear that the tour was off. Mom and I listened to the radio as Prime Minster John Vorster, in his thick Afrikaans accent, said: 'We are not prepared to accept a team thrust upon us by the people whose interests are not the game, but to gain certain political advantages which they do not even attempt to hide. It is the team of the anti-apartheid movement. They are not welcome in South Africa.'

IT DID TAKE NOT LONG to forget Dolly and my cricketing misery. We went to the coast for three weeks that December, heading to East London, where the Indian Ocean was warm and the beaches were golden. Even the journey was thrilling, from the moment we were woken soon after four in the morning so we could dress and eat a quick breakfast. Dad then bundled us into the car. We were on a mission, he said, to break the back of a long journey.

I sleepily thought of Maggie as we raced through the dark. She had gone back to her family in the black location outside Witbank. When we still lived in Dahlia Street we had sometimes driven her home to the bumpy dirty roads and tin shacks of the township. It had none of the wide beaches or rolling breakers of East London. How could Maggie have a holiday in Witbank? She would see her children but she might have been happier if she had stayed in her back room in Germiston so she could look after Shandy. Our dog, instead, had been taken to a kennel. I had cried at the thought of Shandy being locked up in a steel run. Maggie had put her children before our dog.

The Free State sun, streaming into our faces, woke Heather and me just after eight. We were starving and we were bursting. Bursting and starving. Those stock words for a full bladder and a pang of hunger were chanted by the two of us, but we were so close to Bloemfontein that dad would not be diverted. Our holiday schedule was like a military operation.

We made it to Bloemfontein, the Holden finally turning into the courtyard of a Shell garage as we uncrossed our legs, turned down the squealing and raced to the loo. Our summer holiday had truly begun.

The rest of the journey was already mapped out. Dad had a small black notebook in which, every year, he jotted down the exact time and mileage of each leg of our travels from the Transvaal to the Eastern Cape, where we alternated between visiting East London and Port Elizabeth.

Each year the only difference was whether we ended the first day in Queenstown or Cradock. Queenstown was on the road to East London while Cradock led straight down to Port Elizabeth. This year, being East London's turn, we reached our usual stop-over hotel in Queenstown just after 2:30 – bang on schedule, dad said, with a weary grin.

I liked the way our bags were whisked away by a couple of smil-ing and white-jacketed black porters who led us to our rooms. We were looked after even more enthusiastically by the bar boys, who served drinks in the lounge at 6:30, and by our black waiters in the main dining room as we sat down at 7 p.m.

The same service smoothed our three-week stay at the Queens Hotel in East London. We were familiar guests and often asked for the same rooms and the same table so that we ended up with the same maids and waiters who remembered us from two years earlier. They smiled at the way I had my hair plastered down with Vitalis – which was 'The New Greaseless Way to Keep Your Hair Neat All Day!' – while being made to wear a jacket and tie to dinner. Mom said I needed to dress like a little gent if Heather and I were to eat with the grown-ups.

Most evenings, once we had been put to bed, my parents returned to the lounge and mom would sing, for the hotel pianist loved her voice. A few years before, hearing that she had sung professionally in Johannesburg, in *Oklahoma!*, the pianist had persuaded her to warble through a few tunes like 'Out Of My Dreams'.

Her speciality song was 'Little White Dove' – which Heather and I would shred in mock-operatic voices. But we were still stunned that our mom, Jess, who was just over five feet tall in her heels, had the confidence to stand next to a piano and sing soprano to a lounge full of strangers getting tipsy on beer and miniature bottles of Babycham.

On that particular holiday the pianist arranged for us to visit a recording studio in downtown East London so that he and mom could cut a crackly version of 'Little White Dove'. They each received a shiny 7″ vinyl record, a 'seven single', which we could play for fun in Germiston.

All the hotel guests, naturally, were white families on holiday. And all the staff, apart from the manager and his wife, the pianist and two receptionists, were natives. It was a black-and-white picture at the Queens, just as it was across every other hotel in South Africa. We expected nothing less. Our suburbs and schools and swimming pools were reserved for whites only, as were our beaches and parks and cinemas and trains and buses. The natives had their own buses and trains, if not any beaches or hotels. But why would a native want to lie in the sun on Orient beach in East London or anywhere else in South Africa? They didn't need a tan like us.

If they were lucky they got to be maids and waiters at a decent place like the Queens, where people like us, the McRaes, were very kind. We laughed and winked at them and I knew dad always gave them a good *bonsella* [tip] at the end of our holiday.

I actually preferred the natives to the Afrikaners, who were coarse and mean. Their English was terrible and their accents were hilarious. Afrikaners wore safari-suits for style and crew-cuts for pleasure. The *Boertjies* [little farmers] didn't even wince when they walked *kaalvoet* [barefoot] to the local Afrikaans school in Germiston and trod on jagged stones. Their fathers, meanwhile, wore long socks and *veldskoen* [felt shoes] below their khaki shorts. The *ou toppies* [old boys] carried combs inside those brown and green socks. Rows of metal teeth glinted between meaty sand-wiches of ribbed sock and hairy leg.

We saw plenty of Afrikaners most evenings in East London because they tended to stay further down the road from us, near the miniature golf 'Putt Putt' course, at the cheaper Snyman's Hotel. Queens, in contrast, was almost exclusively English. After dinner, and once we had sat in the lounge so my parents could drink coffee in tiny white cups, we would walk along the sea-front. It was a nightly ritual before Heather and I were whisked up to bed. As we passed Snyman's it was obvious that the Afrikaners were dressed less smartly than us. Most of the men were still in shorts. Their steel combs gleamed above the sock-line.

I wore shiny shoes that had been polished by the hotel maid. Little Afrikaner boys, meanwhile, raced barefoot across the grassy banks lining the seaside walkway of East London – or *Oos* London as they insisted on calling it. I was amazed they would even accept going on holiday in a town named after 'London'; for I knew they called English-speaking South Africans like us *rooi-neks* [red-necks] and *sout-piels* [salt-cocks]. They said our necks were red because we were too limey-white to stand the African sun. Yet we were as brown as chocolate buttons. I blushed more shyly at the thought of being a salt-cock. The Afrikaners claimed we wanted a foot in two countries separated by the ocean – South Africa and Britain. They chortled that, with our legs spread wide, our little dicks dangled in the salty waves.

The Afrikaners had cut their own ties with Holland. They had taken hold of a black country and made it their own. But we called them 'hairy-backs' or 'rock-spiders', 'crunchies' or 'Dutchmen'. Dad shook his head when he heard Heather and me ridiculing the Afrikaners. It was wrong, he said, to make sweeping statements about a whole group of people. We were prejudiced, which meant we were unfair. Afrikaners were also people, just like us, and we should respect them.

'Yeah, yeah, dad,' my big sister shrugged, looking across at some shaven-headed Afrikaner kids wrestling on the grass in a dark tangle of arms and legs. 'They're still rock-spiders.'

Dad knew many more Afrikaners than we did. On the breakdown gang at Eskom, back in the early 1950s, before he and mom were married, he worked with rough and tough Afrikaners as they repaired giant power station turbines. He was the only English-speaker on the maintenance team; but the men were sympathetic about how he'd had to abandon his university studies because his parents were too poor to pay his fees.

He told Heather and me sternly, as we giggled along the moon-lit promenade, that those Afrikaners were not rock-spiders. They were good working men – just like Granddad George.

We turned back to the Queens Hotel. Mom would soon fill the hotel lounge with the strains of 'Little White Dove' while dad enjoyed a whisky and maybe even a cigarette. Heather and I would be asleep in our adjoining rooms at the end of the long wooden-floored passage on the top floor.

I noticed two Afrikaans boys as they stalked our seaside walk. They pretended to be soldiers as they crept behind us, trying to hide behind bushes and trees, or leopard-crawling through the more brightly-lit stretches of the front. It was obvious that I was watching them watching me, but they didn't seem to care. They looked as if they were born to be soldiers, as if they were yearning for the day they could finally join the army, and be sent messages on *Forces Favourites*.

Each boy carried a long stick, which looked like a gun as they pointed it at me. They came closer and closer, weaving fast from one bush or tree to another, as if hunting me down.

I was just about to slip my hand into dad's, and show him the scuttling rock-spiders, when their game suddenly ended. They had seen a young black girl walking hurriedly across the road from us. I recognized her. She sold ice creams on the beach every day. Heather and I, and dad of course, must have been her three best customers.

The ice cream girl was always nice to us but it bothered me that she walked on a white beach like Orient. Her bare feet left foot-prints in the wet sand. I always made sure I stepped over her black footsteps. My feet were a lovely golden brown. Her feet were pitch black on top and yellowy white underneath. I was not sure she should be allowed to walk barefoot in the sand – especially when no other black person, apart from a sad cleaner in a blue overall, was seen on Orient beach.

She headed up a side-street where she would catch the black bus to the locations. Her feet were covered in white *tackies* [plim-soles]. She walked faster and faster and then, as she began to run, I saw the soldier boys were chasing her. Their sticks were raised above their heads as if they were about to beat her hard for walk-ing through a white area at night. She shrieked as she ran, but her long legs allowed her to escape the two boys who gave up the chase.

They turned to their parents who were laughing on the small balcony of Snyman's Hotel. '*Kyk na die kaffir!* [Look at the kaffir!]' the stockier boy shouted. '*Sy is net so bang!* [She's just so scared]'. My own mom and dad, leaning over an iron railing along the prom-enade, had not seen anything. I crept between them as they gazed at the ocean.

White breakers crashed loudly before rolling slowly in towards the shore. Tiny lights of fishing boats and container ships glimmered in the distance but the vast ocean swallowed up everything else. And the more I stared into the blackest sea, the less I saw.

Don McRae, Colin Mann Primary School, Germiston, 1970

CHAPTER FOUR

FIGHTING MEN

WE WENT TO PRETORIA early in 1970. As the extended McRae clan gathered for a military journey it felt like the night we all went to hear 'Donald, Where's Your Troosers?' But on a Sunday morning in February there were only nine of us. Outside my grandparents' house on Angus Street, my seventeen-year-old cousin, Brian Statham, was missing. At the outset of his nine months of National Service he had just completed six weeks of basic training at Voortrekkerhoogte.

There were two soldiers in our convoy to Brian's camp: Granddad George and my uncle Frier, who had fought briefly in World War II before he had been captured at the Battle of Tobruk in Libya and kept in an Italian prison camp for more than two years. In September 1944, having finally escaped after a dangerous hike across the Alps into Switzerland, Frier had made it all the way back to Germiston.

On his first Friday at home, there was a ball at the City Hall and Frier asked Laura, my dad's older sister and the girl who had written to him when he was a prisoner of war, if she would be his partner. All those years later, Frier still remembered the pretty blue dress she wore that night.

They were about to celebrate their twentieth wedding anniversary that month, just as they prepared to see their eldest son in army uniform. We were not officially at war in South Africa but there was a chance that Brian could be sent to the border to keep out the black terrorists.

Neither of them spoke about the border war but it seemed as if uncle Frier and Granddad George were quieter than usual as we climbed into the two cars. A war-time chain linked our family together, from my granddad to my uncle to my cousin.

At the end of our hour-long journey to Pretoria we stopped at the Voortrekker Monument. It was one way to kill time before we were allowed into base camp to see Brian. That monument to Afrikaner suffering consisted of a huge slab of cold granite perched on a hill on the southern fringes of Pretoria. Inside, the images of ox-wagons and determined Afrikaners were eerie and scary, as if reminding us that we were ruled by a crazy *volk* [people].

Two hours later, at the gated entrance to Voortrekkerhoogte, we were approached by a sentry. His face looked like it was made out of stone. The soldier ducked his head through dad's rolled-down window. I turned away when his eyes burned into me. He did not smile when he spoke to dad in Afrikaans. Granddad winked at me, as if to say we would be all right. But my stomach tightened. My two cousins on my mother's side of the family, Malcolm and Kevin, would soon follow Brian into the army. Brian's brother, Alan, would be next. And then it would be my turn.

Slowly, the gates opened and we headed up to the camp. The fields around us were covered by red dirt and dry grass. And then we saw them. Standing in straight lines, the new soldiers could not even glance at us. Each one of them looked straight ahead, as if frightened he might be shot if he even dared peek at his family.

Granddad George and my uncle watched the troops parading in front of them. But I stared instead at the amputated stump on Frier's right hand. He had lost the top half of his index finger in an accident with a washing machine, rather than in World War II, but it still looked spooky. I wished we could have been at a picnic instead, playing cricket and eating Peppermint Crisp chocolate.

When Brian was finally allowed to join us I hung back, feeling shy around my big cousin in uniform. His face, arms and the back of his neck were all brown; and the colour of his skin after so many weeks of marching in the hot sun was made even more obvious by the gleaming flashes of white beneath his shirt and high on his upper arms. Brian had a proper *Boere-tan* [farmer's tan]. But, unlike the *Boers* [Afrikaners], he still spoke English as he reassured us that he had survived basic training better than we might have thought. He had decided to enter the Signal Corps which, Granddad George said proudly, was reserved for the smarter infantrymen.

Brian said they were woken up at four every morning because there was a daily 4:30 a.m. inspection. Some of the soldiers slept on the concrete floor rather than their beds because they would be yelled at if the sheet on their bed was not folded so crisply that it made a perfect ninety degree angle at each corner. They had no black servants to help them here.

'I'm fine,' Brian murmured. 'But it's such a waste of time ...'

TIME ALSO SLIPPED PAST slowly at Colin Mann Primary School in Germiston when, studying the state syllabus of Christian National Education, we were shaped into devout young white South Africans. Our history lessons taught us that the country had come into official existence with the arrival of the first white settlers, led by Jan van Riebeeck, the Dutch commander, who reached the Cape on 6 April, 1652. We celebrated that date every year with a public holiday, Van Riebeeck's Day, while the old Dutch founder's face was plastered all over our cents and rands.

The settlers, both Boer and British, had fought the natives, especially the Zulus, before they turned their guns on each other. Our history classes also taught us that the Nationalist government had swept to power in 1948 with the new name of apartheid. These policies helped in geography as we learnt that the people of South Africa could be divided into four separate groups.

We studied ourselves, the Europeans, and cried out 'easy-peasy' when we were asked to fill in the various names of our 'dwellings'. Everyone knew that we 'dwelled' in houses and cottages and flats and hotels. Our 'transport' consisted of cars, taxis, planes and trains while our 'professions' included doctors, lawyers, engineers, architects, accountants and soldiers. We enjoyed 'activities' like sport, church, swimming, *braaivleis* [barbecues], gardening, dog-walking and sun-tanning. Our 'characteristics' saw us being described as wealthy, healthy, religious, educated and kind. We had Dutch and British roots, but our forebears came from all over Europe. We had founded the most advanced country in Africa.

The Coloureds were the closest in colour, culture and language to the Europeans. They were the third largest racial group and they spoke Afrikaans as a home language. Most Coloureds lived in the Cape and had a mix of white and black blood. They were polite and often worked in shops and cafés. On New Year's Day in Cape Town they participated in a colourful festival known as the Coon Carnival when they painted their faces white and danced and sang happy Malay songs.

Indians were the smallest group in South Africa, and they were darker than the Coloureds. They originally came from India to work in the sugar fields of Natal. Some Indians were educated and hard-working, but most found jobs as waiters or in factories. Indians had their own religions and customs and they were shy and reserved people.

We spent less time on the largest group, whom we were taught to call Bantu rather than natives. The Bantu were non-whites who were neither Coloured nor Indian. There were many kinds of Bantu and many different Bantu languages. Each Bantu belonged to a tribe which had its own customs. Bantu people were not educated and so they worked as labourers, cleaners and maids. They lived in locations, mud hats or servants' rooms in our gardens.

I didn't mind school, as boring as our lessons seemed, because at break we played marbles or our new yo-yo craze. We called ourselves the Yo-Yo people of Africa as we stood with our backs to the sun and spun the coloured discs of plastic along blurring strands of string. Twenty or thirty yo-yos, turning together, made a low white hum. Afterwards, like magicians in a circle, we shared our tricks and taught each other how to loop the loop, make a cradle, build the Eiffel Tower, wash the baby and walk the dog.

And then, after school ended at one-thirty, we would pour out onto the fields to do what we loved to do most: play sport. The badge on our green blazers told us all you needed to know about Colin Mann Primary School. It featured a cricket bat criss-crossed with a tennis racquet. A football and a smaller tennis ball were placed neatly above and below the bat and racquet with a logo of 'Play The Game' emblazoned across the bottom of our badge. We were sports-mad.

Every afternoon, except Friday, which was reserved for our own private matches in my garden, there would be cricket or football or tennis or athletics or swimming at Colin Mann – but never against an Afrikaans school. We preferred it that way. The idea of facing Afrikaners seemed almost as foreign as an impossible match against a team of alien black boys.

The only time I dared cross the divide was during school holidays when me and my best friend, Hilton Tanchum, a Jewish boy who lived on Frank Street, stole into the local Afrikaans primary. We both loved rugby and, on crisp winter days, we spent hour after hour trying to kick penalties through the school posts. Sometimes, if a passing Dutchman spotted us, we would get sworn at or told to watch out. They would come back and *donner* [hammer] us.

The bloody Afrikaners had turned the whole world against us. I came home from Colin Mann one late summer afternoon in March 1970 and, while demolishing one of my mother's culinary specials, melted cheese topped by Mrs Ball's Chutney, we listened to the last few overs as a great South African cricket team completed a 4-0 whitewash of Australia in Port Elizabeth. But the reaction to apartheid had become so fierce we were worried that Graeme Pollock, Barry Richards and Mike Proctor might never play another Test match again. The International Cricket Council had called for a vote on the permanent exclusion of South Africa from the world game.

We would eventually be banned and isolated from international sport forever. It was hard to believe that the world could be so cruel.

THE DAY OF THE first rugby Test between South Africa and New Zealand, on 25 July, 1970, was typical of a Highveld winter. Early-morning cold in Pretoria gave way to a cloudless sky and a high sun which, by noon, boomeranged off the bleached grass. Fifty miles away Germiston was quiet as, soon after lunch, I retreated upstairs with my transistor radio. It was too cold to swim in the refinery pool and I was too anxious about the rugby to be anywhere but home that afternoon. I sat alone in my room, looking out at the empty streets below.

It had been a long time since the Springboks had faced the All Blacks. New Zealand's planned tour of South Africa in 1967 had been cancelled after John Vorster's government refused to issue visas to any Maori rugby players. They insisted that the All Blacks had to be all white.

Yet, three years later, John Vorster backed down. He knew that if there was a choice between playing New Zealand and barring all Maoris, most white people would side with rugby. In South Africa an oval ball was the only thing which, sometimes, could seem more important than the colour of a man's skin. The Maoris would be allowed into the republic as 'honorary whites', which meant they could play rugby against the Springboks as well as stay in white hotels and attend white functions. As long as the tour lasted they would be as good as white.

Four 'non-whites' were included in the All Black squad. There were three Maoris in Syd Going, Blair Furlong and Bluff Milner and a nineteen-year-old Samoan wing called Bryan Williams. I was just as excited that the All Blacks included a centre, Ian MacRae, who had the exact same name as my dad, apart from that extra 'a' in his surname. But our newspapers were fascinated by the 'dark flashing looks' and 'brilliant white smile' of the Samoan teenager.

In his first match on tour, Williams appeared as an All Black saviour in Bethlehem, a cold and small town in the Orange Free State. He sliced through some helpless Afrikaners and scored two sparkling tries. Williams was then approached by cheering coloured spectators after the All Blacks won their next game, an easy win over Griqualand West in Kimberley.

We knew why they ran onto the pitch from the small non-white section of the ground. Coloured and black South Africans always supported the overseas team. It was the only way they could beat white South Africa. As Williams shook hands with the happy bunch they were intercepted by a group of Afrikaans fans. A white man hit one of the coloureds before each side reached for bricks, bottles and pieces of wood to use against each other. It took the police ten minutes to separate the usually segregated men.

A spokesman for the New Zealand team suggested later that, 'this hard core of white spectators destroyed two weeks of wonderful welcomes in this oh-so-pleasant land.' We wondered anxiously what Bryan Williams made of it all because we were desperate to be liked.

Dad explained again that people overseas were unhappy because there were no black players in the Springbok side. But our natives didn't even like rugby. How could we select a black boy who had never played the game and might even be frightened of the Afrikaners in his team?

Mof Myburgh and Hannes Marais, our hulking prop forwards, would never allow a black hooker to dangle between them in the front row. In a scrum, sweaty faces brushed against sweaty bottoms. Huge hands and heads were pushed between tree-trunk legs. A great Afrikaner lock like Frik du Preez would never put his head between Mof's legs and those of a black boy.

Hilton and I mocked the Afrikaners at a distance, knowing that they could turn us black and blue. Even when they called themselves names like *'Mannetjies'* [Little Man] Roux and 'Tiny' Naude they couldn't fool us. Rugby meant everything to the Boers. And so behind their backs we called them 'rock-spiders'. But, for eighty minutes against the All Blacks, we loved the Afrikaners madly. We rolled those suddenly gorgeous names round our mouths as if we had been born on the *platteland* [flat-land/rural areas] ourselves, speaking sugary Afrikaans as we said:

'*Man, daardie Mannetjies!* [Man, that little man!]' or '*Ja, net soos Tiny!* [Yes, just like Tiny!]'

Our rivalry with the All Blacks was intense. Boy Louw, a former Springbok captain, had said in 1949 that, 'When South Africa plays New Zealand consider your country at war.' Our sportswriters used that quote in 1970 when revealing that the Springboks had gone into hiding. They developed secret battle strategies while South Africa's hard-bitten coach, Johan Claassen, urged the Boks to die for their country. The All Blacks, meanwhile, were driven to a frenzy by Ivan 'The Terrible' Vodanovich, a suspiciously Russian-sounding surname. He might have been a communist had he not been so obsessed with rugby.

That Saturday afternoon a stray black man trudged towards the station at the bottom of Whitfield Road, which ran adjacent to the street where we lived. As the commentator read out the names of the New Zealand players who would take the field at Loftus Versveld, the walker lifted his black hat in greeting. He held it in the air as if offering his own private salute to the All Blacks. Then he strolled towards the shade of a tree where Maggie answered his wave. She was knitting a red jersey. Holding a ball of wool and two needles in one hand, she used the other to welcome him.

Even through the closed windows I could hear their laughter and the odd shouted word of an African language I didn't understand. Our black and white worlds seemed far apart then as, turning up my radio, I watched them share a cigarette on her blanket under the tree. I doubted that Maggie even knew the Springboks were about to face the mighty All Blacks.

Maggie and her friend kept talking and laughing loudly. She was always chatting and joking with the natives who hung around our corner, opposite the Greek-owned store and the gambling ring which had frightened me on our first night in Germiston. When she was not working, Maggie was far happier sitting on the grass outside our house than spending time in her backroom.

In Pretoria, the two teams ran out. New Zealand were first and then, to a roaring bellow, South Africa emerged from the tunnel. I shivered in anticipation. Just after 3:30, the green-and-gold shirts of the white Springboks crashed into the black shirts of the white, Maori and Samoan-born New Zealanders. The ball was driven forward before, like a hot breath of dry wind from across the border and his native South-West Africa, the Springbok flanker Jan Ellis tore away on a gusting run. He was finally brought down and, from the resulting scrum, his fellow flanker, Piet Greyling, hacked the ball ahead. There was a small explosion on my radio as the commentator screamed. Dawie de Villiers, our golden-haired scrum-half, had reached the ball first and dived across the line. It had taken the Springboks just four minutes to score the first try of the series.

South Africa were soon cruising at an altitude of 6,000 feet with an unbelievable scoreline of 12-0. But the All Blacks fought back. A penalty and a try closed the gap. Bryan Williams, with a devastating jitterbug, intercepted a looping pass and sidestepped a couple of Springboks before flying over in the corner for a try that was then worth three points. I looked out of my bedroom window and over the brick wall, down at Maggie. Her friend had left to catch his township train. She sat alone, oblivious to the breakthrough of the Blacks. A cigarette dangled from her lips as her steel knitting needles flashed in the fading sunshine.

Six points behind and with less than five minutes left, New Zealand were awarded a penalty. Going, the bald Maori scrumhalf, took a tap-kick and set the black shirts rolling forward. And then my and Hilton's favourite player, Syd Nomis, the Jewish wing who had big sideburns and wore flared trousers away from rugby, intercepted a desperate move and hared away from the chasing

New Zealanders. As he ran, the Afrikaans commentator Gerhard Viviers barked out his name again and again: 'Siddy! Siddy! Siddy! Siddy!'

Siddy crossed the Blacks' line with a sparkling plunge. South Africa had won, with the conversion lifting the final score to a resounding 17-6 victory. I did a jitterbug around the radio, only breaking away to see if Maggie had heard the shouts from inside the surrounding houses.

But, on the darkening street below, Maggie had pulled her blanket around her. I watched her slip a bottle out of her bag. I guessed it was gin, for mom and dad scolded her for drinking too much. Maggie took a slug, with no sign she would feel either joy or sorrow if she knew the score from Pretoria

THAT WINTER Hilton and I followed the rugby fervently as South Africa clinched a 3-1 series win, with the final Test a 20-17 humdinger in Johannesburg. The only eerie moment came that evening when I phoned Hilton to hear what it had been like to be at Ellis Park. He and his dad, as Transvaal season ticket-holders, had been at the Test.

Hilton said it had been the most amazing afternoon of his life. But I clutched the phone a little tighter when he told me how the rickety wooden stand to the left of where they always sat had almost collapsed whenever the All Blacks scored. I had been to Ellis Park often enough with the Tanchums to know he meant the small non-white enclosure of a few hundred natives.

He felt uneasy when he saw how the natives danced and whooped, until the stand quivered, in support of the All Blacks. It was obvious that they hated us so much they would rather love a team from the other side of the world. We thought it was incredible they had not been locked up by the police, or *donnered* [hammered] within an inch of their lives by the Afrikaans rugby fans who surrounded them at Ellis Park.

But we didn't linger long over the natives. We moved on to celebrate the fact we were the unofficial champions of the world in both rugby and cricket. It made us feel very proud.

Yet Bryan Williams, who played sensationally throughout the tour, had done something far more exotic. He was almost one of us, an honorary white, and he received 1,500 letters of thanks from South Africa on his return to New Zealand. We owed him that much. Bryan Williams had become a hero in a white country, an amazing feat for a coloured man in a black shirt.

THE DAY AFTER that fourth Test victory was a muted Sunday in Germiston. No-one was sure when we might play international sport again. That afternoon I sat on our garden wall and watched the street entertainment on our corner of Cachet Road. I had long since worked out that the gamblers across the road used their games as a cover for the business they ran from the drains adjoining our garden. Bottles of African beer, of gin and brandy, were stashed underground and sold to passing natives walking to the station. Whenever someone wanted to buy a bottle he would take up a spot in the gambling corner and make that familiar cry:

'*Tsa-huuuhhh! Tsa-huuuhhh!*'

That was a sign for a man that dad called 'The Godfather' to send over one of his boys to the drains. There, the chosen native would lift up the cement covering to the drain and reach down into the hidden depths. He would bring out the brown bottles of home-brew which everyone called '*kaffir-beer*'. If the moaning and groaning from the gamblers grew louder it was a warning that the lookout on the far corner had spotted a blue police van. It was better to be caught running a dice-game than a drinking den – and so there would be just enough time to stash the bottles back in the drain.

My favourite runner to the drains was a native called Cassius. He named himself after Cassius Clay, who had since become Muhammad Ali. On the day I met him he entranced me. Cassius chased after the football I had kicked over our garden ball by mistake. He scooped the ball up with his foot and flicked it onto his knee. Cassius juggled the ball like a black-faced clown, shifting it from his knee to a shoulder before letting it settle magically on his thigh. He pulled faces and sang a strange song: 'Ali, Ali, float like a butterfly, sting like a bee, Ali, Ali, Muhammad Ali.'

And then he flipped the ball over my garden wall and dropped down into a hunched boxing pose. 'Put your hands up, *baasie* [little boss],' he whispered. 'Come on, float wit' me, sting wit' me!' He threw punches at the winter sunshine as his huge feet danced in front of him. His breath snagged huskily at the back of his throat.

'*Jy is die baas . . . jy is die baas!* [You are the master . . . you are the master!]' he said as he boxed against his shadow. His words chugged in a way that made him sound like a train.

The gamblers dissolved into laughter. 'Don't worry, *baasie*,' one of the natives called out to me. 'Cassius is just crazy.'

I waved to Cassius that sleepy Sunday afternoon when he sauntered over to a truck crammed with white men. They were still celebrating the Springboks defeat of the All Blacks. There were four men in the back and two up front. They wore an assortment of safari suits and string vests. Samson often did business with whites on the Sabbath. Everyone knew that, apart from the churches, everything else was shut on a Sunday. Our sewer was one of the few places in Germiston where a white man could buy a drink.

Cassius took their order and soon dragged up the booty – half jacks of brandy and some quarts of Black Label. Afrikaners would not drink '*kaffir-beer*' unless they were desperate.

From the top of my garden wall I watched Cassius float back across the street like he was Ali, or a fluttering black butterfly. The white men in the truck glared at him, as if they suspected he might have cheered on the All Blacks. But Cassius liked boxing rather than rugby.

Cassius handed over the hooch to the Afrikaners with a curious bow. He rubbed his hands together more nervously, as if he was trying to wash them.

Instead of paying him, the driver smashed his head into Cassius's face. As blood arced out of Cassius's nose, the men in the truck jumped out. A knee sank into Cassius's face, splitting his top lip. He fell to the ground. The men kicked him until he looked crumpled and dead.

I slid from the wall and ran inside. Mom and dad would help Cassius. I ran to my parents' bedroom, overlooking the street corner where Cassius had been attacked. He twitched on the tar as the white men circled him.

'Ian,' my mom told dad, 'call the police ...'

Dad reached for the phone while black people milled around silently, watching Cassius lift his head. He had left a flat red pillow of blood on the street. Maggie, inside our garden, spoke softly to The Godfather through the slats of the fence. Eventually, dad went out to join her.

'Be careful,' mom said anxiously.

When they arrived the police turned first to Cassius, lifting him up and dumping him into the back of their van. They then picked out The Godfather and forced him into the same caged hold.

Dad spoke to the policemen. He was told to step aside for this was a police raid on an illegal shebeen. The men who had cracked open Cassius's head watched the van roar off with their two black prisoners. They laughed like hyenas as they climbed into their truck.

When he joined us upstairs again, dad turned my head away from the black natives on the street. 'It'll be all right,' he said, as I began to cry, my tears leaving wet streaks on his pale blue shirt.

Heather and Don McRae, 1971

CHAPTER FIVE

THE FIRE

DOWN IN PARADISE, at the bottom of Africa, life regained its peaceful rhythm. The attack on our street seemed so strange it soon faded into the background. Cassius returned to his corner after a week. He was a more subdued figure, but he still ran the odd job for Samson. The shebeen itself seemed unaffected by either the violence or the brief jailing of Cassius and Samson.

We were more interested in one obvious change. Samson, The Godfather, had become Maggie's new boyfriend. Maggie talked loudly to most of her friends, but with Samson she spoke in a low murmur. She smiled sweetly at him, showing the gap between her front teeth. He often poured a sneaky splash of gin into Maggie's cup to blunt the sweetness of the Fanta Orange she drank on Thursday afternoons.

Maggie worked every Thursday morning and then she would have the rest of the day and that evening free from work. Thursday was known across South Africa as Maid's Day Off, and so Thursdays were popular nights to eat out and avoid the washing-up in the maid's absence. In our house Maggie also didn't work on Saturday afternoons and evenings, unless my parents were having a dinner party, or after lunch on Sunday. Those were the times you were likely to find her at the same spot on the corner of Cachet Road, usually in the shadow of Samson.

The Godfather had a huge stomach. His gut was so large it looked as if he was carrying a giant watermelon inside his bulging shirt. I once saw a button pop off Samson's shirt and hit Maggie on the top of her coloured *doek*. She didn't seem to mind and, instead, kept talking gently to the big man. Maggie also ignored the match-stick which usually jutted from the corner of Samson's mouth while he chewed steadily on the splintering wood, as if eating match-sticks was his attempt to diet.

Our girl and her boyfriend took a big risk together on many nights in the backyard. Once, on a Thursday evening, Maggie and Samson were a little drunk. Dad and I stepped outside as they stag-gered up our driveway. Maggie waved and shouted: 'Samson is walking me home, master!'

The fact that less than a hundred yards separated our front gate from her pavement corner did not matter. Maggie still required a gentleman escort to her room.

Dad reminded Maggie that she needed to be careful. It was almost dark and Samson was not allowed on our property. The gov-ernment had just introduced a new law. Every white suburb in South Africa, including Lambton, had been declared 'White by Night'. This made us safe in our beds because it meant no native was allowed on the street at night. And no black boy or girl could stay on a white property unless they were employed as a servant. Every other black person was meant to go back to the locations, as we still called the townships.

Under the new law, The Godfather and his gamblers had to dis-appear when darkness fell. It was like they had become vampires in reverse. They would surely shrivel and die, or at least be locked up in prison, if they were seen out on a white street in the black of night.

'Samson can't stay here,' dad reminded Maggie.

'Yes, master,' Maggie nodded gravely. 'He is just taking me to my room.'

'And then, Samson,' dad said sternly, 'you must leave.'

'Yes, master,' Samson said with an extravagant bow of his head.

'OK,' dad said, before slipping into the language of the natives: *'Hambe kachle.'*

'Hambe kachle' was Zulu for 'go well' or, more plainly, 'be careful'. I wasn't sure if Maggie or Samson were Zulus. They were just natives to me; but I knew they understood.

'Thank you, master,' Samson said.

'Night-night, masters,' Maggie crooned to me and dad.

We soon heard the iron gates open at the bottom of the garden as Samson left before the first police patrol cruised past.

But some nights, perhaps even most nights, Samson came back once we were all in bed. Dad sometimes heard the squeaky gate open. Jumping out of bed, dad would stand on the balcony in his shortie pyjamas and check it was Samson, rather than a burglar, stealing up our driveway.

Dad often went back to bed when he saw it was Samson. But some nights he would walk down the carpeted landing and into the bathroom which overlooked the backyard. Dad would open the window and wait for the moment when Samson scaled the locked back gate. He'd call down to Samson then, as softly as he could so he didn't wake our Afrikaans neighbours. Dad would remind Samson that, if the police caught him in Maggie's room, he'd end up in jail. And dad would be given a big fine.

Samson's gut hung over the gate as, in mid-air, he listened to dad. And then, because he knew we were White by Night, he clambered down again.

'Yes, master,' he would say before disappearing into the darkness. 'Sorry, master.'

The next morning, dad would remind Maggie that Samson could not sleep in her room. We would all end up in jail if she kept taking such risks.

'Yes, master,' Maggie said softly. 'Sorry, master.'

SUMMER AFTERNOONS on the Highveld could be electrifying. The intense heat of a long African day often built up storm clouds that rolled across the previously pale blue sky like black and grey tanks. They rose up quickly while, as furiously as sudden gunfire, lightning flared and thunder boomed. Heather and I felt small and frightened then, especially one late Tuesday afternoon when the approach of another thunderstorm sent a chill through us. In the spreading darkness we could hear the screams and growls of the two small monkeys our neighbours, the Oosthuizens, kept in a large cage in their garden.

We raced to find Maggie, for she was looking after us that afternoon. Tucked away in her room, with Shandy the cocker spaniel, we gazed again at the sight of her bed stacked high on its piles of bricks. We clambered up and breathed in the fumes of gin and Vicks Vapour Rub.

As the heavy clouds burst open, letting loose giant white hailstones which hammered against Maggie's tin roof, I looked at the photographs of her two children. It was hard to believe Maggie was their mother. We listened to the hail and rain and jumped every time another lightning bolt lit up the yard outside. As a diversion we eventually hung upside down, draped over the side of Maggie's bed, and tried to soothe Shandy as she whimpered.

When the storm finally passed, leaving only the steady drip of rainwater from the old gutters, the air outside smelt fresh and sweet. All the dust and heat had gone. Maggie took us back inside our house – to feed and bath us before my parents returned from an early evening work function.

Late that night, when we were all dead to the world, a different storm broke. We were woken by the sound of Shandy barking dementedly. I sleepily followed my agitated father as he raced past my bedroom to the bathroom window so that he could look down at the commotion below. I stood on a chair behind him as he called out to the blue uniformed men when they vaulted our iron gate. They kept on shouting and shining their torches so that ghostly shadows spread across the white backyard wall.

When they emerged from Maggie's room, having manacled Samson, dad was already downstairs. In his pyjamas, he tried to convince the Afrikaner officer that they should not arrest Samson. The big black man stood silently in the centre of the courtyard, dressed in a vest and trousers with his hands cuffed and his feet bound. He watched the white policeman and Maggie's master, my dad, argue his fate. We all knew who would win the battle. The officer soon pushed past my father and shoved Samson towards the blue van parked halfway down our drive.

Dad knew Samson had broken the law. As the policeman slammed the door shut behind Samson, and the engine fired into life, I watched my father walk down the passageway to Maggie's room, to remind her that, in the civilized suburbs, we were strictly White by Night.

ONE-ARMED GRANDDAD SCOTT, my mother's father, lived with us for more than half my childhood. He was a short, tubby man from Glasgow who had lost his right arm in 1938, when my mother was just ten. Alec Scott had worked then as a rope-maker in a Germiston engineering factory, Haggie Rand. He had slipped on the shop floor and fallen into a giant wire-rope-making machine. It yanked him into its whirring grip and sliced through his upper arm. The limb was left dangling by threads of flesh above the elbow. He was rushed to hospital, while his severed arm was supported by a white-faced co-worker. At Germiston Hospital, the doctors decided on an immediate amputation.

My mother was then at Germiston South, a primary school just a few blocks from the hospital, but she only heard the news when she got home that afternoon. She screamed, and ran to her room. Mom already knew my dad, because they went to the same school, but she would never have spoken to him about her father then. Jess Scott was a year older than Ian McRae and moved in a different world. He had no idea what had just happened to the girl who would eventually be his wife for almost sixty years.

Granddad Scott had been depressed for weeks after the accident. He was only forty-six, but it seemed as if part of his life ended on the day they took his arm away. It was difficult to imagine how he could ever work again because he had always used his hands to make a living. Before he came to South Africa he had been a ship-builder in Renfrew, west of Glasgow. Equipped best for manual work, he and my grandmother, Isobel, had been afraid he would lose his job.

Yet, because he was a practical man, granddad found the strength to overcome his missing arm. Impressed by his courage, his company offered him a supervisory role as a factory foreman. Alec taught himself to write with his left hand and to drive a car with only one arm. I liked the story of how he had always stuck out his artificial arm when he needed to signal a right turn. In those long-gone days, he explained, cars operated without indicators.

We were far more modern. My mother had just given up her spluttering white MG which, when she flicked a switch, shot out a small orange stick on either the left or the right side of the car to indicate the direction of our next turn. She now drove a little dark green Austin which had the same flashing indicators, at the back and front, as dad's grey Holden.

Granddad Scott had since abandoned his artificial arm. When he went out, he wore a navy sports jacket, a white shirt and tie, neatly-ironed grey trousers and black shoes. Granddad would tuck his armless right sleeve into the pocket of his jacket so it never flapped. It was different at home. He wore short-sleeve shirts and the white remains of his right arm protruded nakedly. If he was about to read his latest cowboy novel in the garden he would smother his pale stump with lotion so it wouldn't burn. I always yelped whenever he jokingly asked me in his Glaswegian accent to rub sun-cream into his amputated arm.

Granddad Scott was different from most white South Africans. They would jump in the car rather than take a five-minute stroll; but each weekday morning he walked three miles from our house to the Germiston library. Once there, and having swapped his book, he sat on a bench under a huge oak tree and looked up at the Cenotaph erected in honour of all the hundreds of men from Germiston who had died in World War II. But, most of all, he chatted to the same old men who met him every day on the library concourse. They yakked away and watched the world rush past. At eleven o'clock they would wander over to the Wimpy Bar on Victoria Street for coffee, before granddad set out on his walk back home for lunch.

I didn't know any other white person who would walk six miles a day for pleasure, but granddad didn't mind that every other walker seemed to be a native. He knew he was white because no black person was allowed to sit on the bench, enter the library or drink a coffee at the Wimpy. The signs gave everyone the same stark message: Europeans Only/*Slegs Blanke* [Whites Only].

In 1971, granddad was just a year short of his eightieth birthday but he stuck to his walking routine. He had been living with us for almost three years as he divided his time between our family and that of his son, Duncan, my uncle, who lived with his wife, Bobbie, and my three cousins, Malcolm, Kevin and Gail, on the other side of Germiston.

Malcolm had just lost his toe during his year of compulsory military service. Assigned to the Technical Services Corps in Pretoria, he had been guiding a crane when a heavy container smashed down on his foot. His big toe was crushed and it soon turned so black and *vrot* ['rotten'] that the army doctor decided to cut it off. It seemed as if we were becoming a family of amputees – with my granddad's arm stump, my uncle's lost index finger and my cousin's missing toe. The only consolation for Malcolm was that his injury meant he was assigned to permanent light duty for the rest of his army stint and spared any future camps.

Granddad Scott became the first person to hear of my worry about the army. Sitting next to me on the green garden swing under the berry tree one afternoon, his stump gestured at the black and white football that lay untouched in the middle of the lawn. He didn't need to say anything else for we both knew that, usually, I would be deep in a game of fantasy football, pretending to be playing for one of my two favourite teams – Germiston Callies, in the whites-only South African first division, or Arsenal, closing in on an historic league and FA Cup double in England.

But, that day, I sat mutely on the swing. It was only when Granddad Scott started talking that I opened up. I'd been thinking about Malcolm, and how I didn't want to go into the army. 'Och,' granddad said gruffly, 'that's years away. I wouldnae fret if I were you.'

I couldn't help myself. I was destined to follow my cousins into a dirty brown uniform and be hollered at by an Afrikaner sergeant for a year or more. A big cloud hung over my future.

Granddad Scott told me how different it had been for him when he was young. He had wanted to become a soldier in Scotland. But unlike Granddad George, who was six years younger than him, he had been barred from military service in 1914. Granddad Scott was devastated when he received the order that he had to remain working in the shipyards. It was more important that he helped build battleships. He knew now that they had been right, and Germany had been defeated, but at the time he had felt bitter regret.

It was enough to make my head spin. I had one granddad who had lied about his age to join the army, and another who wished fervently he could have become a soldier. My old granddad from Glasgow explained the difference. He and Granddad George knew who they were fighting. I was less certain about the identity of our enemy. It couldn't be the natives because they already worked for us. So why did all white boys have to go into the army?

'Don't worry about it, wee man,' Granddad Scott said again. And then, to make me laugh, he leaned over and, using his stump like a magic wand, tickled me in the ribs.

I tried hard to stop giggling on the swing but granddad's short arm kept finding a gap between my tightly folded arms. I twitched this way and that, attempting to look serious, but the stump got me every time. It nuzzled and kneaded my ticklish ribs until I thought I would burst with laughter.

ON MY TENTH BIRTHDAY, in April 1971, I chose a special treat. The whole family went to see an old Laurel & Hardy film called *Block-Heads* at the Roxy Cinema in downtown Germiston. Mom was unimpressed by my choice of a 1938 black-and-white slapstick movie but I thought it was hilarious. Even Granddad George stayed awake the whole film when, typically, he fell asleep every Friday night at the Roxy as soon as the MGM Lion roared and the opening credits rolled.

In *Block-Heads*, our ridiculous chums, Stan Laurel and Ollie

Hardy, played the part of two World War I soldiers. Stan had the task of guarding a trench while Ollie went 'over the top' with a lurch and a trip. This was just the start of the farce because, twenty years later, Ollie opened a newspaper to read that Stan has been discovered guarding that same old trench. Granddad George almost tumbled out of his red velvet seat with owlish hoots and chuckles as Ollie rescued Stan.

Six hours later, we were fast asleep. It had been a long and happy day; but we were shocked awake at ten minutes past two in the morning.

The banging made it sound as if our front door was being broken down by murderous burglars. I sat up in bed, goose bumps spreading like tiny welts as I heard my mother cry out to dad that he should call the police. But what if it was the police themselves, storming our house after they'd found Samson hiding again in Maggie's room?

Dad hurtled downstairs, looking more scared, but eerily determined, than I had ever seen him.

He was confused by the time he reached the front door because the banging had stopped. From the top of the stairs I watched him hesitate as mom pulled on her dressing gown. The noise started again. This time it came from the back of the house.

Mom's breath hissed between her teeth as she tried to calm me and Heather. Our attackers were attempting to bludgeon their way through the back door.

The curtains running across the back kitchen window had been drawn, and dad had to pull them open to face the danger. He stepped back in surprise. The face at the window was white. It belonged to an Afrikaner; but Frikkie Oosthuizen was neither a rampaging policeman nor a violent burglar. He was our next-door neighbour, a thin man with a blond moustache. Frikkie shouted but dad could not hear him above a crackling roar. It was only when he turned his head in the direction of Frikkie's finger that he saw the fierce glow.

Our garage was on fire, the flames spreading fast as they curled around the wooden beams and shot over our two parked cars – mom's new Austin and dad's old Holden. An oily rag near the hood of the Holden had started to smoulder five minutes earlier. That morning, after checking the oil and water in our two cars, dad had tossed the cloth onto the workbench. It must have landed on top of the light bulb which, after it had been turned on for a few hours, gave off such heat that the rag eventually burst into flames.

Dad raced back inside to shout instructions to mom. Frikkie's wife had already called the fire brigade but we all needed to escape the house.

Granddad Scott's thin white hair, which was cut very short and normally plastered down in a Brylcreem-topped side-parting, stood askew on his head. He was dressed in pyjama bottoms and a white vest. His small stump waved in the air. Granddad already had a plan in mind. He hustled round the shadowy garden with a hosepipe. Wrapping the end around his stump he scuttled down the back alley behind Maggie's room so that he could reach the garage more quickly.

Maggie had, by then, joined us. She had wrapped a blanket around her waist and pulled a red cardigan over her white night-shirt. It was strange to see her bare head because it was normally covered by her *doek*. Her hair looked like little black peppercorns which she rubbed anxiously as she ran back and forth to tell us what was happening.

Granddad Scott aimed arcs of water into the burning garage but, risking everything, dad had decided to rescue the two cars before they exploded. He made it to the Holden first, yelping in pain as the scalding cement floor burnt the soles of his bare feet. Dad turned the ignition and the engine sparked into life first time, without turning into a petrol-fuelled fireball. He reversed the car out of the garage and sent it screaming backwards down the drive.

Mom shouted, begging him not to go back for the Austin, but dad had made up his mind. 'It'll explode if I don't,' he hollered, ignoring the fact that it could erupt into flames as soon as he reached it. But dad took his chance as Granddad Scott continued his one-armed fight against the fire. Dad ran back into the garage, scorching his feet even more badly, and climbed inside the small green car.

In the driveway we heard the Austin splutter and start. We watched our hero, dad, reverse down the drive. He had made it, but he ran quickly on his blistered feet to relieve Granddad Scott of his hosepipe. Our seventy-nine-year-old granddad switched his attention to the buckets of water Frikkie was filling at the outside tap. Granddad Scott took over at the tap and filled bucket after bucket for Frikkie to hurl at the blaze. Dad, meanwhile, aimed his hosepipe at the centre of the fire. They were still helpless and the entire garage was soon consumed by flames. There were only a few minutes left before the house would start burning.

But Heather and I had begun to dance and cheer because two fire engines, sirens blaring, had swept up the drive. A dozen fire-fighters jumped down and unleashed the giant water-guns which dwarfed dad's hosepipe. Dad and granddad got out of the way as the firemen poured forward in thrilling symmetry, the uniform clatter of their boots and the hissing stream of water on the driveway making them sound like a fire-eating army.

It did not take them long to win the battle. In five minutes the fire had been extinguished. The garage was transformed from a roaring tinderbox into a blackened shell. Smoke swirled in damp clouds around the backyard, and the burnt rafters of the garage roof glowed in the dark.

'You must have forgotten to blow out all your birthday candles,' my old granddad said as his stump wiped the sweat from his face.

In the ghostly light he looked like the small, brave Scottish soldier he had wanted to be more than fifty years before.

A S THE SON OF A maintenance worker, and the son-in-law of a rope-maker, dad had risen to an unexpected place. He was a big shot in the company which his father had served humbly for four-and-a-half decades. Granddad George continued to work as the caretaker and groundsman at our local high school. He still needed the money at the age of seventy-three.

It was different for dad, and he was soon offered his latest job. In September 1971, just days before he turned forty-two, Ian McRae became the first manager of Eskom's Central Generating Undertaking [CGU]. Deep down he felt too young and inexperienced to control the country's generation of electricity, but mom reminded him of his strengths in his new position.

Dad could talk to anyone, and he would listen to the hopes and fears of the lowliest power station worker. He would be away from home more often as he travelled from one station to another in his bid to talk to thousands of workers and capture their support for his new organization.

I already thought dad worked too hard and, secretly, I worried he would fall down dead from a heart attack. We would be lost without him, and he'd just had a lucky escape in our flaming garage. But there was no stopping him. He loved his new job and each week he came back with stories about the ordinary artisans and manual workers he had met at far-off power stations. Dad felt a bond with them because he'd once worked as a fitter and turner. And then, after his degree, he had insisted on completing his apprenticeship as a maintenance man in steaming boiler and turbine rooms. He had done the same rough-and-ready work as his own dad and so it was easy for him to talk to the many men he now managed.

When he was young a couple of natives, Dummy and Big John, had also taught him two valuable lessons. Dummy had been the black groundsman at Eskom's Simmerpan property, where dad had grown up. Everyone called him 'Dummy' because he was deaf and dumb. He looked after the bowling green and the clay courts of the Eskom tennis club.

Dad imitated Dummy for our benefit. He made a haunting moan that sounded like it had bounced back off a wall. It seemed as if dad was trying to say words which never escaped his mouth. They stuck in the back of his throat and, to convey Dummy's frustration, dad shook his head as he made that strangled sound.

'But Dummy was always smiling,' dad said in amazement. Dad made it sound as if a deaf and dumb native was one of the most special people he had ever met.

We also heard the story of Big John. We weren't sure if 'John' was his proper name as this was still dad's favourite nickname for most natives. Years before, Big John and my dad had worked together on the turbines, deep in the Orange Free State. Big John was 'the boss boy', the main native at Vierfontein Power Station.

As dad had just joined the team, he had to endure a two-week stint away from home with the breakdown gang. It seemed disastrous to a newly married man. One Saturday afternoon, while cleaning blades on the stationary turbines at Vierfontein, dad felt sorry for himself. He wished he was back home in Germiston, skippering a fast-moving yacht through the sunlit waters of Victoria Lake, while his new wife waited to join him for a few drinks after sailing.

Dad's mood was gloomy but, alongside him, Big John sang a joyous African song as he worked. Eventually, dad turned in bemusement to Big John. 'Don't you get tired of this job?' he asked.

Big John laughed and exclaimed '*Aikona!* [No way!]' He then spoke firmly. 'I need to earn enough for my family. I must always do a good job.'

Dad felt ashamed to have been so miserable. He knew Big John would never sail a yacht or get a chance to move off the turbine team. Yet he still sang and smiled as he worked. We should remember Dummy and Big John, dad said, and appreciate our good luck.

Maggie heard our dinnertime conversations; but our lessons in understanding and respect had their limits. She prepared and cooked our food. But Maggie's meal would be placed separately on her plate in the warming oven while she waited for us to finish so that she might then wash the dishes. We never once thought of asking Maggie to join us at the table. She was a servant, and it would have felt unnatural if anyone had suggested Maggie might eat a hot meal at our table rather than an hour later on her bed in the backroom once she had finished her chores for the night.

Anyway, we thought Maggie preferred eating on her own, in her linen overall and red slippers. We had our way of living, and she had hers. That's why we were so happy together.

When we had guests for dinner, mom placed a silver bell on our immaculate table. At the end of every course, mom rang the bell delicately until Maggie opened the door and wheeled in the Hostess tray. Maggie would say 'Good evening, master' and 'Hello, madam' if our visitors offered her a greeting. Her task was to clear the plates from the table and load them onto the Hostess, which contained the next course either on the hot tray below or the cool upper shelf.

Occasionally, if it was just my aunt and uncle, or close friends of my parents, Heather and I might be allowed to join them at the table. I'd get a turn then to ring the bell and summon Maggie. It made me feel important as Maggie rushed in, her brown face covered in a sheen of sweat from cooking in a boiling kitchen. And so our normal pattern of life continued, as neat as the pristine white serviette Maggie folded into a perfect triangle next to the little silver bell I loved to ring. It made me feel as if, just like dad, I was the boss.

Ian McRae with a Zulu tribal dancing chief, 1973

CHAPTER SIX

THE DEATH OF A SOLDIER

ON THE FIRST DAY of May, 1973, another stint of family conscription began. My cousin Kevin Scott was taken to Germiston Station early that Tuesday morning to start his national service. I was in my final year of primary school, lost in the bliss of playing football, cricket and tennis every afternoon, of riding my bike and larking around in suburban swimming pools. We also loved movies and pretending we didn't like girls, even if we were secretly smitten by Jenny Allman and Nicola Price. Our biggest problem in life was being caught sneaking another lingering look at Jenny's brown legs or Nicola's flawless blonde bob. The ribbing would be merciless – and we'd flush angrily at the horrifying insult that we might fancy an actual girl.

I was in awe of my cousin because Kevin was a great runner and rugby player. Six years older than me, his life was about to change forever. It seemed bad enough that he faced ten months in the army; but Kevin had been posted to Walvis Bay. Even the name sounded bleak and mysterious.

We knew Walvis Bay was almost 2,000 kilometres from Johannesburg in the forsaken desert of South-West Africa. The distance meant he would only return home once in the next ten months – because it took three days on a slow train to reach the camp which was called Rooikop [meaning Redhead]. Conscripts at the most notorious base in the South African Defence Force suffered more than ordinary soldiers.

At eighteen, Kevin relied on his mother's long weekly letters with their news of family and home. They helped him through basic training. He always wrote back to his parents, telling them he had few problems with the physical rigours of basics out in the desert. The real test lay in the mind.

He described the psychological shock that took hold of him at Rooikop. Kevin said there was nothing to see but sand and sky. He was woken every morning at four and, alongside bleary-eyed fellow soldiers, yelled at by corporals. They were intent on breaking every single conscript. And so they set about stripping away the soft layers that had comforted the boys back home. They made the new soldiers feel raw and vulnerable.

Kevin battled against sleep deprivation and the cold that seeped into his bones. He had been assigned to the armoured division. This meant he would end up on the border, holding back the terrorists from SWAPO, who were trying to wrest South-West Africa from South Africa so that they could declare the independent state of Namibia.

He thought his time on the border, in the Caprivi Strip, a 400-kilometre stretch of land adjoining South Africa, South-West Africa and Botswana, had some perks. Kevin had been promised danger pay and two beers a day. In the midday heat of the desert, Kevin held onto the thought of those two beers.

His parents, and mine, laughed at his quip. 'Kevin is coping,' they said. 'Kevin is coping.'

IN JUNE 1973, on a flawless winter morning, we left home early. We swept past Germiston Lake, headed straight over Power Street and entered a bare area beyond the railway tracks. Large groups of natives hung around a dirty corner shop. Under a straggly tree, a queue of black men waited for their turn at the outdoor barber. The boy on the stool had a white sheet placed over him, with a hole cut out for his head. A barber worked on him with a battery-operated razor.

Dad was familiar with the drab backstreets of Germiston. He used to cycle this way to work as an apprentice at the Eskom maintenance workshops at Rosherville. The two-mile ride was just long enough to remind himself every morning that he did not want to spend the rest of his life as a manual worker. He wanted to achieve much more in the years ahead.

I tried to picture my dad in his early twenties, hunched over the bars of his bicycle as he pedalled past the craggy goldmine dumps which lined the road. It seemed strange to think that, twenty years later, in a new company car rather than on his bike, dad would be the guest of honour at Eskom's annual Tribal Dancing national finals at Rosherville.

We had already been to the local and then the regional tribal dancing competitions during the previous six months. This was our third successive year at the finals. My sister and I were the only white children never to miss a dance-off; and that morning I'd sulked at the thought of another day on a dusty sports field as black Eskom workers stomped their way through the various Zulu, Xhosa, Northern Sotho, Southern Sotho, Venda, Shangaan, Swazi, Pedi and Tswana dancing sub-divisions as one power station team competed against another.

It felt like school, where we were in the midst of learning that the Bantu would eventually be relocated to ten randomly created homelands dotted around the most remote sections of the country. The

Zulus were meant to find political freedom in Kwa-Zulu, the Xhosas were granted citizenship of the Transkei and the Tswana people now belonged to the supposedly independent country of Bophuthatswana, a small area of land in the middle of north-west South Africa. The same principle applied to seven other homelands, meaning that ten different little black states would soon exist within South Africa itself. Natives, after all, were not actually South Africans.

No other country recognized the homelands; but the South African government was undeterred. They planned to open embassies in each newly independent state. Eighty-five per cent of the South African population would find political fulfilment in ten pockets of dry land that occupied less than twelve per cent of the country's geographical area.

Dad appeared to accept government policy, but he focused on the dancers as part of the Eskom family rather than as representatives of the tribal homelands. The company always came first for dad. He treated each day of tribal dancing as if it was his first, and so that morning he waved happily to the Zulu and Xhosa troupes as we were led to the VIP enclosure.

I munched on dainty egg and cress sandwiches and freshly baked scones as mom and dad listened patiently to the scheduled programme for the day. The regional winners of each tribal division would dance in front of the judges, my parents, and a crowd of a thousand spectators. We knew we were in for the long haul, with about forty different dance routines to watch.

I only liked the Zulu dancers and, of course, the gumboot men. The best Zulu teams chanted beautifully as they hunched low in a snaking line. Their shields and assegais made a glinting chain in the sunlight. Heather and I were more amused that, from below the knees, their legs were covered in fluffy white tassels. The Zulu leader, the fattest man, broke away to produce a series of high-stepping kicks which the rest of the group copied in perfect unison, bringing their feet down hard. Small clouds of dust rose up around their mournful singing. Black women in the crowd ululated in praise as the drumming and shrill whistling became increasingly frenetic.

The head Zulu had the loudest whistle of all and, when he wasn't barking out instructions, he blew with piercing intensity to inspire his troupe still further. We grinned along with everyone else when the men pawed the ground and then tumbled and rolled over each other in a blurring rush. The last wild minute of their dance had them whirling their assegais above their heads and stamping their feet as they inched closer to us, their eyes rolling and their mouths widening as if intent on eating us whole. We were tempted to reel back, had we not been already laughing nervously at the sight of the Zulu leader lifting his short but powerful legs above his ears as he reached a crescendo of stomping. And then the whole troupe joined him and the temporary stands shook as the crowd erupted in delight.

We also loved any group who did the gumboot dance. Wearing mining helmets and black gumboots, the dancers started slowly with a call-and-response routine interspersed with grunts and rhythmic handclaps. They used their whole bodies as instruments, slapping their chests and arms like drums before they hammered ever more percussively on their gumboots. We knew that mining boys were always issued with long black boots so that they could work far below the surface of the earth. The mining floors were so poorly drained they were often flooded. The miners dug for coal or gold in the seamed walls while standing in pools of water.

Many men lost their lives every year, dad told us, which made the sound of the gumboot dancers seem sad. But they smiled so warmly at mom and dad after the final echo of a gumboot shuffle had died away that we could only believe they were singing songs for us and Eskom.

The rest of a long day was more tedious as one Pedi dance

merged into another Tswana stomp. Heather and I slipped away to eat chocolate biscuits in the shade of the striped canopy. But we were back for the final presentation when dad spoke for twenty minutes without notes, his right hand casually tucked in a trouser pocket as he talked about the family of Eskom and how we formed a crucial part of the company whether we were Zulu or Sotho, English or Afrikaans. Dad praised the dancers, while mom, wearing a new dress and a smart hat, presented the prizes.

Even in her high heels, she was dwarfed by my father. But mom was dad's equal in every other way. She applauded the dancers and had a special word for all the men. Dad also looked humbled when the winning pot-bellied Zulu from Arnot Power Station gave him a shield, as a mark of respect from one leader to another. The floating trophy was then presented by dad to the man.

They looked very different. Dad wore dark trousers, a white shirt, navy-blue tie and his black Eskom sports jacket. The Zulu chief showed off his huge white feathered head-dress, a leopard skin wrap over his neck, a naked chest and tummy, an animal hide around his waist and those fluffy white leg warmers above his shoeless feet. We could see his bare bottom between the slats of animal hide. He listened to dad's congratulations and, before shaking hands, wiped a sweaty palm on his bare buttock. As our dad and the dancing Zulu king clasped hands, Heather and I giggled helplessly. The big old bum routine never failed to set us off.

THE WORDS LEAPT from the radio the following Saturday afternoon. 'A message for Kevin Scott from Sunnyridge in Germiston,' rang out on *Forces Favourites*. The announcer Pat Kerr's voice oozed sincerity as she sent my cousin lots of love from his mom and dad, his brother Malcolm and sister Gail, and his old friends from Dawnview High.

Kevin was back at base camp after his only pass home. Besides six days of travelling to and from Rooikop by train, he had been allowed a week in Germiston. His break came after six months in the army, with sixteen weeks having been spent at Katima Mulilo, on the border at the Caprivi Strip. Kevin's main task as a gunner was to be part of the patrol guarding the sweepers which cleared the roads of landmines. At five o'clock every morning he followed the sweepers in a small armoured car as they went looking for mines planted by SWAPO and Frelimo terrorists.

He saw only a couple of landmine incidents in his time on the border. And, while he sometimes heard gunfire at night, Kevin mostly worked on his tan and enjoyed his two beers a day while dreaming of life beyond the army. He had decided not to turn his obligatory national service into an extended eighteen months in the army, even though he would be paid and granted exemption from all future camps.

He'd already lost his girlfriend, Eleanor, his future wife, after they had broken up when the reality of him only being home for one week out of ten months seemed too much for either of them. Kevin hated to think of everything else he had given up in the army. And once he had been home he decided that he would face the rest of his call-ups in the future.

His mother's message on *Forces Favourites* was a reminder to keep his spirits up. He only had four more months left before he would be home again. The sound of Kevin's name being said out loud on the radio was, to me, more shocking than thrilling. It made the army seem disturbingly real. It was coming closer and closer.

OUR LIVES WERE CHANGING. You could sense it in me and Granddad George. On the first Sunday in January 1974, in the small house where he and my grandmother lived on Angus Street, we faced our new world with uncertainty. Four weeks earlier I had finished my last day of primary school. I went home with a shiny cup, as sportsman of the year, and a murkier heart. I could not explain my feelings as I entered the unknown tangle of high school.

The old soldier who looked at me with his crinkly gaze had his own foreign terrain to cross. Granddad George had finally retired at the age of seventy-five. He had spent the previous seven years as the caretaker of the school I was just two days away from joining. Unlike my big sister, who was about to start her fourth year of high school, I would never get to see granddad walking around the stately building and huge fields he had looked after for so long. But he was weary after a lifetime of work.

Dad said he wished granddad could have retired properly ten years earlier, but he and my gran were too poor without a pension. But even granddad couldn't go on forever and so George and Netta settled down for their last years together. They would not have much money but they had been careful to save what they could and dad would always make sure they were all right.

I was less sure how granddad felt as his final days stretched out in front of him. He might even have glimpsed the end of his life. Yet he covered up his feelings with kindness to me. Granddad said I had no need to worry. Germiston High was a grand place and he'd told all the teachers about me, his youngest grandson, and so I would see lots of friendly faces. Anyway, I was going to a new school with most of my old pals. We would form a great gang in our butcher's blazers.

Granddad always compared the school blazer, with its thin parallel lines of purple, black and white, to a butcher's uniform. He made me a promise: 'You'll be fine, laddie.'

I knew he was right. I was also excited because we had recently reached a mysterious crossroads. Allan Elgar, a much cooler kid than us, had arrived from Cape Town a few years earlier. He was the boy I had just beaten to the big sporting prize, but he had opened our eyes when he'd asked us in our last few weeks of primary school if we wanted to see an FL. We must all have looked blankly at him because none of us had any idea whether an FL might be a new toy racing car or the name of some obscure new yo-yo – a Fast Looper or a Frisky Lizard?

We looked apprehensively at each other when he led us behind the bicycle sheds. Allan reached into the pocket of his short grey trousers and fished out a strange piece of filmy plastic. Waving it in our faces he chanted, 'Check the FL, chinas, check the FL.'

I had no idea why he was so excited. 'This is a French letter, my chinas,' he crooned.

Even when I screwed up my eyes I couldn't make out any tiny French words on the letter. The sheath dangled emptily in front of us. I could not work out what the little teat at the end was meant to do. It did not look much like the nib of a drooping French fountain pen.

'Would you know what to do with this?' Allan asked as he stretched the French letter until it looked as if it might snap.

I wondered if it was a kind of balloon and was just about to say as much when my friend, David Harris, shrugged knowingly. 'Sure,' he said. 'Don't you?'

'*Ja*,' our FL guide said, sounding a touch less confident, ''course I do ...'

I knew David well enough to guess he might not have been quite so sure what to do with an FL, but he had spared our embarrassment.

It was only weeks later when, between us, we almost worked out the puzzle. A French letter was also known as a condom. When you went to kiss and cuddle a girl you really, really liked, you rolled the FL over your 'manhood'. This curious new word was conjured up by another smart friend, John da Silva, who pointed at the silver fly that zipped up his trousers. The manhood lurked somewhere in our underpants.

The prospect of discovering my manhood at Germiston High, while possibly carrying an FL in my butcher's blazer, eased my anxieties about new teachers and mocking teenagers. I realized then that the future could be exciting rather than just frightening.

Granddad George looked as if he was about to retreat back into his own world. His memories of the war remained locked inside him but the symbols of his Scottish heritage were all over my grandparents' house in Angus Street. The McRae clan's crest was stuck high on a wall of their tiny two-roomed home. Against a backdrop of tartan, a man's hand held a gleaming sword aloft, and the word *Fortitudine* was printed on the circular belt and buckle that ringed the image. The McRae clan were fighting men.

A very British ornament stood on the mantelpiece. The powerful bulldog, with the Union Jack painted on his back, was made out of Royal Doulton china. I was always told to put it down when I picked it up. He had come all the way from Britain, six thousand miles away, and I was warned that Granddad George would be devastated if his bulldog was smashed.

Granddad just shook his head. He had seen too much to fret over an ornamental dog. 'It's all right,' he said softly so that granny would not hear on my last Sunday before high school. And he ruffled my hair and laughed again, as if to remind me that nothing lasts forever.

T HE GRASS BENEATH our feet died and changed colour from green to yellow. Another sun-filled winter settled across the Transvaal. I had just turned thirteen and we had begun to play rugby at Germiston High. Football, our favourite winter sport, was not allowed at any government high school and so we adapted to a much harder game. Just as we would soon be expected to slip into military uniforms and endure marching drills in Youth Preparedness every Thursday, so we were groomed to play rugby rather than football. It seemed a sport more suited to our way of life.

Even our favourite radio commercial captured the rugby-shaped simplicity of our lives. We always sang along when we heard it, and even took turns to act out the advert during school break, with one of us playing the role of 'the announcer' and the rest of our gang being the crowd. The announcer spoke in a catchy twang while the crowd shouted out their one-word answers with conviction:

> Announcer: 'Hey, South Africa, what's your favourite meal?'
> Crowd: 'Braaivleis!'
> Announcer: 'Sport?'
> Crowd: 'Rugby!'
> Announcer: 'Weather?'
> Crowd: 'Sunshine!'
> Announcer: 'And what's your greatest car, South Africa?'
> Crowd: 'Chevrolet!'
> Announcer: 'Let's see … that's braaivleis, rugby, sunny skies and Chevrolet, huh?'
> Crowd: 'Right!'
> Announcer: 'Well, you sure sound like South Africa to me.'
> Crowd: 'We are! We love braaivleis, rugby, sunny skies and Chevrolet … braaivleis, rugby, sunny skies and Chevrolet!'

As the days shortened and became colder it seemed as if rugby might yet offer us redemption.

The British Lions tour had been postponed and rescheduled so many times we could barely contain ourselves when, in May 1974, they played their first match of an epic campaign. My new interest in girls, especially those with long legs and developing busts, switched back to squat and hulking Afrikaans hookers and locks with names like Piston van Wyk and Moaner van Heerden. Once they had torn the Lions to pieces our sporting mastery would be undisputed again.

Rugby also gave us a break from brutality every Friday at high school. The last day of the week was meant to be the best day. But our Friday mornings were so distorted by fear it took the rest of the day to recover from the ordeal of four successive periods of Industrial Arts with Mr O'Kelly. An Afrikaner, O'Kelly frightened us with his furious shouting and terrible canings.

He was at his most chilling when lingering over his choice of victim. O'Kelly would croon softly then, stalking past our desks as he ridiculed our hopeless attempts to make a wooden pencil box, chuckling and giggling as he asked who most deserved to be punished for their ineptitude. He was breaking us in for the army, he told us, because the harder we were treated at twelve the tougher we would be at seventeen when we did our duty for the South African Defence Force. So he was actually doing us a favour, O'Kelly insisted, before picking on his prize idiot for the day. He especially enjoyed humiliating small boys, like Martin Milner, whom he would lift high in the sky and then fold in two as if dividing a sheet of scrap paper in half.

Even when he finally allowed us to leave his class at the end of two hours he made us line up, like toy soldiers, and pass through his open doorway in single file. O'Kelly gave each one of us a farewell 'flap' [hiding]. We soon became artful. There were a couple of ways to divert O'Kelly. The first was for some brave soul to offer up a fawning question which would invite O'Kelly to tell us about his own army days or rugby-playing exploits. He usually fell for it. Instead of *donnering* us he would wave his meaty hands in the air and gush forth, heavy with sentimentality and exaggeration as he reflected on all that the army and rugby had taught him.

I always wanted to ask how a moustached monster of an Afrikaner had ended up with an Irish surname, but, instead, I nodded enthusiastically as he predicted a big Springbok win in the first Test against the Lions.

The opposite happened. South Africa were overwhelmed. Our forwards were obliterated and our backs were smashed into the mud of Cape Town. O'Kelly promised us it would be very different in the second Test, at an altitude of 6,000 feet and on a bone-hard pitch in Pretoria. He was right. South African endured an even more shameful afternoon and the biggest defeat, 28-9, in our history.

For the third Test the Springbok selectors picked some huge men in an attempt to intimidate the tourists at the Boet Erasmus Stadium in Port Elizabeth. Hunched over my crackling radio I gasped as the commentators described a match that became known as 'The Battle of Boet Erasmus' and one of the most violent in Test history. The initially venomous Springboks, sounding like fifteen mad O'Kellys, were savaged.

In the end the Lions, winning 26-9, were only two points away from matching their second Test score. But this defeat was far more crushing, both psychologically and physically, for white South Africa. We were dazed and distraught. Our cherished notions of supremacy came tumbling down in the winter of 1974.

Granddad George did not listen to the destruction of South African rugby by a British Lions team containing four Scotsmen. Like my one-armed Granddad Scott, he was more a football than a rugby man; but he did admire Ian 'Mighty Mouse' McLauchlan, the imposing prop, and Gordon Brown, the giant gingery lock whose home town of Troon, gave him his snappy Scottish nickname of *'Broon frae Troon'*. But, rather than turning up his wireless loud so that he could hear the rugby, Granddad George slept quietly in hospital that Saturday afternoon.

He had fallen ill with pneumonia a few days earlier. There was only mild concern from his doctor but my grandmother said she would feel happier if he recovered in hospital rather than in their cramped and cold Angus Street house. Mom and dad had already been to see him twice and he seemed comfortable. And so when I went to bed that Saturday night, my head full of rugby rather than granddad, we all thought he would soon be back home.

But in the early hours of Sunday 14 July, 1974, George McRae, the old soldier, slipped away. He was seventy-five. I had become a teenager less than three months before, and I couldn't help myself. An hour after my mom told me the news I still felt stricken. I eventually went downstairs to see dad and my Aunt Laura, his sister, after they returned from hospital. I wanted to comfort dad, who sat in a wide-backed chair in the lounge. But, seeing him, I thought of my lovely old granddad. They looked so alike.

My tears came, silently and painfully. I turned away from dad, instead of hugging him. I heard him call out to me but I ran to the kitchen. Maggie moved quickly from the sink and stretched out her arms. I was almost as tall as Maggie but I bowed my head into her chest. The red gingham squares on her overall were like blurring dots pressed against my face. Her black arms wrapped around me. Maggie started to sing, in a throaty hum which turned into a beautiful African lullaby.

As her voice faded she lifted my chin so that, eyes still filled with tears, I looked up into her face.

'Your grandfather was a good man,' she said quietly. 'But you must go to your father now ...'

Holding me by the shoulders she turned me round so I saw dad, standing at the edge of the kitchen. He held out a hand to me. 'Come here,' he said gently, as he nodded to Maggie.

I walked towards dad, remembering the moment on Christmas

Eve all those years ago when, with a black bat flying above our heads, he and Granddad George had sat out on the side veranda. It was the night we had all been to see Kenneth McKellar, and granddad had sung along loudly in the theatre. I could still hear his voice seven years on, laughter rolling through his Scottish accent as he asked: *'Donald, where's your troosers?'* I asked dad if he remembered that night.

'Of course,' he said as he led me onto the same veranda. It felt warm in the winter sunshine. I wiped my eyes as I thought of Granddad George, who had always sung on Christmas Eve, whether he was in a Belgian trench or an African garden.

'We'll never forget him, will we?' I asked dad.

'No,' dad said quietly. 'We'll always remember.'

Six months later, in January 1975, George's wife, Netta, died – of a broken heart, we said. She might have scolded him when he was alive, and despaired every time he made a mess at the table or fell asleep in his chair, but without him she was bereft. It was as if a bomb had exploded inside my grandmother, tearing a hole through her centre.

She returned to the Angus Street house but no longer complained if I picked up granddad's old bulldog from the mantelpiece. And she did not even seem to notice that Heather now had a boyfriend where, once, she would have warned that my sister was far too young to be thinking about boys and parties. Netta McRae, instead, withered away without her husband.

My grandmother died on 19 January, 1975, on the day my cousin Alan turned twenty. His older brother, Brian, a recently graduated engineer, had continued the family tradition by following granddad and dad into Eskom. The ring of electricity around our extended McRae–Scott clan had deepened with my two eldest cousins on my mother's side of the family, Malcolm and Kevin, also joining Eskom after the army.

But, six months and five days after he died, it was as if the last light turned off inside Netta McRae. Dad's parents had gone forever. But he still had us, and his electrifying work at Eskom. I saw that he had also something inside him that helped him go on, even though life would never be the same again. He had faith that, no matter how we all felt inside, we would be happy again.

PART II

REBEL, REBEL
(1975–1981)

Jess McRae and Maggie Thabang (right), 1975

CHAPTER SEVEN

UNIFORM DAYS

ONE THURSDAY MORNING, in the summer of 1975, dad swept into my darkened teenage bedroom as an old song boomed out of him. The door rocked on its hinges as, loudly and out of tune, he sang another favourite from his repertoire of Louis Armstrong ditties:

> *When you're smilin'*
> *When you're smilin'*
> *The whole world smiles with you*

Dad's voice could kill a Satchmo tune at a hundred paces. He enjoyed using it every morning, as a way of waking us up for school and as an instrument of torture when we didn't jump up straight away. At 6:32, having spent two minutes rousing my grumpy sister in the opposite room, dad flung open my curtains. Sunshine streamed through the venetian blinds as he belted out his song:

And when you're laughin'
When you're laughin'
The sun comes shinin' through

I played dead but dad wasn't fooled. Even when I turned over with a theatrical sigh, showing my back to the vivid African morning, he kept on singing:

When you're cryin'
You bring on the rain
So, stop your sighin'
Won't you be happy again?

If it had been down to me, the world could have ended that very minute and I would've been ecstatic. I would have escaped Y.P.

It was another terrible Thursday, another day of Y.P. –Youth Preparedness. We were meant to be preparing ourselves for the onslaught of communist forces intent on overthrowing apartheid and white South African civilization. The army uniforms, and the chaotic marching drills we did at school, were supposed to steel us for military conscription. And so in Standard Seven, in our second year of high school, in the year we turned fourteen, we had begun to sour a little on South African life. If upholding apartheid meant enduring Y.P., some of us were no longer so sure we lived in the greatest country in the world.

My dreaded army uniform was draped over the back of a chair. Solemnly, I eyed the heavy brown shirt and shorts that our black ironing lady, Martha, had ironed in readiness for Y.P. The only signs of normality were the long black socks, with the familiar purple and white Germiston High trim, and the Clarks shoes we wore every day. Maggie had polished them until they glistened.

I was not so different from Maggie and Martha. We had our

uniforms. As domestic servants, Maggie and Martha wore cotton overalls and slippers. I knew I would have to give in and pull on the dark khaki uniform of a schoolboy soldier.

By the time I reached the breakfast table, I was dressed in full Y.P. garb. Dad said hello without looking up to check I was in my brown fatigues. He was too busy listening to the seven o'clock news on the state-run South African Broadcasting Corporation's English radio while poring over our morning paper, the liberal *Rand Daily Mail*. It was one way, dad said, of remaining balanced while he wolfed down his corn flakes, fried egg and bacon and toast and marmalade. Dad was so lost in his paper, and the radio, that Heather and I could do pretty much as we pleased.

I managed to steal the back page, so that I could read the sports news, while feeding egg to our collie called Ginny. She ate the egg I loathed with yapping relish, making Heather raise her eyebrows when dad didn't even notice. My more alert mother moved back and forth between us and the kitchen, so I just needed to make sure that she was out of the dining room when I poured fried egg down Ginny's gullet.

The SABC news that morning focused on the high morale in the Defence Force and government plans to stem the rising force of communist propaganda. We had already heard it was likely that future recruits would spend two full years in the army, followed by months of border camps.

Dad's attention switched to his work at Eskom and, once his last corner of toast and slurp of tea had disappeared, he was on his way. He told us to enjoy our day at school, while Heather and I grunted back, following with more interest the way dad managed to cram still more paperwork into his bloated briefcase. Dad's briefcase was nicknamed 'Bertie'; and we regarded him as a member of the family. It was often said that dad spent more time with Bertie than with us.

Bertie went wherever dad went – to work and back, to meetings and on planes which took them all over the country together. And every night, at home, Bertie would be placed next to dad's chair in the study. While we listened to the radio, dad concentrated on Bertie, rifling through the various compartments. Sometimes dad even scooped Bertie up and sat him on his lap so that he could peer more deeply into the briefcase as he went searching for an old report or a new agenda. One of the last things dad did every night, before walking upstairs to bed, was to check that Bertie was neatly packed for work the following morning.

'Dad,' my sister once cried out in exasperation, 'Bertie's like your boyfriend!'

I thought this was hilarious. My mother was less amused. 'Bertie,' she said, 'is officially married to your father.'

By the time I slung my schoolbag over my shoulder just after 7:30, dad and his new husband had reached their office in Braamfontein, in downtown Johannesburg. I travelled more slowly to school, on my bicycle with handlebars so high, like a Harley-Davidson, I could lean back in the saddle and pedal in leisurely style alongside my friends. We cruised along the long, flat stretch of Cachet Road which was divided into two one-way strips by a grassy island. Near the top we took a right turn down Anderson Lane, one of the prettiest streets in the whole of Germiston. Our brown shirts billowed as, freewheeling down the sloping road, we picked up speed. We flew past rolling green gardens and palatial houses.

It was easy to forget Y.P. for a while and to remember the cricket match we had won the previous afternoon, and to look ahead to the frenetic games of football we played every break. There was also time to drool over the various 'chicks' we fancied, with most of our attention focused on girls too old ever to be interested in horny little pipsqueaks like us.

I liked good-looking and apparently sophisticated girls like Suzanne Price who, at sixteen, was two years older than us and her younger sister, Nicola, whom we used to swoon over at primary school. But my taste in women had matured, or so I said. I now liked the older Price sister because she looked good in a swimming costume and wrote about modern art in the school magazine. I was impressed by her essay on a visit to the Johannesburg Gallery, where she saw a painting of a clown by Picasso:

'This piece of art is a masterpiece of reality,' Suzanne Price wrote of *Tête d'arlequin*, 'the sort of reality that no-one seems to want to face. Pablo Picasso is able to face this reality with a cynical, bitter, yet uninhibited outlook on life . . .'

I didn't know much about Picasso but I was willing to confront the same reality as old Pablo if it helped me catch Suzanne Price's worldly eye. I wished I could go up to her in the school quadrangle and tell her that I, too, was 'cynical, bitter, uninhibited'. I might have looked just like another of her kid sister's gawping classmates but, on the inside, an old devil lurked. She could call me Don Pablo and, together, we would face the rough reality that left Picasso's clown looking, as she wrote, 'helplessly demented and lost'.

Our school lives remained a surreal mix. We were dragooned into wearing our boy-soldier uniforms by our new headmaster, Bob Gouldie, an arch-conservative. But individual teachers opened our minds in illuminating ways. It was different at the top where Gouldie, the miserable old head, lamented in our school magazine that, 'The church is losing its hold, parents' attitudes are slipping and the combined effect is uncommitted individuals who have no sense of loyalty. Traditional values and moral standards are being rejected. It is small wonder that so many young people are confused and uncertain.'

There was no confusion or uncertainty in my preference for the much more obviously smart and beautiful young teachers who bewitched us at Germiston High. Gouldie obviously believed in Youth Preparedness and military service. I looked elsewhere, and specifically at the likes of Miss Murray and Miss James.

Yvette Murray was our form teacher in class 7I and, in her early twenties, she exuded a racy panache which made our heads spin. The boys hooted and the girls sighed when I went up to her and said, without blushing, 'Miss, I want to bed you ...' Miss Murray looked at me calmly. I tried to remain serene. 'Er, Miss, I meant to say I want to beg you to see my homework.' I was that juvenile. I was that dumb. The worldly Miss Murray sent me back to my seat with a cool smile and reminded us to concentrate on our work rather than the lame jokes.

I was even more fascinated by the mysteriously chic Miss James, who taught English to the senior classes. She edited the school magazine and regularly slipped in references to Irish novelists and French philosophers. I had already decided that I was going to become a writer and so I was intrigued when she started talking about James Joyce and Albert Camus. She made them seem like great men in her editorials, on the opposite page to Bob Gouldie's dire warnings.

Miss James also had an impact on my sister's life; for Heather was one of the selected students invited to her flat for the occasional *soirée*. I had no idea how to spell 'soirée', let alone what it meant. But it sounded very exotic as Miss James introduced them to different books and new ideas over soft drinks and peanuts.

Heather was especially influenced by Simone de Beauvoir's *The Second Sex*, which Miss James discussed at one of her first swar-rays. My sister's copy soon became the most familiar item in her bedroom. Whenever I walked in Heather would be reading it avidly, whether lying on the carpet or stretched out on her pink bedspread. She said Simone de Beauvoir showed how women had always been oppressed. And so Heather, thanks to Miss James and Madame de

Beauvoir, announced that she was a feminist. Our parents were mystified but they hoped that it would just be a passing phase. Heather, however, knew her life had changed forever.

I was more interested in the 'sex' in the title. I was ready to become a feminist myself, whatever that meant, if it would allow me to hear Miss James discussing sex at one of her swar-rays. And there were even days, when Heather was out with her boyfriend or canoeing on Germiston Lake, that I picked up the life-changing paperback. The cover, with its image of a blue Henry Moore sculpture of a woman's body, was embedded in my brain. But as hard as I searched, turning over page after page of dense words, I never found anything sexy in *The Second Sex*. I got a bigger kick reading the odd sex scene in one of dad's hard-boiled Mickey Spillane detective books.

But I was amazed by Miss James. I suspected that something far more thrilling lurked beyond the big words. I obviously could not have known then that, within another two years, she would marry one of her students, Dickie Berkeljon, who had belonged to that very same James Joyce reading class and swar-ray group as Heather. He was only three years older than me; but maybe, unlike me, he had already started reading Camus and grappling with existential thought in the addictive company of a teacher who became his wife.

There would be another marriage between one of our teachers and a freshly departed student during my time at Germiston High. In my final year, in 1978, our brash science teacher, Mr Matthews, married the previous year's head girl, Daphne Scott. And so, beneath the surface of a strictly regimented government school at the height of apartheid, illicit relationships lurked.

Back in 1975, however, the contrast was stark every Thursday. Our entire syllabus fell under the doctrine of Christian National Education which was meant to churn out religious patriots who would remain loyal to the ideals shaping the white republic of South Africa. Youth Preparedness epitomized the ethos. But my army uniform chafed and made me wish I could escape two hours of marching and spend them instead at a swar-ray with Mary-Anne James and Albert Camus, with Yvette Murray and James Joyce.

WE MADE SURE our purple, black and white ties were threaded neatly around our necks. My tie felt like a noose as I pushed the knot up towards my throat. I slipped the silky material between the second and third buttons of the brown shirt I tucked into my brown shorts. It was important our ties did not flap as we marched, and that our shirts and shorts looked crisp and smart. Even a hint of untidiness could result in a *klap* [slap] from the older boys leading our platoons.

Pulling on our brown berets, we were even more careful. If they were not placed perfectly on our heads, with a slanted angle to the right and a seamless curve at the back, we could be *klapped* even harder. The beret would fly off our heads and, with scrambled brains, we would have to refit it in front of the whole giggling platoon and our glowering leader.

Youth Preparedness also turned one of our mild-mannered elderly teachers, Mr Webb, into an officious demon. We had to address him as Major Webb and obey his barked commands. Major Webb had fought in World War II, and his military experience was meant to prepare us for battle against communist forces. But the idea that the Soviet Union might invade Germiston High seemed less distressing than the likelihood of another slap.

Everything changed on that particular Thursday in the summer of 1975. Major Webb was joined on the rugby fields by four Afrikaans men in uniform. They were real soldiers. One of our platoon commanders, a menacing kid, laughed softly when he saw our faces. '*Ja*, [Yes],' he cackled, 'now you *okes* [guys] are going to *afkak* [shit off].'

Our lives were so shadowed by the army that we knew huge chunks of soldier slang. We called it 'army *taal* [language]'. We had heard phrases like '*Vasbyt* [Hold on]' and '*Min dae, baie hare* [Few days, lots of hair]' on *Forces Favourites*. But '*Afkak*' and '*Bevok* [Mad/Fucked]' were Afrikaans swear-words you would never hear on the radio. They were sinister army words.

We stood stiffly to attention while a huge army-man studied us. 'Are you joking me?' he finally shouted in thickly-accented English.

He let his ungrammatical sentence hang in the air as he eyed one of my friends.

'No,' my pal whispered.

'No, what?'

'No, I'm not joking you,' my friend said, looking as if had already peed in his pants.

'No, *sir*!' the soldier whooped, his neck thick with purple veins.

'Yes, sir!'

'Yes, dumbo,' the man sneered.

A boy in the same row tittered, either because he wanted to please the soldier or because he was so nervous he couldn't contain himself.

'*Hou jou bek!* [Shut your mouth!]' the soldier hollered.

We hardly dared breathe as he walked up and down, muttering about how '*pap* [limp]' we all appeared. 'What are you?' he finally asked again.

We shifted uneasily in our brown uniforms, toes curling up in fear inside our school shoes. What did he mean? Who were we? It was obvious. We were small and scared. We wished we could crawl back inside our classrooms, even if it meant doing double maths or four consecutive periods of woodwork with the cane-wielding Mr van Rensburg.

'I'll *blerrie* [bloody] well tell you what you're not,' he sneered. 'None of you *moffies* [queers] are G1 K1! Not one of you.'

We understood enough military terminology to know that any conscript who received a 'G1 K1' certificate from an examining medic was considered healthy and fit enough for active duty. 'G' stood for *'gesondheid'* [health], while 'K' meant *'kondisie'* or 'condition'.

'Most of you look like *blerrie* G4 K4s,' he roared, using the term given to any ailing soldier unfit for anything more taxing than a clerical position.

It sounded less like the intended insult than the sweetest compliment. But our angry man had not quite finished. 'Some of you might even think you're G5s!'

A G5 ruling resulted in a complete medical discharge from military service. It was an ambition worth pursuing, but not with a fierce Afrikaner hovering over us. He was searching for a G5 to humiliate and so we all stood a little taller and straighter, staring blankly ahead with a silent prayer of *'Not me, not me!'* echoing in our heads.

'*Ja*,' he laughed, 'no-one wants to be a G5 do they?'

Our silence deepened. 'Do they?' he shouted.

'No, sir!' we yelped.

He told us to stand at ease, then, and spoke more reasonably, explaining that he was about to give us our first taste of the army. The next four years of Y.P. would prepare us for the serious work we would do as soldiers when we left school. He expected all of us to be G1 K1 soldiers who would keep South Africa safe from our enemies both inside and outside the country.

'*ATTEN ... TION!*' he suddenly shouted.

Chaotically, we lifted our right legs at varying angles and brought our right feet stamping down.

The Afrikaans soldier scowled and made us to do it again and again and again. He then showed us the correct way to position our hands and our arms as we marched.

Eventually, we were given a different command. *'About turn!'* he hollered and, like a creaking crab with dangling pincers, we scuttled around slowly until we faced the opposite direction.

'Quick ... march!' he shouted and off we went, chanting, *'Left, right, left, right, left, right, left ...'* as we struggled to move our feet in symmetry with our arms and words.

Marching back and forth, past the rifle range adjoining the swimming pool, we trudged towards mindless oblivion: *'Left, right, left, right, left ...'*

I CAME HOME LATE that Thursday afternoon and peeled off my uniform. Youth Preparedness was over for another week. Pulling on a T-shirt and shorts, I went into my sister's bedroom. Heather was sprawled on her bed, barefoot, listening to music and still reading *The Second Sex*. She was about to turn seventeen and her pink bedroom walls were covered in posters of men who either looked like pretty women – David Bowie and Marc Bolan – or were named after girls.

Alice Cooper sounded like a very English schoolgirl. But he looked more like an American corpse on the huge poster that dominated the wall opposite Heather's bed. Black rings were painted around his eyes and jagged lines, like tears, ran from the lower lids. His eyes were wide and staring, and they were framed by greasy streaks of black hair. He draped a huge python around his bare neck and clung to the microphone with his right hand. In his left hand he cradled a skull which looked white and fragile against his shiny black outfit.

His gravelly voice rang out from the gleaming vinyl that spun around Heather's turntable. *Billion Dollar Babies*, Alice Cooper's 1973 album, had made him the biggest rock star in America. The record had also gone to number one in the UK album charts, but its reception had been less grand in South Africa. Only a few thousand white kids, like my sister, had managed to buy imported copies of an LP that featured songs whose very titles dismayed my parents: 'Raped And Freezin'', 'Sick Things' and 'I Love The Dead'.

That last track echoed around Heather's room as I stepped inside. We always turned up the volume because we knew how much it sent mom and dad crazy. They were devout church-goers, intent on us following the same religious path, and they could not believe we would be in thrall to a demonic man called Alice as he celebrated his fetish for the dead. I waved hello to Heather and looked again at the poster of Alice with his snake and skull as I listened to the words:

> *I love the dead before they're cold,*
> *Their blueing flesh for me to hold ...*
> *While friends and lovers mourn your silly grave*
> *I have other uses for you, Darling.*

Heather was smart enough to know Alice didn't really mean it. And, following her discovery of Simone de Beauvoir, she was also having second thoughts about a man called Alice. But, for now, she reassured me that it was all an act, just as his live performances were more about theatre than reality. Alice hacked off the heads of baby-dolls and covered himself in fake blood and put his neck on the block of a wooden guillotine. It seemed strange, but I liked it because Heather liked it and it made me laugh when mom and dad shook their heads. But I especially liked it because I knew these songs were the very opposite of Youth Preparedness.

Our favourite Alice Cooper song was 'School's Out', which sounded like an upbeat summer anthem but, in reality, as Heather insisted, was about bombing your school to smithereens:

> *School's out for summer*
> *School's out forever*
> *School's been blown to pieces*

It was exactly the kind of message I needed to hear after Y.P., and I told Heather what had happened earlier that day. I said it made me want to avoid the army forever.

'Good for you,' she replied, knowing she would never confront the same conscription blues. The girls at Germiston High were even spared the uniforms and marching. Heather was one of the luckiest girls in all the school. As she was a member of the first team in tennis she and Linda van Niekerk, her best friend, were allowed to play a couple of sets together on the school courts while the boys marched every Thursday.

The rest of the girls, meanwhile, were given extra Domestic Science lessons. They were taught to sew and cook so that they could look after their soldier boys once we all grew up. Heather said this proved we lived in a country which treated women either as domestic servants or sex objects.

David Bowie was still the king, or the queen, of my sister's bedroom. Over the previous year Heather had played his 1974 song, 'Rebel, Rebel', at least once every day. Even more than Alice Cooper's shocking lyrics about murder and death, Bowie's words captured the illicit blurring that made Heather's world seem so thrilling and different.

> *You've got your mother in a whirl*
> *She's not sure if you're a boy or a girl*

Hey babe, your hair's alright
Hey babe, let's go out tonight

Rebel Rebel, you've torn your dress
Rebel Rebel, your face is a mess
Rebel Rebel, how could they know?
Hot tramp, I love you so!

I would have hated wearing a dress myself, and would never want to wear make-up like any of Heather's glam-rockers. I also loved playing football and rugby and cricket and tennis. But I felt at home in my sister's bedroom, surrounded by her records and posters and books.

I felt I was definitely maturing as, sitting on the carpet, listening to 'Rebel, Rebel', I updated the English football league ladders I'd got from *Shoot*, the magazine that took six weeks to be shipped over to the CNA from Britain every Friday. There were four separate tables with the name of every single English football club printed out on a different coloured piece of small cardboard which could be moved and slotted into its latest position on the ladder every week. After a few midweek games in England the previous night I spread *The Star* newspaper out in front of me and, taking note of the scores and new positions, I switched the teams around.

I loved Arsenal, as they had won the league and FA Cup double in 1971, and every Saturday afternoon I would huddle over the radio while an English match was broadcast on the BBC's World Service. I liked the way the roar of the crowd wrapped itself around the voice of a commentator, usually Peter Jones, and swayed across the static of six thousand miles as I listened to football being played at Highbury or Anfield, Elland Road or Stamford Bridge. On those Saturday afternoons I would imagine living in London rather than Germiston.

The same feeling took hold of me again after Y.P. and I wondered if we would not have been happier living in England rather than South Africa. Dad laughed when I suggested the idea to him at the dinner-table that evening. Unlike me, dad had been to England. He did not think of it as the country of Charlie George and David Bowie, of Marc Bolan and Kevin Keegan. Dad had experienced the miserable rain and dark days. England was also dragged down by union strikes and IRA bombs. All four of our grandparents had come from Britain but, as far as dad was concerned, there was something old and grim about life in the UK.

We lived in the best country in the world, a country of sunshine and hope. The outside world might not believe us but South Africa was special. South Africa was like nowhere else on earth.

DAD WAS RESPONSIBLE for electrifying white South Africa. The rest of the country remained in darkness but the cities and towns, the suburbs and farms, were ablaze with light. Since he had been appointed as the Head of Generation at Eskom in 1971, dad had transformed the country's electricity supply utility. He had been instrumental in separating the company into two distinct entities. Dad headed a powerhouse within Eskom called the Central Generating Undertaking [CGU] which focused exclusively on providing all the electricity that South Africa needed. The second division was responsible for the distribution of that electricity.

There were some nights when the full miracle of electricity became evident to dad from the air. Flying back from Durban or Cape Town, or one of the distant power stations in a remote corner of the country, Dad always put his briefcase away near the end of his flight. In his window seat he stared into the African night. And then, as the plane banked towards Johannesburg, he leant forward. Dad picked out the distant pinpricks of light first, marvelling at the way they broke up the empty sky. The gleaming city rose up slowly as if one layer of darkness after another was being peeled from the eyes of a blind man who could finally see.

When they hovered over Johannesburg's vast galaxy of electricity, with illuminated skyscrapers shining down on the brightly-lit streets and houses, dad felt pride surging through him. 'Look at this,' he called out to his colleagues, encouraging them to join him at the small window so they could also see how their everyday work helped light up the largest city in Africa.

Dad never tired of that magical sight. Looking down, his gaze always turned east, as he searched for Germiston. He could picture mom, Heather and me waiting for him. Sometimes he even tried to imagine which house might be ours as he stared at row upon radiant row of streets where lights were blazing, ovens were cooking and heaters were warming hundreds of thousands of people.

He only felt slight unease when he looked further south, and to the west, towards Soweto, where a million black people lived. The township appeared to be covered by a blanket at night. Only a low glow here and there, coming from smouldering coal-fires, punctuated the blackness. Dad was reminded again that Eskom supplied electricity mainly to the white minority. He knew that seventy-five per cent of South Africans were denied electrification.

Dad did not talk much about the glaring contrast between black and white South Africa. He said his generation had been lucky because South Africa had been tranquil for decades. Dad had been far too young to be called up for World War II, and he was only sixteen when it ended in 1945. He had also fallen seriously ill with nephritis at eighteen and so avoided national service forever.

But his division of Eskom into two distinct parts had been a direct response to the increasing isolation of South Africa. Overseas companies which had once invested in the country were gradually withdrawing their funds and personnel. It had become too controversial to retain their association with a country ruled by apartheid.

Dad still led the largest expansion programme of any power utility in the world in the early 1970s. He had used his own new department, the CGU, to generate enough capital to fund that expansion instead of relying on foreign investors. To encourage conservative power station managers on the *platteland* to support his vision of a central unifying structure, which would manage the generation of electricity around the country, dad needed to be as encouraging as he was resolute. He maintained his rota of rolling visits to ensure he went in person to each and every power station in South Africa on a regular basis.

I thought dad was like a preacher because, talking about electricity, he lit up on the inside. He glowed as he spoke about his electrifying faith in the future. Dad wanted us all to be believers in the power of electricity. He tried to make us understand how almost everything we did depended on a current that came directly from an Eskom generator.

Dad made us look at the light switches we had on walls all over our house. It just needed a flick of a finger to transform a darkened room. He pointed at the oven and the toaster and the kettle and the fridge and the freezer and the washing machine and the iron and the heater and the hot water tank and the hair-dryer and even the turntable where we played our Alice Cooper and David Bowie records that so bewildered him. Imagine a life without electricity, dad said, imagine how hard it would be without light and warmth, without hot water or frozen ice lollies?

'Yeah, yeah, dad,' Heather and I sighed. We'd heard the sermon from the lit temple of electricity so many times it made us want to crank up the volume on 'I Love The Dead' or 'Rebel, Rebel'.

'Lighten up, dad,' we'd say, rolling over with laughter at our blinding wit.

I didn't tell dad this but I missed the way he no longer had time to sing 'Hello Dolly' to me in the car like he used to do every Saturday morning when I was a small boy in Witbank. Life had become far more serious when I reached high school. Every Saturday morning saw us sitting at opposite sides of the dining-room table, glaring at each other.

In September 1975 dad had just turned forty-six and I was in the early flush of teenage life. It made for a volatile clash over the tangled enigmas of algebra and geometry. This was my father's world, and it left me dazed and stupefied. I loved words instead of numbers, books instead of angles and formulae, and knew I would never become an engineer. I thought I might have disappointed dad but I wanted to write more than anything. At fourteen I was in thrall to *The Catcher in the Rye* and *To Kill a Mocking Bird*, which made my mom happy. She was an ardent reader of literature while dad liked American pulp fiction, especially cheap paperbacks by James Hadley Chase where the detectives were tough and the women were hot.

On Saturday mornings we slaved over a hapless sequence of sums and shapes that invariably reduced him to anger and me to tears. If his typical week was a streamlined model of progress, our mathematical and scientific scraps were frustrating affairs. But dad banged away until I gave in and tried to get my head round meaningless problems and equations. He watched over me, trying to remain positive but finally shouting when I made another careless error.

'Stop shouting at me!' I yelled.

'I'm not shouting,' he shouted.

We fought over something more fundamental than maths or science homework. I wanted to be a writer, rather than an engineer. I wanted to escape rather than accept the army. I wanted to do something else with my life and not just follow my dad and my granddad, and three of my cousins, into Eskom's illuminated world.

'Wake up, chum,' dad said, more gently, trying to convince me that it was time to grow up.

We looked at each other and the truth hit home. It suddenly felt as if we were, in so many ways, opposites of each other. The divide between us had become clear.

Kevin Scott, Don McRae's cousin, in the army

CHAPTER EIGHT

COMMUNISM BY NUMBERS

Y SISTER MIGHT HAVE BEEN a sucker for pop music but she also read difficult books and sang opera. I nicknamed her 'Small' because she was only five feet tall, but there was a lot going on in her mysterious world. Heather had singing lessons twice a week in Johannesburg with a flamboyant Swedish diva called Nina Zuberki. I didn't like opera, but I was secretly proud of Small.

Nina wanted Heather to move to Europe so she could study opera and pursue a singing career. Heather was already looking for a way out of South Africa, and, even though she had no raging ambition to become a diva herself, opera offered an escape. She imagined herself living a life of freedom in Italy, Germany or Sweden. But dad, instead, saw Heather working as a teacher or a typist in Germiston before she settled down with a decent man, got married and had children.

My parents couldn't bear the thought of their eighteen-year-old daughter ending up on her own in Europe. I would have missed her terribly but I still castigated my parents. Heather could have been Germiston's answer to Maria Callas.

She never sang again after she was persuaded to stay in South Africa. Not one note soared from Heather ever again. Nina, whom she loved, died soon afterwards. There was such finality in Heather refusing to sing that her silence spoke of some deeper discontent.

The more she read *The Second Sex*, the more dad tried to convince Heather that femininity, rather than feminism, should be her path in life. She became especially upset when dad sometimes brought a copy of his Bible into her bedroom so that he could read extracts to her which proved it was God's will that a woman should nurture the needs of her family.

'I'm not going to live a life like mom,' Heather shouted one day. My mother's face flushed with hurt.

Heather was not willing to be subservient to any man. But she had an eye for good-looking boys, especially those who rowed, and they liked her. Once she had recovered from breaking up with her first boyfriend Heather did the obvious thing and hooked up with another crew member, a German rower called Jürgen. He was not a fan of David Bowie or Alice Cooper and he had certainly not heard of Simone de Beauvoir, because Jürgen was a jock who admired his own physique.

Heather wanted to become a rower herself but our parents said it was too masculine a sport for a teenage girl. They thought she might develop huge muscles and end up looking a little too butch for the good men of Germiston. 'But you're such a pretty girl,' mom would say when Heather complained. Dad was even more certain. It was important Heather retained her femininity. Why didn't she ever wear a nice summer dress? Dad loved girls who wore dresses and had long hair. His only daughter preferred jeans, T-shirts and short hair.

At least she won her struggle with dad to go to university instead of heading for teacher training college or typing school. Heather swore to me that, one day, she would become more than just a prospective secretary or a wife. She enrolled at the University of the Witwatersrand, where dad had obtained his mechanical engineering degree. Heather, who was primarily interested in zoology and animal conservation, registered for subjects like English and Sociology, because dad felt a Bachelor of Arts degree would help her find a job teaching English.

Wits University was very different from Germiston High. In 1976 protests against apartheid were a regular part of university life. Heather was too smart to claim that her personal conflict, as a young white girl growing up in a male-dominated society, was akin to racial repression. But her understanding broadened at university. It became easier for her to grasp why she was dismissed as a 'chick' or a '*poppie* [doll]', who apparently needed a husband to justify her existence, when she realized how apartheid brutalized so many lives.

'The whole country is fucked,' she said bleakly to me one night.

Yet her boyfriend was elated by white South African life. In February 1976 Jürgen and Heather remained a couple despite being separated by the army. She had kissed him goodbye early the previous month, her sadness intensified by his excitement at spending a year in the army.

Jürgen's return home on a weekend pass after almost two months of basic training coincided with the end of Heather's first few weeks of varsity life. Her new world was a direct counter to his military regime. He embraced the stark rituals of basic training as if he had been born to serve in the army. Jürgen told Heather happily that, as an aspiring radio operator in the SADF, he had a good chance of being sent to the front line. His ambition to fight on the border repelled her.

Gung-ho Jürgen was oblivious to his girlfriend's sexual politics and her attitude towards apartheid. Instead, he spoke about the way in which he had learned to treat his rifle as if it was his 'wife'. Hours of basic training were spent caring for a recruit's new 'wife' as he disassembled, cleaned, reassembled and polished his rifle until it gleamed. Jürgen was a masterful husband. He could whip through his gun routines at dazzling speed.

Heather felt like giving him a quick pistol-whipping around the head. She shuddered when he spoke of his desire to beat up some 'munts' [a white South African version of 'nigger']. Jürgen and a few of his friends were tempted to return to Germiston High and find some of the 'munts' who worked there. These were the same men who had been so loyal to Granddad George. Jürgen wanted to teach them a lesson because they smoked 'dagga' [marijuana] behind the toilets.

Six weeks in the army had apparently transformed a cheerfully uncomplicated rower like Jürgen into a disturbing presence. Heather broke up with him that very night.

'But why?' a suddenly confused soldier lamented. 'What have I done?'

KEVIN SCOTT KNEW how the army worked when it broke a conscript. It tried to turn soft and muddled young civilians into soldiers of hardened certainty. Discipline and fighting spirit needed to replace doubt and diffidence. At the age of twenty, and three years since he had completed his initial ten months of military service, my cousin could see the reason for all the army's talk of '*rooi gevaar*' [red danger], the threat of communism and terrorists. Kevin and his fellow soldiers were led to believe that a black 'terr' [terrorist] would want to slit their white South African throats on the border. They were made to feel the severity of the threat so that, unquestioningly, they would be ready to crush any opposition.

Once a national serviceman had been broken, and accepted commands automatically, the reverse process began. He was built back up again, and praised as he underwent specialist training. Kevin had been through it all, and he was a good soldier, as practical and dedicated as he was strong and fit. But he was also worn down by the prospect of returning to uniform. In January 1976 he was called up for the first of three three-month camps. He would turn twenty-one on the border.

Kevin was settled and happy at Eskom, where he underplayed the fact that he was the nephew of the head of the company's generation division. He had not been married for long, to Eleanor, with whom he had broken up during his first stint in the army, and just before his next camp he found out that she was only a few weeks pregnant. Kevin knew he would miss his wife, and the important first few months of her pregnancy. He prepared reluctantly for duty.

Border conflict had become increasingly serious, and before he rejoined his platoon Kevin was told to get all his papers in order. He needed to be fully insured, in case of injury or death.

Four of the five countries surrounding South Africa were at war. Rhodesia, South-West Africa, Mozambique and Angola were seething with the struggle of black liberation against colonial rule. Botswana remained quiet but the pressure elsewhere was intense. Even Rhodesia's crack army units could not hold back Joshua Nkomo's ZAPU and Robert Mugabe's ZANU forces forever. ZAPU and ZANU were also backed by the Soviet Union, while Rhodesia had become isolated from Britain and America. The rise of Zimbabwe was inevitable.

The previous year, Mozambique and Angola had won their battle for independence from Portugal. In March 1975, Frelimo had taken control of Mozambique while eight months later, in November, the MPLA became the new ruling party in Angola. There was more trouble in South-West Africa. The South African army were trying to quell a different acronym of 'terrorists' in Swapo [the South-West African People's Organization]. Skirmishes near the border between South-West Africa and Angola did not amount to a full-scale war but Swapo were becoming belligerent. They had begun to launch attacks from bases within Angola. At the same time the MPLA had been dragged into a post-liberation civil war against the rival and South African-backed factions of Unita and the FNLA. After fourteen years of armed struggle against the Portuguese, the three rival groups all pursued overall control of Angola.

Kevin suspected the South African army operated deep in Angola, despite emphatic denials from the government in Pretoria. The truth was confirmed when he re-joined his armoured division as a gunner. They headed first to Oshakati, the largest town in the northern region of Owamboland, where the SADF based itself. Kevin realized that he was in the midst of one of the biggest military offensives the South African army had attempted since World War II.

Operation Savannah had begun three months before, in October 1975, with the express purpose of assisting the rebel forces of Unita and the FNLA against the Soviet-funded MPLA. John Vorster's desire to curb the MPLA meant that the South African prime minister had already ratified the provision of arms, worth $14 million, to Unita and the FNLA. By December 1975 around 3,000 South African soldiers were active, covertly, in Angola. At the same time 4,000 Cuban troops had arrived to assist the MPLA in bolstering its new government.

When Kevin moved from Oshakati to Ondangwa, where fighting with Swapo was intense, he became even more aware that the SADF were effectively at war in Angola. He moved across the border and spent his twenty-first birthday guarding one of the small Angolan towns the SADF and Unita had captured. It was not much of a day for him, so far from home, but he was fortunate to be considered one of the '*ou manne* [old men]' and spared front-line duty.

The SADF made its eighteen-year-old national servicemen bear the brunt of the action because, in terms of adverse publicity and insurance payouts, it was worse to lose a married civilian attending a three-month camp. Kevin was assigned to a troop responsible for guarding the Ruacana Power Station on the South-West African and Angolan border. He watched the SADF blow up a bridge crossing the Kunene as they attempted to limit the chances of an attack on the power plant from MPLA and Cuban forces in Angola, and to prevent their escape route being cut off. It was a tactic which the Angolans themselves had used previously when trying to slow the South African invasion. They had destroyed Bridge 14 on the Nhia River as they and the Cubans were pursued by the SADF. The South African reaction had already entered army folklore.

Despite constant enemy fire, sappers had rebuilt Bridge 14. Armoured columns from the SADF had poured across it into Angola where they had routed the Cubans who had been waiting to ambush them. The soldiers themselves were convinced that they would take Luanda from the MPLA but, politically, South Africa could not proceed without American support. Forty-nine SADF soldiers had been killed in Angola or, officially, gone 'missing'. For the sake of public morale it was considered best to arrange a strategic withdrawal – while continuing to support Unita's efforts to destabilize the MPLA. A different kind of war had begun.

OUR INNOCENCE ENDED in April 1976. I had just turned fifteen and the prospect of a week away from home was exhilarating. We were ready to escape our parents on a school trip in the wide open veld. A gang of us took up the three back rows of seats in the bus early that Monday morning. Dave, John, Pashe and

I sat alongside Russel, Norbert, Albie, Eddie, Robert, Milan, Basil, Mauricio, Hannes and Moreno. We were a mini-United Nations of cultures and nationalities – Jewish, Portuguese, Greek, German, British, Afrikaans, Dutch, Hungarian, Czech and Italian.

With a name like mine, and four grandparents who had been born in Aberdeen and Glasgow, I was obviously of Scottish descent. But I didn't feel Scottish at all. Like everyone else I felt as South African as biltong and boerewors. I loved 'braaivleis, rugby, sunny skies and horny girls', the song we sang dementedly as soon as we turned out of the Germiston Lake school grounds, replacing the plug for Chevrolet with a celebration of the lusty Lolitas we hoped to meet at Schoemansdal Veld School.

'Ag, don't be so *dof* [stupid],' some bright spark shouted. 'There's gonna be nothing but *okes* [guys] there. This is gonna be like Y.P. – not a *blerrie* [bloody] porn movie.'

I hid my sudden unease by singing even more loudly. My best friend, Hilton, had already convinced his parents that it would not be in his interests to make the trip to Schoemansdal. Hilton was more thoughtful than my other friends, who were generally as loud and swaggering as me, and I trusted his judgement. He was the only boy in whom I confided my true thoughts about the army. With everyone else I played the role of a '*joller*' [a party-going dude] – and so I was never going to duck out of Schoemansdal myself. It was easier to remain one of the boys.

Our 280-mile journey took seven hours, and we were dazed with dusty fatigue when we arrived. The surrounding mountains and the lush bush were beautiful in the late afternoon light. But Schoemansdal itself, with an iron gate and barbed wire fencing, looked like a prison camp.

'Welcome to Schoemanshell,' someone muttered, accentuating the 'hell' in his made-up name.

Our coolest teacher, Mr McGettigan, whom we called 'Tim' in

his more relaxed moments, told us we would be joined by Mr Lightfoot, the camp commander. Apparently he liked to be known as *Oom* [Uncle] Lighty.

What a scream. *Oom* Lighty? Uncle bloody Lighty? Only an Afrikaner, a thick Dutchman, would want to be called *Oom* Lighty.

Eventually he appeared, Oom Lighty himself. '*Goeie middag, manne* [Good afternoon, men]', he said as he heaved himself up the stairs and stood at the front of the coach. 'Welcome to Schoemansdal Youth Camp. My name is *Meneer* [Mr] Lightfoot . . .'

He eyed us solemnly, before smiling with queasy sincerity. 'But listen, *manne*, you can just call me Oom Lighty . . .'

Our bus rocked with incredulous laughter. But we soon fell silent as Oom Lighty stressed the disciplined Christian principles of the camp and explained that we would be tested both physically and psychologically at Schoemansdal. We would camp under the stars on three of our four nights at Veld School and face various trials that would prepare us for a dangerous world.

All our excitable hopes that a few girls might spice up a week in the veld were ruined. We could see a snaking line of spotty-faced boys from Benoni High staring dolefully at us as we left our bus. It was more disturbing to see the army fatigues and grim expressions of Oom Lighty's bearded pals – *Meneer* Viljoen and *Meneer* Keuen.

We were marched to some low-slung brick dormitories and completely bare rooms.

'Where are the beds, chinas?' a hopeful soul asked plaintively.

We were holding them. Our sleeping bags were meant to be unrolled onto the hard floor rather than on top of any soft and feathery mattress.

Our exhaustion became obvious only an hour later. At a veld school version of dinner, we stared at our plates. We were meant to be eating spaghetti and egg, and the horribly mangled slop in front of us made us shudder.

'*Heerlik army-kos, kerels!* [Lovely army-food, guys!],' Oom Lighty chortled.

'Our girl wouldn't eat this crap,' someone complained, thinking of his black maid at home, 'never mind the dog.'

The tin plates and old forks and spoons seemed exactly like the kind of crockery and utensils that our maids used every night. But at least Maggie ate our food, and I knew that back in Germiston a tastier dinner would be waiting for her in the warming oven as she washed the dishes.

In one of the many lectures we endured at Schoemansdal, Oom Lighty advised us to maintain a close relationship with our domestic servants. We should try to get to know our black maids and gardeners better so that, through them, we might pick up information which could help combat unrest. Oom Lighty handed out printed leaflets which summed up the challenge confronting white South Africans.

'*Today, South Africa is facing a silent war against communism and terrorism. They are trying to get you. You are the youth of the country – you are the leaders of tomorrow. The communist says, "Give me a child and I will win the war." They want the whole world. The so-called freedom fighters on our borders are not fighting for freedom – but for communism. There are also thousands of terrorists at work in the locations and townships around our country. Be aware of them. Speak to your servant – she will tell you. If you notice anything strange about her, don't be afraid to tell the police. We must make use of our superior knowledge to outwit the communists. How do we get this knowledge? Listen to the radio. Read the newspapers. We must be spiritually prepared. We must be militarily prepared. We must be like David against Goliath. We will defeat communism and terrorism and live peacefully in our beautiful country.*'

It was so ridiculous that we barely paid attention to Oom Lighty and his disciples as we sat around a camp fire. But there was enough fear to make us nod whenever we were asked if we understood the looming gravity of the *rooi gevaar* [red danger] and the *swart gevaar* [black danger]. There was no point antagonising Oom Lighty's glowering henchmen.

We only showed outright disdain when, during the most ludicrous lecture of the week, our holy trilogy of Afrikaners tried to teach us the meaning of numbers and symbols in communism. It was impossible not to laugh out loud when they warned us never to get involved with a girl, no matter how beautiful she might appear, if she wore a T-shirt emblazoned with the image of a butterfly or the number 69. Indulging in a bout of sixty-nine with a butterfly-loving girl was one of our purest fantasies, and we would have worn red satin hammer-and-sickle underwear if it would bring us closer to that delicious honey pot. We loved the idea that the communists might use women to seduce us. We were ready to be used and abused.

'This is no laughing matter,' Oom Lighty warned. 'You don't know how these people think.'

If this was how they thought, in dirty dreams of free love and oral sex, we were raving Marxists already. But of course we had to sound sensible beneath the baleful glare of Afrikanerdom and so we politely challenged the curious logic of Oom Lighty and his men.

They jumped on our doubt with religious zeal, pointing out how naive most of us were in failing to see the link between ordinary numeracy and communist subversion. We thought it amusing that a whole bunch of us were already wearing T-shirts with numbers written on them, for it was considered fashionable, at least in Germiston in 1976, to pay homage to the American jock. Most of us wore strange v-necked T-shirts which featured a wide variety of apparently meaningless numbers, like 5, 17, 88 and 99 that sounded like the digits dished out to a big squad of American footballers.

Our lecturers lingered over their own mocking laughter. Did we really have no idea that each number was linked to a specific prophecy or event in the history of communism? Pointing to the number 5 on one boy's shirt, Oom Lighty was aghast to think we had not picked up a direct reference to Stalin's five-year plan. Did we not know that the communists always worked to five-year plans?

Oom Lighty pointed at another shirt and another number. What was the significance, to the communist, of the number 17? We stared blankly at Oom Lighty. He clapped his hands, as if to wake us from our stupor. The Russian Revolution had begun in 1917.

We set out to demolish Oom Lighty's theory, picking out two numbers ourselves that went beyond the obvious historical curve. What could 88 mean, apart from two fat ladies playing bingo in Benoni? 'Eighty-eight?' Oom Lighty said slowly, thinking hard, trying to remember if anything significant had happened in 1888, at least in his working knowledge of Russian history.

'Don't you know?' Oom Lighty finally said. 'Eight. Eight. What is Afrikaans for "out"?'

'*Uit,*' we said, hearing the word sound exactly like 'eight.'

'*Ja* [Yes],' Oom Lightly exclaimed. '*Uit. Uit.* They are saying: "Out! Out!" They want us to get the hell out of Africa.'

Someone stuck his hand up amid the stunned hush. '*Ja, Meneer,* [Yes, Sir],' Oom Lighty said.

'How long have they have been speaking Afrikaans in Moscow?'

Oom Lighty stroked his chin thoughtfully. 'The communist is very clever. He takes control of people who can speak our language.'

We threw one last number back at him – the 99 I wore on my shirt. I'd persuaded my mom to buy it for me from Edgars because there wasn't a 69 in the whole store.

'Ninety-nine is their final aim,' Oom Lighty said bluntly. 'They want to take over the whole world by the end of this century. 1999 is the end of the world, if the communist gets his way.'

On our second night we had to survive out in the bush on our own, relying on ourselves and a small platoon of boys. Each group was provided with a tent, a compass, a torch and a whistle. We would be led deep into the bush by an experienced commander who'd then leave us to pitch camp for the night. At dawn we would be expected to find our way back to the base.

The long slow march into the African blackness was conducted in silence, apart from the occasional nervous giggling at the sound of an animal in the distance or a stray curse when someone snagged themselves on a thorn bush. We walked for an hour, heading further into the unknown, until we were finally allowed to stop. All our teachers and commanders had retreated back to base and so we were alone.

There had been enough mosquitoes and ticks on our first night to ensure that we spent a long time examining the ground for scorpions and snakes before we spread out our sleeping bags. It was freezing in the bush and we shivered when we heard, according to our resident wildlife expert, a chatty red-headed boy called Hannes Oosthuizen, a couple of hyenas.

In an effort to take our mind off the hyenas we asked each other questions. What was fucking old Oom Lighty thinking? Wasn't this the most terrible week of our lives? If we could have any woman in the world join us in our sleeping bag who would we choose? Miss Murray from Germiston High or Farrah Fawcett-Majors? And what would we have for breakfast if we could escape Schoemanshell and find ourselves back in the comfy warmth of our homes?

We woke in a grey dawn feeling sore after a night on stony ground. But we were alive at least, uneaten by scrawny hyenas or hairy rock-spiders. We were also starving. It had taken over an hour to trudge this far, with a guide who knew the way, and so we feared that it might take twice as long to get back to camp. The more sensible members of our platoon hunched over the compass, trying to pinpoint the way south because we had been told we were marching north the previous night. They agreed, after some bickering, to head through the trees about a hundred metres from where we had slept. The rest of us shrugged sleepily, tagging along because compasses and camp commandos existed outside our sharply focused interest in girls and sport.

Slowly, we picked our way through the trees and bushes and blinked blearily at a surreal sight. Schoemansdal was right in front of us. We gaped at the roaring faces of Oom Lighty and his men. They slapped each other on the back in delight as we shuffled in embarrassment.

'*Ja*,' Oom Lighty chuckled, 'you *manne* thought you were walking straight into the bush last night. But we had you going round in circles. You stayed right inside the camp the whole time!'

And then Oom Lighty held up his hand to make a serious point. At least we had faced our fears. We would make it as soldiers, one day, Oom Lighty promised.

The next night we were taken to a bare field where giant obstacles had been assembled. It was an army survival course where we had to scale hulking contraptions and work out ways to help each other climb over dizzyingly high obstacles. We had to cross a river using two ropes, one of which worked as a knotted pathway for our feet while we held onto the other with our hands as we inched across the black waters below. And after we had leopard-crawled and run hard and reached the end, we were told to feel proud of each other and of ourselves.

Oom Lighty asked us to join him in prayer. I kept my eyes open as he thanked '*Liewe Here* [Dear God]' for the lessons we had learned in renewing our commitment to the future security of South Africa. We would fight with all our might to keep our country a place of freedom and faith.

I looked around the campsite, winking back at my friends who were also ignoring Oom Lighty's call for united prayer. I also saw Tim McGettigan, and recognized from the look in his eye that a teacher really was on our side.

As we prepared for our departure from Schoemanshell the following morning, we sat in a bus parked alongside the Benoni High coach. We felt drunk with the anticipation of fleeing Oom Lighty and seeing our parents again. Both buses rocked with chanting and we swapped jokey insults with their boys. The mood soon soured. One of their *brekers*, a big mug, showed us the dreaded zap sign, sticking the end of his thumb between his index and middle fingers, as his way of telling us to fuck off. And then, reeling through a cosmopolitan array of gestures, he gave us the finger, thumbed his nose and raised his forearm in a provocative flurry.

'Fuck you!' he yelled. 'Your mom's a bloody *poes* [cunt]!'

Oom Lighty had clearly not brought serenity to the boys from Benoni. But the *breker* had picked out our biggest kid, Eddie Paoli, who was coolly staring at him from a side window.

'What you looking at you fat *moffie* [queer]?' the *breker* shouted.

'You,' Eddie said quietly. He was on his feet before the Benoni boy could say anything else.

'*Ed-die ... Ed-die ... Ed-die ...*' we chanted as our hero walked along the gangway, down the stairs and stood in the grassy patch between the vehicles. The *breker* joined him.

I had seen enough school-ground fights, and had had a few myself, but this felt menacing. The size of the two boys, who were big enough to pass for eighteen, made it seem serious.

As they circled each other, I felt a little afraid for Eddie.

They flew at each other, and were soon rolling on the ground, flinging punches as the blows bounced off heads and smacked into faces. But Eddie, our champ, was too strong. He soon got the Benoni boy in a headlock and dragged him to the side of their bus.

Slowly, systematically, he began smashing the boy's head against the bus as we chanted '*Ed-die ... Ed-die ... Ed-die ...*'

I stopped after a while, turning to look at the boys screaming around me, as Eddie continued his retribution.

It needed McGettigan and a few other teachers to pull Eddie away from the bashed-up Benoni boy. The fight was over and we had won, but I just wanted to get away from Schoemanshell.

Late that Friday afternoon, I was the last off the bus. Mom was waiting for me, her face alight with happiness. I could have cried when I saw her but, instead, I just hugged her and told her how glad I was to be home. And then, stepping back, I shook my head. 'I'm never going,' I said.

'Where?' she asked.

'The army,' I said softly.

'Don't think about it now,' she replied. 'You're home.'

Soweto Riots, 16 June, 1976. Mbuyisa Makhubo carries the
dead body of Hector Pietersen, the first child to die in the riots.
Hector's sister, Antoinette, runs alongside them.

Chapter Nine

THE REVOLUTION WILL
NOT BE TELEVISED

THE BLISS OF BEING HOME became complete early the following week. At the age of fifteen I finally lived in a house
with a television set. It seemed as if, having escaped the backwoods
of Schoemansdal, we had reached the modern world. We were free
at last.

Television had been banned for so long I had almost given up
hope that the day would ever come. When I'd been a small boy
living in Witbank, Prime Minister Hendrik Verwoerd had compared television to the atomic bomb. He warned that: 'They are
modern things – but that does not mean they are desirable. We
have to watch for any dangers to our people, both physical and spir-
itual.'

Even after Verwoerd was assassinated, the Minister for Posts and
Telegraphs, Albert Hertzog, remained adamantly opposed to 'the
devil's box'. Hertzog believed that, 'inside the pill of television

there is the bitter poison which will ultimately mean the downfall of civilization'. He saw television as 'a deadly weapon' that could be used to 'undermine the morale of the white man and even to destroy great empires'.

Hertzog had been disgusted by a subsequent softening of apartheid. Making even the draconian Prime Minister John Vorster sound like a thoughtful liberal, Hertzog was incensed by his own removal from the cabinet in 1968. He left the Nationalists to form his own party – the even more right-wing *Herstigte Nasionale Party van Suid-Afrika* [Reconstituted National Party of South Africa] which called for a return to strict Calvinism, the adoption of Afrikaans as the only national language and a far stricter separation of the races.

The HNP believed that black domestic servants should be returned permanently to their 'homelands'. They endorsed pure racism and were contemptuous of government attempts to blur their policies by trying to rebrand apartheid as 'Separate Development'. Hertzog's breakaway party relished the rigorous isolation of apartheid, and a readiness to live without black servants.

Most white South Africans felt differently. We needed our black maids and cleaners and gardeners and labourers and dustbin men and petrol pump attendants. And so we were happy to allow natives in our suburbs if it meant that they did all our dirty and boring chores. Yet we were still aggrieved to be considered pariahs by the outside world – and pined for television.

In July 1969 Neil Armstrong had became the first man to set foot on the moon. My parents had listened to the historic moment on radio; and I'd pasted newspaper pictures of the moonwalk in a scrapbook. The rest of the world watched Armstrong walk across the moon on television.

White South Africans felt as if they had missed out terribly, and even government ministers expressed disappointment. It seemed curious that the most powerful and technologically advanced country in Africa was locked in the past when it came to television. Fifteen other African countries, including Rhodesia, already boasted their own national TV stations. Hertzog and the HNP argued that Rhodesia's fate proved their point. Television had been introduced to Rhodesia in 1961 and, since then, the country buckled under the threat of black majority rule.

South Africa was controlled by the Broederbond [Brotherhood], a less-than-secret organization of Afrikaans leaders who promoted their own *volk* [people], culture and language. Every single prime minister and state president since the emergence of apartheid in 1948 had been a senior member of the Broederbond, and that pattern remained unbroken until Nelson Mandela came to power in 1994.

One of Hertzog's first decisions when he became Minister of Posts and Telegraphs had been to appoint Piet Meyer as the head of the South African Broadcasting Corporation. Within two years, Meyer also became chairman of the Broederbond. Meyer emerged as a more sophisticated propagandist than Hertzog. He believed, in the mid-1970s, that television could be used as a weapon on behalf of Afrikanerdom. 'We must harness all our communication media in a positive way,' Meyer told the general council of the Broederbond. 'This will allow us to gather up Afrikaner national political energy in the struggle for survival.'

We were oblivious to the machinations of the Broederbond. We just wanted to join the rest of the world in watching TV every night; and so there was great excitement when television was formally unbanned and a national service began on 5 January, 1976. One of my friends, Pascali Paschalides, and his go-ahead Greek family had their television installed in time for the opening broadcast. We were thrilled to be in their living room, whooping and eating his mom's baklava, when the first glorious pictures were screened. It seemed daring that the SABC had decided to launch television in brilliant colour rather than in regimented black-and-white.

My parents waited a couple of months, as if to ensure that the government would not shut down the broadcasts, before they splashed out on our first set – a little Sony TV that looked like a box of magic in our study. The SABC only screened two hours of television a day, between six and eight every evening, and there was just a single channel. One hour of the daily broadcast was in Afrikaans with the other half being in English. It still felt like Christmas/*Kersfees* every day.

We were ecstatic to have left the Dark Ages. Life seemed sweeter than ever.

THE MORNING OF 16 June, 1976, was typical of that winter. On a bitterly cold Wednesday the steam rose from a long line of black walkers as, leaving the township trains, they trudged up the hill to the white homes where they would work for another day. I pulled on my black school jersey and, from my upstairs window, watched the procession. My bedroom was warm but the black people outside looked frozen. The men wore balaclavas against the icy chill, while the women wrapped themselves in blankets. Misty puffs of breath slipped from their mouths.

Downstairs, in the kitchen, Maggie Thabang glanced over her shoulder and said hello. She held her hands over one of the hot plates on our electric stove. Maggie looked bleary with weariness as she tried to warm herself. Our two furry dogs, the collie and a German Shepherd, leapt around me excitedly. They left muddy paw prints all over the kitchen floor that Maggie had cleaned the afternoon before, and she clicked her tongue in irritation.

She shook her head and retreated to the sink where she would soon wash our breakfast dishes. I wondered if Maggie had another hangover because she seemed surly, whereas usually she was cheerful. But I made a point of not shooing the dogs outside and allowed them to follow me into the dining room where my parents and Heather were having breakfast.

Dad's radio, as usual, was cranked up loud and his head was buried in the morning paper. Mom was in the midst of planning her schedule for the day which, after Wednesday morning tennis at the Eskom courts, was crammed with charity work. She was organizing a book sale to raise funds for the Simmer Sanatorium, or the 'loony bin' as I called it, and arranging a theatre evening to benefit the local orphanage. Heather was even busier at university with mid-year exams in between activities at the various societies and clubs to which she belonged. She had moved into a strange new world that meant little to me as I stayed in the same old school routine.

The usual gang of us met outside my house on our bikes and, wearing balaclavas and gloves, we liked to think we resembled a spooky gang. But we were so caught up in chattering about what we had seen on television the night before that there was nothing menacing about our weaving roll through the chilly suburban streets.

By mid-morning, with the sun streaming through the classroom windows, we took off our blazers in double English with the delectable Miss Horne. She was another young and pretty teacher. As boys at the back of the class, we eyed her with such relish she often could not help but blush. But we liked Miss Horne, rather than just lusted after her, and her literature lessons were my favourite of the week. As she led us through our set book for the year, *Animal Farm*, she made George Orwell sound like one of the most interesting writers who had ever lived. The 'four legs good, two legs bad' mantra echoed around our class as Miss Horne explained the political backdrop in a way that made it seem as if Orwell was not just attacking Stalinism but all totalitarian states.

English merged into History which, in Standard Eight, our third year at high school, had become far more interesting. Rather than being force-fed Afrikaner nationalism, we studied Napoleon's epic attempt to invade Russia in 1812, which ended in such disaster, as well as the rise of Hitler. Our history teacher, Miss Zeiss, was much older than Miss Horne, and a friend of my mother. She did not make it onto our list of teaching babes, but she gripped our attention. It was too risky for her to draw any obvious parallel between Nazism and Afrikaner nationalism but her historical echo made us think more clearly about South Africa.

I felt strangely engaged by school that day, by Orwell and history. The memory remains vivid because it is tied to the momentous events that were already unfolding ten miles away, in Soweto. I had no idea that, in the middle of the morning on 16 June, 1976, black school-children my age, or younger, had just taken to the streets in a bloody protest that would change South Africa forever and mark the beginning of apartheid's collapse.

Instead, oblivious to the township struggle as children were shot and killed, I rocked on my chair and spoke about sex and transvestites with Beverley Ackermann. We had only four girls in our class of twenty-five, and Lynn Shepherd and Beverley were the funky pair with whom we could flirt and sometimes kiss at the next party in the garage of some kid's family home. Beverley loved *The Rocky Horror Picture Show*, which had just been released in South Africa. There was outrage that such a decadent film had slipped through the censors' net. It had been passed with a u-18 certificate which meant that fifteen-year-olds like us were too young to gain entry.

We still managed to blag our way into the 20th Century cinema on President Street, just down the road from the Shul where I had been to three of my friends' bar mitzvahs. The 20th was the best movie-house in Germiston and the Jewish girl at the ticket-kiosk gave us a wink whenever we sneaked into an over-age film.

Beverley and I had both seen *The Rocky Horror Picture Show*. She laughed huskily as she stretched out in class and told me she was being driven wild imagining what it would be like to meet a man as hot as Tim Curry, who played the lead role of a transvestite in his ruby red lipstick, pearls, latex corset and gloves, black panties, suspender belt, fishnet stockings and high-heeled boots. Beverley narrowed her big green eyes and told me that he was definitely the sexiest man she had ever seen.

I was mildly shocked that a Germiston girl could have a steamy crush on a transvestite – and pointed out that, as Dr Frankenfurter, Curry wore suspenders and stockings. 'That's what's so sexy about him,' Beverley sighed. 'Did you see his legs? And those luscious lips? He's gorgeous.'

Susan Sarandon was more to my taste. I regaled Beverley with my own drooling take on how the most arousing scene in *The Rocky Horror Picture Show* centred on the transformation of the very prim Janet, played by Sarandon, into a shamelessly wanton woman. '*Ja*,' Beverley said, 'but Tim Curry is even hotter.'

We were never going to go out together, because I was still a sucker for older girls and Beverley knew I was not Germiston's answer to Tim Curry, but there was a little frisson between us when she suggested we see the movie again that afternoon. There was a matinee at 2:30, and we could just about make it as school finished an hour earlier.

The idea of sitting in the back row of the 20th Century with Beverley, who might even let me slip a hand inside her bra as she ogled a British transvestite, seemed scarily enticing.

'I can't,' I gulped. 'I'm playing rugby this afternoon.'

She laughed and said Dr Frankenfurter would be disappointed. He was definitely not a rugby player.

Amid all the contradictions and contrasts, between the deep repression of white South Africa and the fleeting emancipation of Germiston High, I felt a jolt of happiness. I knew I would never forget those days, no matter what happened in the years ahead. I was entranced by literature and history, by sex and Susan Sarandon, by sport and even school.

And that afternoon, I played rugby with pure abandonment and had a rare stormer of a game. By the time I climbed onto my bicycle just before five I felt sore but elated. The hurt felt good. I could have done with seeing Alison Fleischer and Lucinda Robinson, or Beverley Ackermann fresh from another titillating encounter at *The Rocky Horror Picture Show*, to show off my battle wounds in the imagined hope that they might strip me down and clean me up. But I really needed a real woman, the Orwell-quoting Miss Horne or the Camus-inspired Miss James, to tell me to chuck my bike into the back of her car, so that she could give me a lift back to her place.

I amused my friends with my fantasies as our shadows meandered up a long hill. Anderson Lane was a killer. But we pedalled steadily. Our small crew leant back in our saddles and steered the high handle-barred machines home. We were the dudes in *Easy Rider*, we were the *peloton* in the Tour de France. We were preparing ourselves for great things – from our first hangover to our first woman.

As we climbed that dappled hill I saw the helicopters. I pointed just as someone shouted 'Check the choppers!' The leading helicopter was followed by another and another and then two more. There were five of them, flying tightly together, heading to the south-west of a darkening sky. They were police helicopters. Silhouetted against the end of the day's streaks of blue, red and yellow, they looked beautiful.

The surrounding streets were quiet, and our breathless chatter rang out. We turned into Cachet Road and freewheeled down the long street where I lived. I eventually shouted out 'bye!' and 'check you tomorrow' and skidded into our drive. I had forgotten about the helicopters arcing through the winter sunset. Ginny and Lindy, our dogs, yapped as I got off my bike. I was glad to be home. I could see mom and Maggie in the kitchen, working behind a steamed-up window.

Mom's face was even more clouded when she saw me saunter into the kitchen. As she said hello, I noticed that Maggie looked away. 'What's wrong?' I asked my mother. She poured me some juice and sat me down at the kitchen table. Mom said that she didn't really know the exact details, except that there had been trouble all day in Soweto.

Maggie walked over to me. She put her hand on my arm and squeezed it. I looked up in puzzlement. 'There has been trouble for the children,' Maggie said softly.

There was such sadness in Maggie's brown face that, suddenly, I felt afraid. It was if she was worried most about me, as if Maggie was like another mother to me. I was no longer the cool cat swinging on his chair at the back of the class as I answered questions about George Orwell or pretended to know what I was talking about when discussing transvestism. I was just a boy looking up uncertainly at the two women who knew me better than anyone: mom and Maggie.

My mother explained the facts she had heard. The schoolchildren of Soweto were rioting. Some of them were younger than me. The township was burning, and the police had shot many black children. They said they had no choice. The government were about to send the army into the township. I thought of the helicopters, and my mouth felt dry. More than a million black people lived in Soweto, just fifteen miles away. Other townships, like Natalspruit and Katlehong, were even closer. The day had come. This was the black revolution they had warned us about in Schoemansdal. Oom Lighty had told us to prepare ourselves for war.

I longed for dad to walk through the kitchen door with his bulging briefcase, Bertie, so that he could tell us everything was going to be all right. But dad never got home before six. Heather was due back at any moment and mom said she would be relieved to see her.

I was still confused. Why were the children in Soweto rioting?

Maggie remained silent as I turned to her first. I thought she would know the reason better than my mother. Maggie shook her head and looked at mom: 'Madam,' she said, 'it's terrible.'

'I know,' my mother nodded.

My question remained unanswered until Heather eventually arrived. 'At last,' mom said. 'I've been so worried.'

Heather knew more than both mom and Maggie, because the news she had gleaned about Soweto at Wits University was different from the censored reports on state radio. It had been a day like no other at Wits, Heather said, because the whole university was enflamed. There had been no work done after the news from Soweto broke around mid-morning. A mass meeting had been arranged in the Great Hall and hundreds of students planned to march into downtown Johannesburg in protest at the shootings. Heather had heard the death toll was mounting and that the rioting was likely to escalate. Nervous policemen had arrived on campus that afternoon but, barracked and threatened, they had kept their distance from the main throng of students.

Student leaders, using megaphones, had shouted out the reasons for the riots. Apartheid was the cause of the unrest; but the violence had been sparked by a specific protest against the change in Bantu Education policy which insisted that black children would have to have fifty per cent of their subjects taught to them in Afrikaans, with the remainder in English. It was, again, puzzling. Why would a black child have to learn maths or history in Afrikaans?

Heather had brought home a pamphlet which provided a few choice quotes of explanation. In 1953, as Minister of Native Affairs, Hendrik Verwoerd had said: 'There is no place for the Bantu in the European community above the level of certain forms of labour ... What is the use of teaching the Bantu child mathematics when he cannot use it in practice? That is quite absurd. Education must train people in accordance with their opportunities in life, according to the sphere in which they live.'

This policy of downgrading education for black children was a cornerstone of apartheid. Punt Janson, the Deputy Minister of Bantu Education, said: 'I have not consulted the African people on the language issue and I'm not going to. An African might find that *"die grootbaas"* [the big boss] only spoke Afrikaans or English. It would be to his advantage to know both languages.'

Maggie shook her head in disgust. She paid for all her children's school books; but Heather and I received free, and far superior, education. My parents helped Maggie by giving her extra money to cover the costs. This latest indignity, however, cut deep.

I tried to imagine what it would be like to have trigonometry and algebra taught in Afrikaans. How would I feel if Miss Zeiss switched to Afrikaans as soon as she started teaching us about Napoleon or Hitler? I could imagine our howls of protest.

Heather said that it was another deliberately provocative act of state oppression and so thousands of black schoolchildren had gathered in Soweto that morning. The police blocked the students at the top of one of the township's dirt roads, just in case they really tried to march all the way into Johannesburg. A standoff ensued. The black children sang protest songs and stamped their feet, causing small clouds of dust to rise around them. They waved their banners at the white policemen. And then they started. The children moved towards the police.

They kept singing as the police raised their guns in warning. Some of the older students bent down to pick up stones. As they sang, they threw those same stones at the thick lines of blue. The police fired back. Small black bodies fell; but others began running towards the police, their stones and songs soaring through the air.

The rioting lasted all day, and it was hard to know what might happen next.

Even dad seemed uncertain when he returned home. Soweto was, apparently, 'quiet'. But I could only imagine the worst. I went to bed early that night and said a hushed prayer for us all; for mom and dad, Heather and Maggie and me.

WHEN WORKING PARENTS returned to Soweto on the night of 16 June, having travelled back from the city and suburbs on packed township trains, they saw the bodies. 'It was like war,' one father said. A single photograph captured the cost. Published in *The World* newspaper early the following morning, it showed a fifteen-year-old boy, Mbuyisa Makhubo, crying and running, his fingers digging deep into the crumpled black bundle he carried in his arms.

The dead boy he held was thirteen-year-old Hector Pietersen, the first child to be killed in the riots. Hector's sister, Antoinette, was two years older than Mbuyisa and me. She was seventeen. Antoinette looked on the verge of hysteria, her grief held back by disbelief. She ran as fast as her short and chunky legs allowed, holding up a hand as if to plead for the nightmare to stop.

They ran from Theuns Swanepoel, the Afrikaans police commander who gave the order for his men, twitching behind their guns, to open fire on the singing schoolchildren marching towards them. Swanepoel, the most notorious policeman in South Africa, liked to be called 'Rooi Ruus' – the Red Russian. He seemed ready to turn Soweto's dirt streets red with blood.

The rioting spread to townships all around the country. Hundreds of people were killed, with thousands more wounded, as clashes between black students and white policemen and soldiers flared in Port Elizabeth and Cape Town, while intensifying in Soweto and across the Highveld. It became impossible for the world to look away from apartheid, for the killing of children illustrated the brutality of the South African government.

It seemed incredible that, a week later, the All Blacks arrived on another controversial rugby tour. John Vorster welcomed them by insisting that there was 'no crisis' in South Africa. The New Zealanders discovered a different truth. Bryan Williams, a Samoan hero to us on the All Blacks' visit six years earlier, had already tried to justify his reasons for returning again.

'Apartheid does get me down,' Williams told the *Auckland Star*. 'Knowing that I'd probably be in the same situation as South Africa's blacks if I lived there is not a very nice thought. I do get depressed about it. But if you fight the problem by boycotts, by bullying someone, you get resented. If you go there, and discuss it with people, you do get communication.'

But Williams, Ian Kirkpatrick and two New Zealand journalists were amongst those tear-gassed in the middle of Cape Town when the police dispersed rioting students. Two other All Blacks, Tane Norton and Andy Leslie, the captain, were asked by a Durban mother, Lynette Philips, if they would visit her son at Voortrekkerhoogte's military hospital near Pretoria. He had been on the border, 'fighting the terrorists', when he had stood on a landmine. The boy's chest 'looked like meat waiting for the *braai*', his mother told the shocked All Blacks. Leslie declared that, 'South Africa is at war.'

The pictures on our television screens ripped away the layers of blindness from my eyes. I stared at the nightly news footage as armed white men, in police and army uniform, cut down children like they were stripping fresh bark from an old tree. Dad looked up from his reports and files and watched quietly, while mom was more vocal in her dismay.

It became harder to skip easily over the 'Whites Only' signs that surrounded us. It seemed as if there was nothing I did which did not involve remaining on the white side of life. We were on one side of a pane of glass; on the other side, smudged and blurred, the rest of South Africa remained. We kept going to our white schools and offices, our white shops and stadiums, driving in our white cars and eating in our white steakhouses; and all the while a black country burned.

By the time the All Blacks tour had creaked to a close on 18 September, with the Springboks winning the Test series 3-1, the rioting had still not ended. Three days later, the *Rand Daily Mail* reported on the findings of the country's Christian Institute which had discovered that, since 16 June, the students' death toll had passed 300. A further 5,200 people had been arrested; and 900 were still detained without trial. The police used eighteen different kinds of torture on the detainees and at least three of their prisoners had died in custody. Forty-six new security laws had been introduced by the government as they cracked down on the townships.

My eldest cousin, Brian, already knew he had to be careful. His latest army call-up began that week and he and his girlfriend, Alison, had devised a code that would enable them to communicate once he was on the border. Heather and I watched in fascination as, across the table from us in Germiston, my cousin and his girlfriend worked out how he would dupe the army censors and smuggle messages back to her in his correspondence. They hit upon a simple technique. He would use the first letters in a series of words of a paragraph about family members, either real or imagined, to spell out the name of the place where he would be working 'over the Red Line' – army slang for facing military conflict on the border. Brain would mention Auntie Jess and Uncle Ian, or Aunt Orla and Uncle Simon, or ask how Win and Hilda were, as he also wrote more general messages to her parents and his own mom and dad. And the key point would be for Alison to pick out the made-up relatives and use the first letters of each unfamiliar name to build a sequence which would reveal his whereabouts.

I could see how the code worked, but you needed to belong to our family to know who was a real or fake person. Jess, Ian and Win belonged to us; and so we had O for Orla, S for Simon and H for Hilda spelling out the first three letters: O-S-H. That would already be almost enough but, lower down in the letter, in another paragraph about family members Brian would add more bogus names beginning in A, K, A, T and I. And so the full name would be spelt out: Oshakati.

It felt like we were spies; and I was gripped by the subterfuge. But the seriousness of his three-month camp was hard to ignore when Alison pressed Brian to dream up some more code-words to tell her how safe, or otherwise, he felt. The unrest in the country, and the war on the border, lent an edge to the code. It also felt as if we were intimately involved as Brian had asked my mother if she would drive him to Kensington early the following morning. His own parents were overseas on business and he did not want Alison to take him to the drop-off point on her own.

He would spend his first four days at a camp in Soweto. After patrolling the township streets around Orlando, which had seen some of the worst rioting, he would take the 'Troop Train' with the rest of his platoon up to the border. Brian was twenty-four and he should have moved beyond the army. He wanted to concentrate on his career with Eskom and on his personal life. Having already bought her engagement ring, Brian and Alison had been forced to delay making any formal announcement until he returned from the border just before Christmas. The army had taken over his life, again.

My mother dropped him off in Kensington just after dawn, realizing that, in a few more years, it would be me who would make the same journey. And, four days later, she and Alison went to see Brian at Johannesburg station as, having survived Soweto, he climbed aboard the border train.

Brian made the most of what he hoped would be his last stint in uniform. Based at Oshakati, where he helped man the command centre, Brian spent six hours at a time in the radio tent. He encoded and decoded messages for battalions trying to keep the terrorist cadres from crossing the Angolan border. In between six-hour shifts, the signalmen officially had a twelve-hour rest period; but, usually, Brian and his colleagues were required to keep moving amongst all the infantry units in the region to adjust their radios or re-establish communications. His platoon was occasionally under fire but, inside northern South-West Africa [later Namibia], the biggest dangers were being ambushed or hitting a landmine. Brian had to cross landmine-strewn territory and it became a matter of instinct whether their Unimog all-terrain vehicle travelled down the side of a road or drove bang down the middle. They sat on a flat base at the back of the Unimog, with sandbags beneath them to absorb the worst impact.

The pressure on his platoon was intense and, rather than the usual forty-five-day tour of duty, they spent almost three months on the border. Brian completed eighty straight days across the Red Line, which meant he was awarded a Pro Patria medal; but he was too exhausted to really care. His platoon of thirty-two men, all but one of whom were graduates like him, were replaced by a signal battalion of 132 soldiers. The war was escalating, both in and outside the country.

EVEN DAD, whom we mocked as the most positive man in South Africa, talked of 'challenging times' and 'difficult days'. We took this as a sure sign of looming apocalypse, after the world had changed on 16 June.

Overseas investment in South Africa had shrunk still further and it had become increasingly difficult for dad to recruit enough skilled operators from abroad to fill all the specialist positions Eskom needed at their new power stations. For many potential candidates, the lure of African sunshine and a pampered lifestyle was offset by concerns about apartheid and rioting.

Dad, as always, saw an opportunity buried inside a problem. Eskom and South Africa were lurching towards a crisis, and yet a solution appeared like a vision to him. It was no longer sufficient to rely just on white workers. The country had enough people to do the work, as long as they were judged on their potential rather than their colour. Dad increasingly believed it was morally wrong to endorse government policy. In his own way, he began to think like a revolutionary. My sister and I, being teenagers, did not realize the significance, but dad planned a radical departure from normal business practice in South Africa in 1976. He began to consider how he might train black workers for skilled roles which were reserved exclusively for white South Africans.

The impoverished education his black employees had received meant that they had few academic qualifications. But a plant operator did not need much more than a year or two of high school and so dad saw a way forward. In the longer term he could even imagine a competent black operator becoming a shift engineer if the requirement for a more academic technical certificate was removed. As an engineer who had learnt most when he was working with his own hands, rather than in completing his university degree, dad decided the discriminatory policies of Bantu Education could be overcome by a black worker gaining practical experience.

He shared his thoughts with us, around the dinner table, and relied heavily on my mother's judgement. While Heather and I said little, apart from making the odd spiky comment, mom knew he had made the right choice. Yet it was too politically risky for him to discuss the idea with his colleagues in senior management at Eskom. He knew it would be gunned down as soon as he mentioned the bare outline of his plan. Conservative figures in the boardroom of a public utility would not consider flouting state policy on the whim of an English-speaking manager.

Dad told us he would not have long before news leaked out and he was blocked by senior executives, some of whom were already suspicious of the way he had turned his generating division, the CGU, into Eskom's most powerful department. He decided to broach the idea with a small group of power station managers in an attempt to gauge the levels of hostility or support before he took on the white trade unions and Eskom's board.

He moved cautiously at first. Explaining that they would have to think more practically than before, dad said they should encourage promising white plant operators to apply for further training so they might eventually become shift supervisors. At the same time, intelligent and responsible black labourers should be given the opportunity to better themselves so that, after adequate preparation, they might be ready to work as plant operators, replacing the white men who had moved up into positions as shift supervisors.

The expressions around the table confirmed that dad had made a scandalous suggestion. Ben Lategan, an Afrikaner, who revelled in his status as the strongest character amongst all South Africa's power station managers, was emphatic: 'You cannot do this. It goes against all our principles – and it's completely illegal.'

Asked for alternative ideas to solve the glaring lack of skilled manpower, they responded with shrugs. Dad urged them to accept that unless they adopted a more flexible approach then their own power stations, and the big 600-Megawatt sets that were soon to be introduced, would struggle to match the growing demand for electricity.

Lategan looked hard at my dad before he shook his head defiantly. 'We'll never go down that road,' he said. 'Never in a hundred million years.'

Dad praised the work Lategan had done as the manager of one of Eskom's most important new stations. It was less flattery than a sincere appreciation of his technical excellence. But, after that compliment, he asked Lategan if he would do him just one favour.

'What?' Lategan asked suspiciously.

'Think about this again tomorrow,' dad said.

'You know how I feel,' Mr Never-In-A-Hundred-Million-Years said gruffly. 'The answer is no.'

Dad was not surprised. Lategan was a deeply *verkrampte* [reactionary] Afrikaner whose power station, Camden, was not that far from Witbank, where we had once lived. It was a far right-wing area where people believed in hard-line apartheid. There was little talk of Separate Development from Lategan and his crew. The future of white South Africa was all that mattered; and *'die swarte'* [the blacks] were expected to know their place at the bottom of society.

There was no disillusion in dad as he set about plotting a new way of convincing other power station managers to adopt his thinking. He expected it might be easier in the Cape or Natal than in the *platteland* [flat farmlands] of the south-eastern Transvaal.

He was startled, however, when Lategan called him a few days later. The big man said he had done as dad had asked. He had thought carefully about all they had discussed. Dad expected another echo of his 'never in a hundred million years' mantra; but Lategan shocked him. 'Ian,' Lategan told my dad, 'I've changed my mind.'

Lategan was not only ready to support the radical proposals. He argued that the programme should start at his own power station. Lategan would ensure its success and, once it proved workable at Camden, it would be easier for dad to convince his other stations to follow their lead.

Dad, for one of the few times in his life, was stunned. But he was also elated. Ben Lategan was a man of conviction. If that conviction had once bolstered his unshakeable prejudice, it promised to drive through a different way of thinking in a heartland of Afrikanerdom. Dad trusted Lategan and, buoyed by the transformation, he visited every other power station in the country.

His most difficult moments came in the supposedly liberal Cape, with an English-speaking manager at Salt River. Dad was told that, coming from the Transvaal, he did not understand the mentality of the 'Cape Coloureds', and that the scheme would never work. In the end he had to return with Lategan, who had managed the Hex River power station in the Cape for years, and allow an Afrikaner to convince an intransigent English-speaker to proceed. No-one could tell Lategan that he didn't 'know' the coloureds and so he steamrollered through the reluctance. Salt River became the final power station to agree to this initial form of affirmative action.

At the same time mom and dad decided to attend a safety awards function for coloured staff at Salt River. They had to apply for permission from the security police to attend, as it was in the coloured area of Athlone. My parents were effectively breaking the law as laid down in the Group Areas Act and so the security police demanded a copy of the speech dad would make to his coloured employees. Even when he said he never wrote his speeches, but spoke spontaneously, he was told that he had to write down exactly what he planned to tell his staff.

Eventually, mom and dad were given permission to attend the event but were warned that white and coloured people would not be allowed to dance at the same time. It was also made plain that security police would be present to monitor proceedings.

My parents left Salt River for Athlone, and they had a great night. Dad made his speech, mom gave out some awards and they even took to the dance floor alongside the coloured workers in a spirit of goodwill. It was another risk, but the watching security policemen obviously decided that there was no point taking any action.

By the time they had flown home, dad decided he had better have a quiet word with his chief executive, Jan Smith, and the senior manager of personnel, Jannie van der Walt. Dad revered Smith, but he knew that van der Walt, who belonged to the Broederbond, did not harbour the same feelings towards him.

'Ian, what the hang are you doing?' Smith asked.

Dad laid out his plans as methodically as he could. Smith did not say much, which dad knew was a good sign. Finally, Smith said, 'OK,' and, far more thrillingly, 'It's amazing.'

The only proviso Smith laid down was that van der Walt should accompany dad when he met the white trade unions and that he should also be present during some of his discussions with Eskom's black staff. Otherwise it was up to dad to keep pushing forward – boldly but carefully.

Serious reservations emerged during his encounters with the union representatives. There was particular distaste at the thought that some of their members might eventually be asked to change into their work clothes alongside black plant operators. It was an outrageous image that would invite police scrutiny. Dad appeased the unions. He would never ask his employees to break the law, and of course it would remain a legal requirement for Eskom to maintain separate changing rooms and toilet facilities for whites and non-whites. The unions were uneasy but agreed that they would allow their members to at least listen to his proposals.

Black trade unions were banned, and so dad asked Edward Setshedi, a famous black runner, and Eskom employee, to accompany him as he went from one power station to another to meet his 'non-white' staff. Edward was charming and open, and dad trusted him implicitly. Together they set about convincing Eskom's black workers that they would have the opportunity to become more than just labourers or maintenance men. The main obstacle was the fear among staff that, if they failed to show the necessary aptitude to progress, their existing jobs would be lost. Dad had to reassure them that they would not be penalised, and that he actually expected, with the right training, all of them would succeed rather than fail.

It was draining but exhilarating, and dad and Edward forged a strong partnership. Yet, as a tumultuous 1976 slipped away, they were reminded of the true nature of the country in which we lived. When Edward was refused entry into the white dining room at a rural power station, Dad intervened. He would not eat with his white staff unless Edward was allowed to join them. Reluctantly, the power station manager nodded. Edward could have lunch with them.

These were momentous days for my father; but, at home, he could not ignore everything that had already happened beyond his working world. Heather finished her first year at Wits University and came home with a reminder that, while dad might have eaten lunch with a black man, 600 people had died in the deadly crackdown on the townships.

Black students remained defiant. As the year wound towards its end, Prime Minister Vorster warned white South Africa that the future would be even bleaker. 'You must fasten your seat belts because the storm has not struck yet,' he said, thrusting out his chin. His small eyes glittered on television. 'We are only experiencing the whirlwinds that go before it.'

On the beach in the 1970s – whites only

CHAPTER TEN

DIFFERENT GIRLS

In the witching hours of a cataclysmic year, late on a summer night in December 1976, I stepped out into the darkness. My room at Humewood Mansions, our usual hotel on the sea-front in Port Elizabeth, was at the end of a long corridor. Every floorboard creaked as I crept past my sister's room. My parents slept opposite the staircase, in a double-room overlooking the beach, but I was sure they would be asleep before eleven at night. Yellow light seeped from beneath Heather's doorway and I guessed she was reading as I went for my nightly jaunt. If she heard me, and stuck her head out of her room, I would have blushed guiltily.

'Where are you going?' she might have asked.

I would not have known how to answer. Even after two weeks I was not quite sure where I would end up on the streets. I did not even really understand what I hoped to find in the dark. Instead, I just walked, at first along Beach Road, staring at the inky Indian Ocean and breathing in the salty night air. Heading towards town, I followed the lights of the ships out at sea. It was one way of beating the boredom that, at fifteen, swallowed up most nights of a family holiday.

Every morning I loved body-surfing the big heavy rollers at Summerstrand, in between reading and eating ice cream as I turned a dark nutty brown in the delicious sunshine. Dad, Heather and I went surfing together for an hour at a time. Even mom took to her boogie board, her yellow cap bobbing in the surf. After lunch, back at the hotel, I would sleep deeply, exhausted by my nocturnal ventures and a long morning on the beach. I could then cruise through the ritual afternoon drive and tea-and-scones with my parents.

The nights were different. Once we'd had dinner, and coffee in the lounge, and gone for a walk down to Happy Valley, where carved dwarves were illuminated by Christmas lights, it felt too early to go straight to bed. I felt restless and curious. But my parents were in their late forties and content to have an early night, especially as they were up for a 6 a.m. swim at Kings Beach every day while Heather and I slept for a couple more hours.

My nightly walks were inspired most of all by the vague hope that, eventually, I would summon the courage to duck into a bar and order a beer just before midnight. It would be one way, the only way it seemed, I might meet a girl. But I was still a year away from shaving, and I did not dare risk the laughter if I tried to buy a Castle or Black Label in a dingy bar.

I had started drinking, occasionally at least, a year earlier, when I was just fourteen. At parties we would sneak in cans of beer, or take a quick *dop* [drink] from a bottle of cheap wine, and be amazed by how much prettier the girls looked and how easily we suddenly danced with them. At home, when my parents went to a business dinner, and Heather was out with her boyfriend, I would sometimes open up the liquor cabinet. I would take a swig or two from their creamier bottles of liqueur – shockingly sweet stuff like Cape Velvet or Baileys or, if I was really rocking, a very fruity

Amarula or coffee-tinged Tia Maria. A couple of healthy glugs got me tipsy and I only felt guilty a week or so later when dad noticed how low he was running with his liqueurs. He and mom always suspected the clandestine drinker was Maggie, because she had been caught often enough having a tipple from the cabinet.

But the lure of a seedy bar was wrapped around the fantasy of meeting a girl from Port Elizabeth who just happened to be on the lookout for a shy fifteen-year-old boy from Germiston. Sneaking in an illicit drink at the same time, as a means of advertising my availability to the fallen women of P.E., was a mere incidental. But I never made it. Perhaps I could have slunk inside one of the more rundown joints, near the docks, where the men outside looked too smashed to care whether I was fifteen or fifty; but I always turned and ran the couple of miles back to the hotel.

On this night, however, just before Christmas in the fateful year of 1976, I took the opposite direction. Instead of aiming for town I turned right out of Humewood Mansions and walked towards Summerstrand. The Christmas lights, strung up high across Beach Road, glittered in the sultry dark. I passed the Dolphinarium and the pier at Humewood Beach, where we had seen a shark fin glide past the nets that very morning. Beyond Happy Valley and the tennis courts, I reached the swanky Beach Hotel opposite Summerstrand.

And then I saw her. She strolled into the late-night shop on the corner. I followed her inside.

She was in her early twenties and I heard her ask, in Afrikaans, for a packet of Peter Stuyvesant. I never had more than the occasional puff and gasp on a cigarette at a party. But I was still a sucker for the glamorous Peter Stuyvesant adverts we saw at the movies most weeks. They were American cigarettes, which were especially popular in South Africa, and the commercials were shot with a shimmering sheen. The women were beautiful and the men looked smug as they went sky-diving, Alpine skiing and deep-sea-diving before popping up on a huge yacht to light up a couple of Peter Stuyvesants, for him and her, while they watched a gorgeous sunset sink into the ocean. It seemed as if they were about to indulge in fantastic sex as soon as the woman, drawing deep on her cigarette, had blown the final strand of pre-coital smoke down her flaring nostrils.

I looked at the young woman. She was very pretty. Her dark auburn hair was cut in a bob and she wore a summer dress and sandals. Despite the simplicity, she appeared much more striking than most Afrikaans *poppies* [dolls] we eyed up in Germiston. She shook her head, so that her bob gleamed in the light and her dangly earrings jangled, and she said, now mixing Afrikaans and English together: '*Nee*, [No], sorry ... *die rooi* [the red] soft-pack, *asseblief* [please]. Twenties.'

Having asked for a pack of twenty filter cigarettes, she turned to me. My helpless gaze must have been obvious, but her challenging look softened when she saw that I was just a young pup rather than another old bastard ogling her. I felt the blood rush to my face and I pretended to be more interested in the chocolates on display.

I reached out blindly and picked up a Crunchie.

'They're also my favourites,' she said, in Afrikaans-accented English.

I looked at her in mild panic. We often called Afrikaners 'Crunchies', so why else would I pick that very chocolate bar right in front of her?

She stretched past me to pick out a Crunchie herself and I breathed in her lightly perfumed scent. '*Ag*, let me take one of these too,' she said to the guy at the counter.

The girl paid for her cigarettes and chocolate and stashed them in the bag she had slung over her shoulder. 'Bye,' she said as she walked out of the shop without a backwards glance.

'Not bad, hey?' the middle-aged man drooled, as I dropped twenty cents into his hand while his eyes followed her outside.

I didn't answer, instead watching her twirl her car-keys as she strolled towards a battered old yellow Beetle.

'A VW girl, *nogal* [as well],' the man said, looking at the Volkswagen. 'I wouldn't mind getting inside her bonnet.'

I left the shop and began walking. I made it to the next corner before I looked back. She had just switched on her headlights and her indicator flashed as she waited for a break in the traffic.

If she had been an English-speaking woman in her early twenties I would not have stuck my thumb out, hopefully, as if I was a regular hitch-hiker who just happened to be waiting for a lift. But the fact that she was Afrikaans made me feel bold. And, *nogal*, as the man said, she drove a funky Beetle and smoked Peter Stuyvesant. She ticked quite a few of the sex boxes we had drawn up in our heads at Germiston High. We'd decided that any girl who smoked was definitely not a virgin. For us, a girl lighting up a cigarette was a clear sign that she loved sex. An Afrikaans girl who smoked was even wilder because she had flung off the shackles of her *verkrampte volk* [reactionary people].

'For the ride of your life you should *pomp* [fuck] an Afrikaans chick who wears glasses and has acne,' a friend said knowingly, arguing that she would overcome her physical and cultural imperfections with a sexual performance of gymnastic fervour.

We were excited enough by the suggestion to cycle past the local Afrikaans high school in Germiston at least once a month in the hope that we might find a girl who matched our apparently more experienced pal's description. This was how cruel and hopeless we sometimes were at the age of fifteen. We even shouted out occasionally to an Afrikaans girl we saw walking home. 'Howzit *Skattie*, [Honey], fancy a *pomp*?' Most of the time we made sure that she was just out of ear-shot, but it was another example of how apartheid shaped us.

English and Afrikaans-speakers lived such separate lives that, to us, the 'bloody Dutchmen' were as alien as most black South Africans. I felt more comfortable chatting to Maggie or to Boltman, the smiley but intelligent young black waiter who served our meals at Humewood Mansions. All those half-formed thoughts whirled through my head as I looked at the yellow Beetle and held my hand out in front of me, my thumb pointing in the direction of Humewood. The Afrikaans girl didn't seem to notice because she drove slowly past, her gaze fixed on the road ahead.

As I began to walk to the hotel, I realized that the Beetle had actually slowed to a halt. It was hard to tell if she had stopped to light a cigarette or if she was waiting for me. I was breathing fast by the time I reached the car. She leant over to open the door.

'Hello, Crunchie-Boy,' she said coolly. 'Where're you going?'

'Humewood – the hotel.'

'OK,' she nodded, tossing her bag casually onto the back seat. 'Jump in. A *lightie* [youngster] shouldn't be walking around this late.'

I slid in next to her. A tape played on her cassette deck and, as she drove, she hummed along to the biggest-selling single of that year – Elton John and Kiki Dee's 'Don't Go Breaking My Heart'. I usually pretended to be too cool to like any record by Elton John but, as her little Beetle speeded up and she cranked up the volume, I listened to the choppy guitar riff and the catch in her voice as she started singing the Kiki Dee parts as if I wasn't even there. She sounded as if she was crooning directly to Elton during their call and response routine as, in a suitably smoky voice, the Afrikaans girl answered 'I gave you my heart, whoah-hoar, I gave you my heart'. Tapping the steering wheel lightly as he pleaded, 'So, don't go breaking my heart', she replied with another breathy promise: 'I won't go breaking your heart.' The song churned on until, as we neared the hotel, she and Elton reached a small crescendo which consisted of them repeating that same refrain over and over again, with her voice sounding soft but husky.

'I like your voice,' I said, when her car idled outside the hotel.

'Really?' she said, as if she'd heard it all before.

There was a long pause, as I tried to work out what to say next. Her compilation tape came to my rescue. The eerie guitar, and the spooky moaning, was unmistakable. I had heard the song hundreds of times before, resounding from my sister's bedroom.

'I love this,' I said.

'Do you even know who this is?' she asked.

'Of course,' I said. 'It's the Rolling Stones – "Gimme Shelter". I've been listening to this record the last five years.'

'*Ja?*' she said, rolling her eyes. 'Since you were ten?'

'I'm eighteen,' I lied.

'And I'm thirty-six,' she laughed. 'So how old are you?'

'Sixteen,' I lied again, just as Mick Jagger sang in his muffled falsetto.

War, children, it's just a shot away

It's just a shot away

I thought of how often Heather had played this song over the last few months. It seemed to echo all that had happened in South Africa in 1976.

As if acting on impulse, she switched off the engine, reached for her bag and brought out the unopened packet of Peter Stuyvesant. She peeled off the cellophane, picked out a cigarette from the box, slipped it between her lips and lit it. It looked, in the flaring light, as if her eyes were closed beneath their dark lashes as she cupped the little flame in her hands. She rolled down the window, and blew smoke out into the humid summer night. I was relieved she had not offered me a cigarette. I would have ended up taking one, trying to look nonchalant until I started coughing after my first puff. She took a drag and said: 'Where are your folks?'

'In the hotel,' I said. 'Asleep.'

She asked me where I was from, and she told me that she came from Pretoria. But, rather than being on holiday, she was a student at the University of Port Elizabeth. She had just finished her degree. 'And now I'm going out into the big wide world ... ,' she said.

I hoped she wouldn't ask me anything about school, and so, to beat her to the next embarrassing question, I asked if I could buy her a drink.

She laughed. 'How old do you think I am?'

'I dunno,' I mumbled. 'Twenty-six?'

'Hey,' she exclaimed as she punched me on the shoulder. 'I'm only twenty-two!'

'You look good,' I said, helplessly.

'Good for twenty-six, hey?' She snapped off the cassette player. 'Tell me,' she said. 'What sort of kid tries to chat up a woman he thinks is twenty-six?'

I wasn't trying to really chat her up, and so I shrugged awkwardly.

She looked out to sea again and, switching to Afrikaans, she told me it was her last night in Port Elizabeth. After four years in P.E. she was on her way home first thing in the morning. She would be back in Pretoria in time for Christmas and she'd start working early in the New Year.

'So,' she said, talking in English again, 'this is a weird night for me.'

She wrapped a finger around a strand of her glossy hair and twirled it thoughtfully. Her bob was too short for her twirling to really work. So, instead, she pointed down the road.

'My flat's just down there,' she said, 'third road on the left.'

I sat mutely in my seat, peering in the direction she had pointed. 'Do you want to come back for a while,' she said, sounding shy for the first time. 'We can listen to some records.'

'*Ja*,' I said. '*Ja*, please!'

I must have sounded either desperate or excited because she laughed again. 'Cool it, mister . . .'

She turned on the ignition and, as if to tell me to relax, she leaned over and gave me a chaste kiss on the cheek.

I was shocked. She was gorgeous, and smart, and twenty-two years old. I was on my way to heaven, with a stunning Dutchwoman, a female rock-spider, a Crunchie-eating girl from Pretoria.

'I'm Sonja,' she said, 'but you can call me *Tannie* [Auntie] . . .'

It was my turn to laugh, for the first time in the ten minutes we had been together. Afrikaans girls, apparently, could also be funny.

Inside her small flat, after she had kicked off her sandals and switched on a tall lamp in the corner of her front room, she brought out a couple of beers.

'Just the one for you,' she said, handing me a bottle of Amstel. 'I don't want you getting drunk.'

I already felt drunk, even before my first sip. My hands trembled against the green bottle and, to occupy them, I picked aimlessly at the label. This was the moment I'd dreamed about for the last two years, and I couldn't believe I might lose my virginity to an Afrikaner. But Sonja was no ordinary Afrikaner. I scanned the books that were left on her half-empty shelves, with the rest packed away in boxes. As she lit another cigarette, I put down my beer and picked up the closest book. It was in Afrikaans: *Rook en Oker* by Ingrid Jonker.

'Smoke and . . . ' I said, trying to translate the title into English.

'*Rook en Oker,*' she said. 'Smoke and Ochre . . .'

I didn't know what 'ochre' meant, even in English, and I knew nothing about Ingrid Jonker. For a while I forgot about sex and my nerves, while Sonja told me about the Afrikaans poet. She told me how Jonker, despite coming from a poor and broken home, wrote her first collection of poems when she was younger than me. Jonker's father was a Nationalist Party M.P. who became the head of censorship in art and culture.

Denouncing her father, and apartheid, Jonker became a leading member of *Die Sestigers* [The Sixties]. I must have seemed very young in that moment. I had never heard of Jonker, or *Die Sestigers*, and I must have looked shocked when Sonja told me Jonker's father denied, in parliament, that she was his daughter.

She told me about the affairs Jonker had with other writers in the Afrikaans literary movement against apartheid, and how she had ended up in Valkenberg Psychiatric Hospital, where her mother had died years before. Jonker did not die in the asylum. Instead, in the winter of 1965, she walked out into the freezing sea at Three Anchors Bay in Cape Town and drowned herself.

I had never heard of an Afrikaner who did not believe in apartheid. 'You should read her,' Sonja said.

'My Afrikaans is *baie swak* [very weak],' I said.

Sonja smiled wryly. All the best writers in South Africa were Afrikaners. She chanted out the names: Breyten Breytenbach, Etienne Leroux, J.M Coetzee, André Brink, Ingrid Jonker.

I had not read any of them. And, in 1976, I had not even heard of any of them.

'You've got time,' she said.

She finished her beer and stood up, holding out her hand to me. Sonja slipped her fingers between mine and pulled me towards her.

'I've never kissed an Afrikaans girl before,' I said.

'Have you kissed any girl before?'

'Once or twice,' I said, remembering the only two previous occasions I had kissed an English-speaking girl at a Friday night Germiston garage party.

She kissed me then, and I forgot all about her being Afrikaans. I forgot about Ingrid Jonker and The Rolling Stones. I forgot about everything as, gently, she took my hand again and slipped it up inside her summer dress. I might have fainted had I not instructed myself to savour each moment so that I could tell everyone in

Germiston how I discovered the sweetest meaning of life with a twenty-two-year-old Afrikaans girl in a one-bedroom flat in Port Elizabeth.

And later, when I was inside her, I tried desperately to count backwards in Afrikaans, from the *Sestigers* downwards, from *sestig* [sixty] to *nege-en-vyftig* [fifty-nine] to *agt-en-vyftig* [fifty-eight] to *sewe-en-vyftig* [fifty-seven] to stop myself from coming too soon. I didn't even reach *vyftig* [fifty].

She kissed me again, and spoke in English, telling me how glad she was I'd hitched a ride back with her. I swore to myself that I would never judge another Afrikaner again. I was ready to read the collected works of Ingrid Jonker the very next morning. I was determined to master the art of sex and to count all the way back from sixty to zero and back again, and again, as long as it took, in Afrikaans.

We kept on kissing and, being fifteen, it did not take long before I was ready to start counting in Afrikaans once more. Afterwards, we lay together and listened to Steely Dan and ate chocolate, while she made headway though her Peter Stuyvesants.

But she was a kind girl and insisted on driving me back to Humewood Mansions just after 4 a.m. I felt exhausted, and uncertain what to say outside the hotel. Sonja knew. She reached for her bag again in the backseat. And then she gave me one last kiss and slipped a book into my hands. When we broke away I looked down to see the dark blue Ingrid Jonker collection: *Rook en Oker*.

'Smoke and Ochre . . . ,' she said. 'Read it,' she murmured, 'and think of me.'

I ATE BREAKFAST the next morning in a stunned stupor. My parents might have said something about how sleepy I seemed, but for the fact that I could not stop grinning. 'I'm not a virgin,' I said blissfully to myself as I ate my cereal. 'I had sex with a woman called Sonja,' I congratulated myself as I ate my bacon and scrambled eggs on toast. 'I had sex twice this morning,' I almost shouted out as I knocked back my coffee.

'You are very happy this morning,' our waiter, Boltman, noticed as he topped up my cup.

'Shows you what an early night can do,' dad said. 'We should get some good surfing this morning.'

'Do you surf, Boltman?' I asked dreamily.

'No,' Boltman laughed. 'I'm not allowed on the beach.'

'I'm sorry,' I said, suddenly snapping awake and remembering the Whites Only/*Slegs Blanke* sign on all three beaches near our hotel – Kings, Humewood and Summerstrand.

'It's OK,' Boltman shrugged. 'I have lots of studying to do.'

My parents had already decided that they were going to help pay for Boltman to finish his high school education. I was so happy I wished I could share the good news with him. But mom and dad had decided we would tell Boltman in a couple of days' time – on Christmas Day.

I shook hands with Boltman as we left the table, exchanging the African handshake he had taught me, and drifted out of the dining room. It was incredible. I was no longer a virgin. I was a fifteen-year-old sex-machine.

It was only when we were on the beach, and I put aside my book so that I could close my eyes, that I really started to think about Sonja. I lay in the sun, my eyes closed shut tightly, as I relived everything that had happened the night before. And then it hit me. I had been so excited I had forgotten to even ask her for a telephone number in Pretoria.

I knew she was leaving P.E. that day, and driving all the way home in her Beetle, but I didn't know anything else about her. I didn't know her surname or her address or the job she would begin in a few weeks. The rest of the morning dragged past in a slow blur, and I kept asking mom when we could go back to the hotel. I wondered if Sonja had left a note, or a number in my Ingrid Jonker book. The thought of not seeing her again made me feel ill.

My mother eventually persuaded dad that I was looking 'out of sorts', and we left the beach fifteen minutes early. I just about made it through lunch, hardly eating anything because there was no message for me anywhere in *Rook en Oker*. Soon after we had retreated to our rooms, I slipped outside and ran to her flat. I hammered on the door and was met by silence. Finally, an old man climbed up the stairs from the basement. He was the caretaker.

'I'm looking for Sonja,' I said.

'Sonja's gone,' the man said. 'The new people move in tomorrow night.'

He had no number or forwarding address for her in Pretoria. Even worse, he did not even know her surname. 'She was a good girl,' he said. 'No cheques. She always paid in cash.'

I fell asleep that night, just after eight, having escaped the usual walk to Happy Valley. 'We want you to be right as rain for Christmas,' mom said, tucking me up into bed. 'Sleep tight.'

T HE NEXT AFTERNOON, on Christmas Eve, I returned to Sonja's flat. I raced up the stairs to the second floor, dodging the black cleaner who was polishing the red floor of the narrow corridor. The door to Sonja's flat was open, but a security gate blocked the entrance. I could hear a baby crying inside, and a couple arguing in Afrikaans. My hand slid through the steel grill and I rapped on the wooden door.

A man appeared, wearing tight shorts and a dirty yellow vest. He could not have been more than twenty-two, Sonja's age.

'*Ja?*,' he said.

I told him I was a friend of Sonja. I needed to contact her.

'Sonja?' he said blankly, scratching his armpit. 'She's long gone.'

The man's wife joined him at the door. She carried a tiny baby on her hip. The baby's face was red and scrunched-up from crying. I asked if Sonja had a left a number or an address.

'*Nix* [Nothing],' the woman said flatly.

She moved to shut the door and I blurted out one last request. Could I leave a telephone number with them – in case she called?

'No, china,' the man said.

His wife cackled, and the baby started crying again as soon as she slammed the door.

Late that night, walking back to Summerstrand, I drifted in and out of the Christmas Eve revellers and even went back inside the shop where I had first spoken to Sonja. The same man sat at the till, looking doleful in an Xmas hat.

I retraced my steps, drawn magnetically past the Humewood hotel and to the street, the third on the left, where we had ended up forty-eight hours earlier. The futility of standing forlornly outside her flat seemed acute, and I did not spend more than a minute before I turned back.

I only looked up, after a couple of blocks, when I heard a low whistle. It came from out of the dark and I hesitated, seeing the shape on a low wall. My pause was enough for the shape to stand up and approach me. Emerging from the shadows, the black maid was much younger than Maggie, but she still wore the usual maid's uniform. Her head was also covered by a scarf.

In a soft voice, she said: 'Hello, master, how are you?'

I told her I was fine and, before I could walk on, she gestured for me to follow her. It was nothing more than a sharp tilt of her head, but the message was plain. She wanted me to walk up the dark-ened road with her. I thought she was a little older than Sonja, about twenty-five at a guess. Despite my heartache, I walked towards her.

Before I could get too close she nodded and moved ahead of me. I followed at a discreet distance because, after almost sixteen years of South African life, I knew how suspicious it would look for a teenage boy to walk alongside a black maid just before midnight. I also knew I was acting crazily, and heading for danger, but I couldn't help myself. Each time I thought about running in the opposite direction she looked over her shoulder and encouraged me. It was as if she knew my every doubt and fear.

At the top of a side-street she turned right down an alleyway. A dog barked and she turned to raise her fingers to her lips. I stopped walking but, again, she coaxed me forward. I was now close behind her, feeling even more apprehensive. She motioned for me to stop, pointing at a gate a few yards ahead of us. Walking quietly on her slippered feet, she carefully opened the squeaky gate and looked around the corner to see if anyone had heard us.

I followed her into a suburban garden. The white house was dark. We were at the bottom of a strip of lawn and the black girl had walked ahead and unbolted the door to her room. I thought of Maggie then, and felt oddly desolate. What was I doing? The maid hissed, anxious for me to disappear from view by joining her in her room. I ducked inside, as if dazed and unable to escape. Once she had lit a small candle and made sure the curtains were drawn, she locked the door.

Removing her scarf, she came close to me. She was not like any black maid I knew in Germiston. I could smell the drink on her breath as, stretching her hand out, she whispered 'Twenty rand?'

I suddenly understood. I was meant to pay her.

I shook my head. 'Sorry,' I said, 'I don't have twenty rand.' I wanted to turn and run.

'How much?' she said, smiling at me. I knew I had ten rand

on me. I fished it out of my back pocket and handed it to her, while backing away towards the door. 'Take it,' I said. 'I must go now.'

She slipped the money into her breast pocket and started to unbutton her tunic. I saw that she didn't wear a bra as, with another lazy smile, she bared her breasts.

All the years of apartheid crowded in on me, and I stared at her in bewilderment. She didn't seem to understand that I had to get out, that I suddenly remembered I was a white boy and she was a black woman. If I touched her, and her master or madam suddenly opened the door, they would call the police. We would end up in jail for a very long time. At least once a month I read a story in the newspaper of a white man and a black woman, or the opposite, being charged with breaking the Immorality Act. It was not only immoral but highly illegal to engage in sex, as the newspapers called it, 'across the colour line'. There was hardly a more serious crime under apartheid, short of murder.

The woman was a little drunk but she was cooing softly, telling me that it was all right, that she wanted me to stay. She promised a nice time in exchange for my ten rand.

'Keep the money,' I said, 'but please let me go.'

She stopped, as if she suddenly saw, for the first time, how scared I looked. 'OK, *baasie* [little master],' she shrugged. She buttoned herself up and reached in her pocket to return my money.

I felt even worse then, and shook my head. 'Keep it,' I muttered. 'I'm sorry ...'

And then, gently, she touched the side of my face. 'It's OK,' she said, stuffing the R10 note back into my hand. 'You are a little boy.'

She spoke tenderly, but I still bolted from her room without another word when she unlocked the door. I ran down the path and clattered into a dustbin, sending the lid flying and setting off the neighbourhood dogs in a frenzy of barking. I heard the woman click her tongue in dismay. I ran down the alley, as if the police were already chasing me, plunging along two darkened streets until I found Beach Road. Crossing over, I took the stairs leading down to the beach. I disappeared into the blackness and headed towards the sea. I was crying, but I didn't know why.

The funeral of Steve Biko, 3 October, 1977

CHAPTER ELEVEN

THE OBJECTORS

T HE YEAR HAD HARDLY BEGUN when, in January 1977, our future clouded. Military conscription, the government announced, was about to be doubled to two years. The new Defence Amendment Act also stipulated that, after national service, each white male would be required to attend one camp a year for the next eight years. Camps would last for anything between thirty and ninety days.

It felt like a life sentence. I took the news badly, even though it had been predicted for months. The only consolation was found low down in the details of the Act, which confirmed it was still possible to defer military service by going to university first. It offered the best incentive to work a little harder at school to escape the army for another few years.

Three weeks later Major Webb marched into our classroom with some brown envelopes which soon became distressingly familiar. For the next eight years those same envelopes, containing conscription papers, provided haunting reminders. The army was onto us.

Our English teacher, Miss Brinkman, a passionate advocate of literature and free-thinking, made her scorn apparent. She not only objected to her lesson being interrupted but to the very principle of our having to fill out military papers as fifteen-year-old school-boys.

'It is the law, Miss Brinkman,' Major Webb responded tartly. As the man responsible for our Youth Preparedness marching escapades, the cantankerous former soldier relished making sure we all registered for military duty in the year we turned sixteen.

In a classroom where, unusually, we outnumbered the girls by six to one, silence descended. Major Webb went from desk to desk. Only the four girls were exempt from conscription. Even those boys born outside the country, and whose parents were still not South African citizens, were compelled to register with the SADF. The army was angling to catch them as well. Webb told us he would be back in a couple of days to collect the forms. Miss Brinkman raised a perfectly disdainful eyebrow as she watched him strut off to his next class of victims.

She had already collared four of us, the quartet supposedly most equipped to gain distinctions in English at our final exam the fol-lowing year. Alongside my two Jewish pals, Hilton and David, and our gay friend, Robert, I was told by Miss Brinkman that she wanted us to read much more voraciously than our prescribed set works. She suggested additional books and arranged for us to visit the cinema in Johannesburg on some school afternoons so we might watch subtitled movies.

This was the kind of teaching to which I responded best; being sent to French and Italian films by a young and intriguing woman who resented our militarized state. Miss Brinkman was my kind of educator, unlike Major Webb or *Meneer* van Heerden, our Afrikaans teacher. Rather than introducing great Afrikaans writers, van Heerden enjoyed making individual boys stand close to him as he marked their work at his desk. As often as he could, he would slip his hands between the legs of his chosen boy and whisper '*Nou sal jy dans* [Now you will dance].' Van Heerden would then pinch hard, remaining po-faced, as he twisted the fleshy area of inner thigh with such venom that the boy danced and squealed as the rest of the class brooded or chortled at the absurdity of it all.

Veering between pinched repression and expansive thinking, the divisions were pronounced. The pinchers and the oppressors were obviously aligned with the military and so I was scandalized when dad appeared to side with Webb and van Heerden. He insisted we obey the call of duty. The only alternative to the army was the possibility of him using his government contacts to help me find a place in the navy.

'At least the navy would be better than the army,' my mother said encouragingly.

I refused to even consider the option. The army, the navy and the air force were all the same. 'I'm not going,' I said, even as dad made sure I filled out the conscription form accurately.

'You're going,' dad said firmly. 'You've got no choice.'

One boy thought differently. Mano Gougoumis, a big, burly Greek kid with a fast mouth, was a likeable huckster who had been in a few of my classes over the years. He was a brilliant artist but he also harboured a seemingly contradictory passion for George Orwell and becoming a successful businessman in America one day. Beyond the complex façade, courage must have coursed through him. We were shocked when Mano said he would never submit a returned conscription form to Webb.

Our army rebel shrugged, his dark skin and black hair making him look suddenly exotic.

'You won't get away with it,' someone warned.

Mano Gougoumis shook his head. He told me he had known since he was six years old that he would never go to the army.

Later that day, Mano and another of our friends, an Italian boy called Fernando Patrizi, formed a continental bond as they walked to the bottom of the sports fields and, out of sight of any teacher, shredded their army registration papers. We couldn't work out whether it was an act of staggering bravery, or stupidity. It was akin to burning the orange, white and blue national flag.

We feared for Mano and Fernando. But, secretly, I envied them. I wished dad and I had forged a pact as unbreakable as that between Mano Gougoumis and Fernando Patrizi. We had surrendered instead.

That same day, Miss Brinkman taught us Japanese poetry in the form of the *Haiku*. She showed us how the brevity of a three-line poem could contain lyricism and mystery. The translations seemed strange but they hinted at the hidden meaning behind a traditional *Haiku*. Even war and death, Miss Brinkman said, could be written about in a three-line poem.

We were encouraged to attempt our own *Haiku*, and both Mano and I wrote poems which were published in the end-of-year schoolbook. Consumed by the army, and thoughts of how Granddad George had fought in World War I when he was just sixteen, I offered up a clichéd little poem:

> *The dove flies up, up*
> *above the gunfire,*
> *and agony*

Mano was different, as always. This was his *Haiku*:

> *Exposed on St Valentine's Day*
> *a crimson rose lies dead*
> *in a lapel*

All these years later, it seems significant that a boy a year older than us should have written the last published *Haiku* in 1977's collection. Robert Whitecross, with whom I played hockey at Germiston High, would soon become a security police spy. He would infiltrate white underground resistance movements at university and be responsible for jailing a classmate of mine in Political Science for ten years on a charge of treason. But, in his last year of school, Robert Whitecross wrote a strangely prophetic *Haiku*, one that might have been a poetic prediction of the collapse of apartheid, the system he would fight so hard to maintain in his early twenties:

> *Great empires are*
> *like antheaps;*
> *they crumble.*

Mano Gougoumis objected bitterly to the white empire. The reasons for his hurt were obvious. He and his family were Greek, and his skin was swarthy. Mano did not look like one of South Africa's chosen people. His father came from Mozambique and had fought a lonely battle as an immigrant.

Mano was born in Primrose, a suburb on the edge of Germiston which was less pretty than it sounded. His family then moved to the gritty neighbourhood of Germiston South – where my parents had also grown up. Mano spoke, piercingly, of how he had been persecuted as a dark-skinned boy. Unlike my other Greek friends, Pascali Paschalides and Basil Lazirides, who lived alongside us in a swankier English-speaking suburb, Mano was surrounded by Afrikaans families.

He had often walked to the local park. Once, a big Afrikaans boy had asked him if he wanted a ride on the back of his bike. As Mano was a gregarious child he had nodded enthusiastically. But, as soon as he climbed aboard, the kid bucked his bike so that Mano went flying.

'*Ja, jou Griek* [Yes, you Greek],' the rider sneered and then kicked him. Lying on the yellow grass, Mano looked up in bewilderment. '*Jy is net soos 'n kaffir*! [You're just like a kaffir!]'

The boy kicked him again. '*Vokking Griek!* [Fucking Greek!] *Vokking see-kaffir!* [Fucking sea-kaffir!]'

Throughout his childhood he was called a 'sea-kaffir' – a term of abuse aimed at swathy immigrants who had apparently sailed across the seas to reach South Africa. Mano forged a sombre bond with black people. He looked at the country with clear eyes, absorbing the unjust signs all around him. *Slegs Blanke*/Whites Only was emblazoned across park benches and bus stops, on library walls and swimming pool counters.

His father's restaurant, The Gondolier, was on President Street, close to the 20th Century cinema, the synagogue and Kansas Roadhouse where they served burgers, hot dogs, Dagwood triple-deckers and milkshakes on a metal tray that attached itself to your open car window. Mano's dad employed black kitchen staff and Indian waiters to serve his white customers. He was most fond of Isaac, a black man who also came from Mozambique. It felt as if, just like Maggie did to us, Isaac belonged to the Gougoumis family. And so Mano was upset when he witnessed a police raid on the restaurant. Isaac, coming from Mozambique, was in trouble. He did not have the requisite pass book and, despite protests from Mr Gougoumis, Isaac was taken away.

It happened again when, late one night, the Gougoumis family were woken by banging and barking. Mr G led them out into the backyard. A gang of policemen, holding back a yelping Alsatian, hammered on the door leading to the room where their maid, Helen, lived.

'Open up, Helen,' Mano's father instructed her. 'You have to ...'

The police crashed in and soon returned, dragging out a black man who had been hiding under Helen's bed.

'What has he done wrong?' Mr G asked in his accented English.

'Pass book,' a policeman said curtly as he bundled the black man into the back of a van.

As the years passed Mano thought of Isaac and Helen's boyfriend whenever he saw another pale blue Ford covered in police insignia. The abiding image he would take with him when he finally escaped overseas would be a South African police van where, in the caged hold, black fingers laced through the wire. Mano never saw the faces of the black men on their way to prison, but their fingers, clinging to the steel mesh, represented the injustice and repression he felt so deeply.

America, for Mano, really was the Promised Land. His father, having escaped majority rule in Mozambique, wished he could have emigrated to New York rather than Germiston. At school assembly, where we had to sing the national anthem, 'Die Stem' [The Call of South Africa], Mano would softly hum 'The Star-Spangled Banner'. And so the dream of America enveloped him. He kept telling us he was on his way to the United States, home of the brave, land of the free.

'*Ja*, Mano, of course,' we said, as if we didn't really believe him.

WE KNEW LITTLE about Steve Biko until, on the morning of Wednesday 14 September, 1977, we read of his death in the *Rand Daily Mail*. The front page report was written by Helen Zille, who thirty years later would become the leader of the opposition. Zille was just twenty-six, but she conveyed the significance and the suspicion of Biko's death in detention.

As mom drank her tea, and ate a slice of toast, she also read out a portion of Donald Woods's accompanying tribute to Biko. Dad sat and listened, and I was struck that, at five minutes to seven, he did not make his usual dash for work. Woods was the editor of the *Daily Dispatch*, which we read every other December when we were on holiday in East London, the sleepy coastal town which produced a newspaper as critical of the government as the *Mail*.

'I have just received the news that my most valued friend, Steve Biko, has died in detention,' Woods wrote. 'He needs no tributes from me. He never did. He was a special and extraordinary man who, at the age of thirty, had already acquired a towering status in the hearts and minds of countless thousands of young blacks throughout South Africa. In the three years I knew him my conviction never wavered that this was the most important political leader in the entire country, and quite simply the greatest man I have known.'

Mom looked up at dad. He shook his head. None of us knew enough about the dead man. Yet dad did not rise from the table. He listened instead to mom, as she read that forty-five people had died in detention, with twenty of them losing their lives in the last eighteen months.

'Biko was detained more than once,' Woods wrote. 'He experienced solitary confinement more than once. He always came out of such ordeals as tough as ever, and as resiliently humorous about the interrogation sessions. Any contest of wits between him and the Security Police was an absurdly one-sided mismatch. The only thing that could bring him down was death.

'The basic facts are that barely three weeks ago, when he was detained, he was completely fit and healthy and that this strong young man was imprisoned without trial, and that he died three weeks later in captivity. The government quite clearly never understood the extent to which Steve was a man of peace. He was militant in standing up for his principles, yes, but his abiding goal was a peaceful reconciliation of all South Africans, and in this he was a moderating influence. Therefore, to the racists who have gloated over my grief today in anonymous phone calls and telegrams, even twisted scriptural texts to coat their venom, I reply in the same vein: "Weep not for me, but for yourselves and for your children."'

We sat around the table in silence, and then dad stood up. Life had to go on. He needed to be at work and I had to get to school. I tried to forget the words we had just heard.

But we could not escape for long. Day after day Zille and Woods chipped away at government denials of violence against Biko, while offering insights into the man they described as the leader of South Africa's Black Consciousness Movement [BCM]. We learnt that Biko had been a founder of SASO, the South African Students Organization which brought together blacks, coloureds and Indians, and that he had been one of the main organizers of the protests which culminated in the Soweto uprising fifteen months earlier.

The newspapers also revealed that Biko, banned from leaving his hometown of King William's Town, had been detained on 18 August at a roadblock set up by one of the country's most notorious security forces – the Port Elizabeth branch. On 6 September Biko was eventually moved to the Sanlam Building in Strand Street in downtown P.E.

The building was less than five minutes from where I had driven down Beach Road with Sonja.

In Room 619 he was interrogated and tortured by the security police for twenty-two hours. He was naked and chained to a grille. Eventually, he slid into a coma while the police worked out what to do next, which resulted in a decision to transfer Biko to Pretoria.

Sonja had covered that same 800-mile journey to her home town in her yellow Beetle a few days before Christmas.

Biko barely survived the same journey, in the back of a police van. He died soon after arriving in Pretoria on 12 September.

The government insisted that a self-inflicted hunger strike had caused his death. But Biko's name flashed around a disbelieving world and Port Elizabeth, the boring 'Friendly City', our holiday haven for years, suddenly became internationally infamous.

Jimmy Kruger, the taciturn Minister for Police, was unmoved. Asked at the National Party's Transvaal Congress for his reaction to Biko's death, Kruger shrugged: '*Dit laat my koud* [It leaves me cold].' His contempt seemed even more obvious when Kruger and a party delegate, Christoffel Venter, attempted some banter.

Praising 'the democratic principles of our Minister of Police', Venter sent sniggers rippling around the conference hall when he said Kruger was so even-handed he allowed detainees 'the democratic right to starve themselves to death'.

Kruger nodded cheerfully. 'Mr Venter is right. That is very democratic of us.'

But, as the pressure increased, he backtracked. 'I didn't say he died of a hunger strike,' Kruger protested a few days later, attributing Biko's severe head injuries to a 'scuffle'.

Woods reported from Biko's funeral, where a few hundred whites had joined 20,000 black mourners at a segregated graveyard in King William's Town. Describing the five-hour-long ceremony as 'a fittingly sad and solemn occasion', Woods admitted he had harboured fears he and his wife might be attacked by Black Consciousness supporters.

Yet the funeral had made it possible to believe 'in the kind of country South Africa could become – with people judged as human beings rather than as members of a race group ... [Biko] would say the reason why there was no racial incident at his funeral is that people were there in friendship; they were intermingled and not standing in separate racial groups. Just as hostility grows from separateness and isolation, so love grows from closeness and contact. The opposite of apartheid.'

On 19 October Woods was banned for five years, which meant he could not work as an editor or journalist. He had to remain in East London and could not leave the area for any reason. That same day, the government shut down the Soweto newspaper, *The World*, and detained its editor, Percy Qoboza.

Helen Zille was still allowed to work and it did not take her long to discredit the government. Under a *Rand Daily Mail* headline of 'No Sign of Hunger Strike – Biko Doctors', Zille demolished the state's deception. She revealed that an autopsy proved Biko had suffered massive head injuries, consistent with an attack, and that he had died of a brain haemorrhage.

Graphic photographs Woods had taken of Biko in the morgue were published in the *Daily Dispatch*, and showed the damage done to his head, face, wrists and ankles. The world was incensed, but John Vorster appeared unmoved. 'The world can do its damnedest,' Vorster said.

Reporters witnessed a blistering cross-examination of the Security Police in court by Stanley Kentridge, the Biko family's lawyer, during a thirteen-day inquest. Kentridge concluded that: 'The verdict which we submit is the only one reasonably open to this court – that the death of Mr Biko was due to a criminal assault upon him by one or more of the eight members of the Security Police.'

Yet on 27 November, 1977, in the Old Synagogue building which had been converted into a Pretoria courtroom, the presiding Magistrate, Marthinus Prins, announced his findings:

1. The deceased was Bantu Stephen Biko, a black man aged thirty, who died on 12 September. The cause of death was brain injury which led to renal failure and other complications.
2. The head injuries were probably sustained on 7 September in a scuffle in the Security Police offices in Port Elizabeth.

3. On [the basis of] the available evidence, the death cannot be attributed to any act or omission amounting to criminal offence on the part of any person.

Steve Biko was dead, and there was no-one to blame.

MY PARENTS DROVE DOWN to East London, home of Donald Woods, early the following week. I stayed behind in Germiston with Maggie. Our lives were changing and it was obvious that we would never again share an ordinary family holiday either in East London or Port Elizabeth. Heather had gone away with her new boyfriend, Ross, who would become her husband, and I had stayed at home to play cricket for a week.

On the opening day of the Biko trial I'd attended a regional trial for the South-Eastern Area schools in Bedfordview. It was one of those net sessions where every ball I faced looked huge. I seemed to know instinctively when to defend and when to drive or cut or hook the ball into the mesh netting. When the regional team was picked for the Beckwith Week, which was itself a trial before the selection of the Transvaal schools side, I was one of eleven boys who made the cut.

I was nowhere near good enough to ever be considered for the provincial team that would play at Nuffield Week, where Transvaal faced the likes of Western Province and Natal. The real reward was to miss the first eight days of our usual family holiday. If we had returned to P.E., rather than East London, I might have wanted to spend the entire three weeks with my parents, on the off-chance I'd find Sonja again. But even the idea of walking the streets around the Sanlam Building, where Biko had been tortured, was less appealing.

Maggie had agreed to delay her return to Witbank so she could look after me, and she knew she would gain an additional week's holiday in early January. We got on famously, me and Maggie, and she even curbed her drinking to make sure that I was up every morning in time for breakfast.

Each evening, even though we'd lost badly against boys who were a year older than us and went to posh private schools in Johannesburg, I was happy to come home to Maggie. She cooked my supper as soon as I arrived, and asked me how I'd done, and she even sat with me while I ate and we spoke about her children, and how she longed to see them again. There were times, during those exchanges, when I thought of the black maid in Port Elizabeth, on the night after I'd met Sonja. I felt tempted to tell Maggie what had happened. But she was old enough to be my mother, and I knew she'd be shocked to hear I might have slept with a black girl. So, instead, we spoke about cricket and Witbank, about her family and mine.

I never invited Maggie to eat her dinner with me and, as our family ritual dictated, I allowed her food to remain in the warming oven. It was only when I had made myself a coffee and sprawled in front of the television, and after Maggie had washed my dishes, that she popped her head around the study door to say good-night and to tell me she was going to eat her meal in her room.

One morning that week my stomach tightened at breakfast. I had begun at the back of the paper, poring over the Beckwith Week scores that were printed in a small box on the second last page. I was thrilled, but utterly shocked when, turning to the news pages, I read about Anton Eberhard.

His name leapt out at me when I saw he had been sentenced to a year's imprisonment in military detention for refusing his army camp call-up. Eberhard was the first conscientious objector to cite political reasons for rejecting his conscription papers. There had been other 'peace' protesters, mostly Jehovah's Witnesses, whose religious beliefs prevented them serving in military uniform. But Eberhard had already done his national service. He had been called up in 1970 and, based in Kroonstad and Bethlehem with the Engineers Corps, he'd completed the then statutory nine-month period.

But, early in 1977, after receiving his latest military summons, he had written to his commanding officer: 'I acknowledge receipt of your call-up papers,' Eberhard wrote, 'but for reasons of conscience I am unable to attend this camp. I have given the matter much thought and I am fully aware of the consequences of refusal. But it is my belief that the present government has no right to remain in power; and any organization which enables it to do so cannot be supported.'

Eberhard had been politically naive when he first entered the army, having accepted conscription as soon as he left school. In the intervening seven years his awareness of apartheid had increased dramatically. He had been a student at the University of Cape Town where, for the first time in his life, he met black people on an equal footing. He became friends with a black student called Vusi, and he began to consider the inequities of South African life from a personal perspective.

Travelling with Vusi to Mooi River, and the black township where his new friend's family lived, Eberhard was struck by the racial divisions on the train. Black passengers could only travel in third class, while whites were permitted to buy tickets for either the first or second class carriages. Eberhard smuggled himself into third class, in order to remain with Vusi, but he had to be hidden from the conductor. They covered him with a blanket on the top bunk.

Their friendship deepened and the two men eventually shared a house in Johannesburg – in direct contravention of the Group Areas Act. Eberhard explained in court that he had been particularly affected by the events of 16 June, 1976, and spoke of his distress when he read a *Rand Daily Mail* headline of 'Soweto Burns'. The hundreds of deaths which followed, and the detention of Vusi, hardened Eberhard's resolve. Early in 1977, receiving his conscription papers, he knew it would be impossible for him to wear an army uniform again.

Eberhard had three options. He could go on the run, and keep on switching addresses to avoid the military police, or he could leave the country forever and accept a life in exile. For Eberhard, neither choice was acceptable. He had only one alternative: a refusal to serve.

Chained as he left court, Eberhard was taken by military train from Port Elizabeth to Voortrekkerhoogte. As South Africa's first political Conscientious Objector, he was handcuffed throughout a journey that echoed the route Steve Biko had made during the last hours of his life.

The following night, having packed away my cricket kit and said goodbye to Maggie as she headed back to Witbank, I flew on a plane for the first time. It took just over an hour to travel by air from Johannesburg to East London. My parents were waiting for me at the airport, and I realized how much I had missed them. I told them about the cricket, and Anton Eberhard, while they told me to forget about the army and to make the most of my two weeks by the sea.

In East London, at night, I did not follow the same pattern as the previous year. Rather than walking the streets in the impossible hope of finding another Sonja, I read in my room night after night, ripping through a book list Miss Brinkman had suggested in preparation for our final year. I knew how important it was to get to university and, in so doing, secure a military deferment.

I also thought of Donald Woods, because it was hard to ignore him when his *Daily Dispatch* was delivered with our early morning coffee at the Queens Hotel every day. He was not allowed to edit the paper, or write his syndicated column. The government had muzzled him.

On the evening of Thursday 28 December, 1977, Woods made his last move in South Africa. We had already returned to Germiston when his wife, Wendy, reversed her car out of the family garage in East London. Woods crouched on the back floor so that he could not be seen by the security policeman posted outside his house. Having dyed his hair, and disguised himself as a Catholic priest, Woods slipped from the car outside East London. He said goodbye to his wife and, calling himself Father David Curren, hitch-hiked three hundred miles to the Lesotho border.

Woods had planned to cross the Telle River but, after heavy rains, the banks were flooded and he had no choice but to use the false passport he had obtained. He managed to pass the border patrol and enter Lesotho, where he was able to arrange for his wife to be called. The coded message told Wendy Woods that he had arrived and, soon afterwards, she and their five children drove to the Lesotho border. They made it across and, with the help of the Australian embassy and the British High Commission, they flew from Maseru to Gaberone, in Botswana, and then onto Luanda, Zambia, on United Nations passports. Kenneth Kaunda, the Zambian President, welcomed them as white Africans fleeing apartheid.

On New Year's Day, 1978, the Woods family arrived at Gatwick Airport. They had been granted political asylum in Britain and Woods explained why he had opted for exile from South Africa. 'I could no longer function there as a journalist,' he said. 'I was no longer able to oppose the government, as I have been doing for many years, within the limits of the laws which were already highly restrictive.'

Woods pledged to resume his opposition to apartheid from London, where he would write a book about Biko. But he also made it clear that it was no longer safe for his family to remain in South Africa. Shots had been fired at their home in East London and his youngest child, five-year-old Mary, had been sent an acid-impregnated T-shirt through the post.

'We are not dealing with normal people,' Woods said as the massed cameras around him popped and flared. 'These are desperate people who will do anything to maintain apartheid.'

THE ABSENCE OF over a thousand conscripts from the January 1978 call-up, exactly a year before I was due to begin my own national service, briefly encouraged me. There were no principled political objectors, like Eberhard, but the number of draft-dodgers still made a significant protest.

It did not take the government long to react. The Defence Amendment Act Number 49 increased the punishment for religious conscientious objectors. A twelve- to fifteen-month sentence in Detention Barracks [DB] was lengthened to three years. Any conscript who refused military service, for ideological reasons, would face two years in DB. That prison term, and a R2000 [then £1000] fine, would be repeated the next time the political objector refused another call-up. The pattern would recur until the objector turned sixty-five. Facing such an oppressive clampdown, most of the missing thousand reported for duty. There was no escape.

The McRae family, Germiston, 1980

CHAPTER TWELVE

SNOW IN SEPTEMBER

DAD KEPT MOVING UPWARDS. He had become the Head of Operations at Eskom and, in his new role, he ordered a confidential report into the living conditions of his black power station staff. Their compounds, as the 'non-white' quarters were called, were based on crude gold-mining facilities which used tightly-packed dormitories to house migrant workers. Thin mattresses were placed on concrete shelves as men were jammed together, twenty or more in a small room.

There had to be change and dad ordered the refurbishment and expansion of most black quarters in the Transvaal and the Free State. Actual beds were moved into the rooms, which would hold no more than four men at a time, and cupboards were introduced in place of wire lockers. Dad began to feel a little better, until he was told that conditions at two stations in Natal were so bad that a report could not be submitted. He was advised to travel down to Congella and Umgeni, just north of Durban, so he could see how some of his men were living. The white power station managers were surprised by his request to view the compounds. 'Our boys are happy,' he was assured, but dad insisted. At Congella, the walls of the non-white quarters were painted black and never cleaned. Fifty or sixty men were squeezed into each stinking dorm, adjoined by a few cold-water showers and toilets whose seats were either broken or missing.

When dad asked to see the kitchens he was told that there weren't any because the boys had to buy their own food and they preferred cooking on open fires. He was taken into a yard where some bricked fireplaces and metal grills were being used. But they were so filthy and encased in thick palls of smoke it was hard to approach them without joining in the coughing.

'This is how they prefer it,' the power station manager suggested. 'They like to cook in smoke.'

Dad turned to an old black man who was hunched up against the smoky clouds. The man looked at dad with rheumy eyes, surprised that a big white *baas* [boss] in a suit had offered him a hand to shake. Dad asked the man if this was how he liked to prepare his food. He received a wry smile in return. 'No,' the man said. 'But the chimney is blocked.'

When dad asked how long the chimneys had been clogged, the old man hesitated. 'A long time, master,' he eventually said.

At Umgeni the compounds were slightly better, but instead of functioning toilets there was just a trough which had been dug into the ground. A thin stream of water ran along its length to wash the piss and shit away into a sewerage container. The men were expected to squat over the trough in full view of each other.

Dad was angry, and ashamed. He made sure the walls were painted white at Congella. The chimneys were cleaned and unblocked and a kitchen and additional dormitories were built. The men would no longer have to provide their own food, and health and safety checks were introduced. Separate toilet cubicles were installed at Umgeni and the importance of hygiene and privacy was underlined to the castigated power station managers.

Even black workers, dad said, had rights and needs. Some of his white staff looked at him as if he had gone crazy but, because he was the boss, they gave in to his unusual demands.

I knew little, then, of dad's work. And he told me less and less because he imagined I would leap on talk of the conditions he had just seen as further evidence of evil in the country he loved. Dad knew I had already gone to war against him because I accused him of being in cahoots with the government. My father, I complained bitterly, was turning into a fascist.

T HE END WAS NEARING. In our twelfth and last year of school we were down to the final weeks. 1978 had passed by in a blur. But Mano Gougoumis still saw evidence of apartheid all around him. Whether it was the sight of black prisoners working in the fields alongside the railway track, or the signs which divided the bridge and the train station into separate white and non-white entities, Mano felt sickened. He took it upon himself to make a statement.

At four o'clock one morning, Mano covered his face with black shoe polish. He knew our small local train station was unmanned at night, but there was still an awful danger to his plan. Clutching his can of spray-paint, the black-faced boy ran from his home to Germiston Lake station.

He checked carefully that no-one else was around. And then, bravely, he went to work. Mano aimed his hissing sprays of paint at the signs that angered him. There was something curiously satisfying about the way he blackened out the words '*Slegs Blanke*/Whites Only'. Up and down the bridge and along the length of the platform he sprayed over every racist sign he saw. It was considered treason, and to be caught would mean a certain jail sentence.

In an era before closed circuit cameras, he got away with it. Mano felt a surge of pride the next day when, catching a train, he saw one blacked-out sign after another.

I was not as courageous. Instead, I played the reluctant part of a prefect at Germiston High or, more cockily, a first-team jock in football, cricket, tennis and hockey. A certain kind of girl liked a sporty boy and life was often thrilling at weekend parties. But school itself seemed more serious. Unless I could muster a strong university entry I'd end up in an army camp at Upington, on the outskirts of a desolate town in the Northern Cape. I had received my first call-up, for the second week of January 1979, and from that point onwards I read and swatted and revised.

I was strangely serene when, in November 1978, I sat the ten matriculation exams which would decide my future. Even in subjects like maths and chemistry my head stayed surprisingly clear. At the end I was sure I'd done enough to escape the army just a little longer.

The last day of school, early in December 1978, felt unexpectedly poignant. In the heart of the grounds which my old soldier of a granddad had tended as a caretaker, my gaze lingered over the black men who had worked under him at Germiston High. They raised their hands in salute.

'*Hambe kachle* [Go well],' they said, before telling me how much they missed old George.

I missed him too, and I told them I would also miss them. I said the same words to friends I knew I would never see again, and to the few teachers who had lit up our world. We climbed aboard our old bikes one last time, but it felt more like a beginning than just the end. The rest of my life, out in the real world, was about to start.

THE LAST DAY of school coincided with the end of Maggie Thabang's life with us. After a dozen years as our maid, as the black woman who had lived with us in Witbank and Germiston, Maggie had had enough. She had made our beds and polished our floors and shoes year after year. She had scrubbed our toilets and made sure there were no rings of grime around our gleaming sinks and bathrooms. The vegetables she had peeled and the dishes she had washed would have made mountains. She had laid tables and cleared plates, dusted rooms and shone cutlery, and looked after our additional rota of gardeners and washerwomen, the more fleeting 'boys' and 'girls' who slipped through their part-time jobs at our house while she remained in her permanent live-in-the-backyard position.

There was a jolting intimacy to our relationship which made her more than a black servant ghosting through my life. Sometimes, when I had fallen ill and if my mother was out, Maggie had wiped up my sick. She has also picked up my dirty socks and underwear from my bedroom floor. It was against Maggie that I rested my head and allowed my tears to fall when Granddad George died. She had also hugged me, unexpectedly, when I explained that dad and I were fighting about the army. Maggie had told me not to forget that my dad was a good man.

I just felt bad as I watched Maggie pack her bags in the old back-room. Her tin plate and mug stood empty on the bedside table. Little black chips in her crockery, where the enamel had faded, glinted in reminder of how many years she had lived with us.

'Can I make you a coffee, Maggie?' I asked as she tied a fresh *doek* around her head in the last few minutes before dad piled her suitcases into the boot and drove her to the bus-stop.

She shook her head, looking puzzled as to why I should suddenly offer her a domestic favour.

'You can use one of our mugs,' I said.

Maggie smiled her gap-toothed smile and reminded me that she was like madam, my mom, and couldn't drink anything before a journey. There were no toilets on a crammed black bus.

It was strange to see Maggie dressed in her smart church clothes, and shiny patent leather shoes, rather than the old overall and slippers I would always remember. She was on her way home for good, leaving our family for her children. Maybe that's why she had stopped drinking the last few weeks as the moment of her departure approached. The problem she'd had with drink over the preceding years, and her struggle to stay sober long enough to get through another day, had cleared mysteriously. Perhaps she had been drinking to forget everything she had left in Witbank.

Her eyes shone brightly when the moment arrived. She made one last check under the bed to ensure she had not left anything behind. Maggie knew she would never come back to this room, her home for eleven years in Germiston, a backyard refuge which had been raided twice by the police as they carried out their passbook checks and guaranteed that we stayed White by Night.

Ours was a sober parting. Maggie thanked my mother, who slipped her a little more money, and gave me one of the long African handshakes she knew I loved.

'You must be a good boy,' she told me as if, rather than being seventeen, I was seven again. 'You must listen to your parents.'

My childhood seemed to end with Maggie's leaving. But I suddenly felt as shy and stricken as a little boy. I mumbled goodbye as she climbed into dad's company car. He reversed down our driveway and out into Cachet Road. Maggie leant out of the window and gave me and mom one last wave. The expression on her familiar face, disappearing forever, was impossible to read.

P.W. BOTHA, the former defence minister, had become our latest belligerent prime minister. A staunch admirer of the

Nazis in his youth, and the man responsible for the forced removal of Coloured families from District Six at the foot of Table Mountain in Cape Town in the late 1960s, P.W., or Pieter Willem, was also known as *Piet die Wapen* [Pete the Weapon] and *Die Groot Krokodil* [The Big Crocodile]. He had a huge bald head, a wobbly face, perpetually wet lips, a bullfrog double-chin and a habit of waving his scaly finger in dire warning of a Total Onslaught.

The war against us, according to Botha, would be absolute. It had been planned in intricate detail by the Soviets – who were apparently determined to seize control of the mineral wealth and strategic gateway of southern Africa. Using terrorists, as Botha described all black liberation movements, the Soviets were massing hostile forces to swamp us with their violence and subversion. The only possible response to a Total Onslaught was a Total Strategy that completed the transformation of South Africa into a militarised state.

Apart from intensifying call-ups and engaging in concentrated battles with Angolan, Cuban and SWAPO guerrillas, Botha's Total Strategy would prepare a white nation for war and subvert a worldwide arms embargo. South Africa, under The Big Crocodile, needed to become wholly self-sufficient in armaments supply. A homespun arms industry was soon the eleventh largest in the world with an annual turnover of R3 billion [then around £1.5 billion].

Whenever P.W. appeared on television, which was often, dad would look up from his paperwork as I ranted at the screen. 'Hey, hey,' he'd say quietly, peering at me over the glasses he'd just to start wearing in his early fifties. 'You don't need to talk like that.'

But I needed to shout to stop my head from bursting. At Wits University, my old school friends had followed traditional routes into medicine and engineering and accountancy. It was noticeable how consumed they were by taking their first steps towards a profession. They had less time than me, an English and Politics student, to be incensed by apartheid or entranced by music.

I was still in thrall to groups we read about in our copies of the *New Musical Express*, which were six weeks out of date by the time they were shipped and delivered to CNA branches across the country. Reading Paul Morley, Ian Penman and Barney Hoskyns, I was besotted with The Fall, Wire, Gang of Four, Public Image Ltd and Joy Division, and their American predecessors like The Velvet Underground, Captain Beefheart, Television and Pere Ubu.

But I was affected by one local group in particular. Corporal Punishment came from Springs, a neighbouring town on the East Rand even more desolate than Germiston. Their lead singer, James Phillips, was said to have become a conscientious objector and gone on the run from the army, having refused to attend any camps after everything he had seen during two years as a conscript.

Another rumour insisted that the band members had met each other in a psychiatric unit of the South African Defence Force. I just knew they spoke my language: East Rand English with an echo of the working-class Afrikaners surrounding us.

Their name, Corporal Punishment, matched the black-and-blue memories of my school years and all the beatings we had taken. We called them the Corporals, mocking the low-ranked moustached men in uniform who loved shouting at spoilt suburban kids like us.

The Corporals were not preachers. They did not resort to slogans or rhetoric but, rather, James sang in the voice of a Springs boy who understood how fucked up we were in white South Africa. Our favourite Corporals' song was called 'Darky':

> *Oh, Darky's gonna get you*
> *With a right and a left, with a right and a left*
> *Oh, Darky's gonna get you*
> *With a knife, with a knife, with a knife, with a knife, knife, knife*

The small crew of us who followed the Corporals felt jubilant when we sang those words aloud – for the fear was not ours. The fear belonged to the suburbs and shopping centres of white South Africa. We heard it every day in the voices of the masters and the madams, our politicians and parents, our teachers and neighbours, as we were told about the dangers that 'they', the overwhelming majority of South Africans, posed to us, the ruling minority. There was also insecurity, because merely opposing apartheid did not mean we belonged to the wider mass movement. And so there was a plaintive edge to our rebellion.

At Wits, South Africa's most radical university, an ideological divide became obvious. James Phillips was one of the very first 'new' South Africans, because he called himself a white African a decade before it became fashionable. He also dealt in grittier realities which grated with the dogma of the student left. Singing 'Brain Damage', he lampooned the racism endemic to a mining town like Springs, and the chorus featured a mocking line: *'It takes a lot of skill to be in charge of 40 kaffirs.'*

He had no qualms about repeating that South African word 'kaffirs', although he left no doubt he was ridiculing the white mining managers of the East Rand. But, to some, Corporal Punishment were distasteful, and broke the self-styled militant white students' Stalinist policy of what could be said in opposition to apartheid. A few suburban rebels on campus walked out of a Corporals gig in protest. I decided that I was with the Corporals, and the wasted boys and pretty girls who followed them from one grimy venue to another.

I started a fanzine with a cool and almost beautiful English literature student called Gillian. If I called myself Big Croc, in a supposed piss-take of P.W. Botha, Gillian's alias was slightly more literary. She wrote under the name of Pitty Patti; as her favourite poet and singer was Patti Smith.

Tall and angular, Gillian piled up her long black hair on her head in a wild birds-nest held together by brightly-coloured clips and Ndebele-style beaded grips. She had gone to a posh girls' school in the northern suburbs of Johannesburg, where she had been alone in her musical tastes. But in backward Germiston we had friends like Matthew Krouse, a sophisticated gay Jewish boy who had introduced me to Patti Smith long before anyone else. Matthew also explained Smith's relationship with Robert Mapplethorpe, who had taken the iconic black-and-white photograph which made the cover of *Horses* look strikingly iconic.

Germiston sounded suddenly intriguing to Gillian, who knew that Corporal Punishment came from Springs. Maybe, she reckoned, a bumbling East Rand boy like me would be more interesting than some slick Johannesburg hipster. Without Patti Smith, Matthew Krouse and Corporal Punishment, Gillian would not have given me a second glance, and so I silently thanked each of them every time G and I went to bed in her tiny flat in Braamfontein.

We had some grand plans about becoming writers and cultural dissidents. If we had been musical we might have started a band because G looked like a compelling singer. But she couldn't sing and I couldn't play guitar. We briefly considered the idea of me setting up a William Burroughs or Cabaret Voltaire-style collection of found voices and noises, over which she could talk like Laurie Anderson. Gillian had a lovely, husky speaking voice and I fancied the idea of being a genius mix-master in a trench-coat splicing together loops and burbles and stolen beats to accompany her words as the Transvaal's first performance artist. But it was far too hot in Johannesburg to wear a trench-coat and the best I managed on the mixing front was a badly recorded melange of radio commercials and the garbled voice of P.W. Botha.

So we abandoned the two-person group idea and settled on

fanzines instead. We called our first sixteen-page literary masterpiece *Smoke & Ochre*. It was my memento to Sonja. We had little money between us and managed to pay for just fifty-two Xeroxed copies which we sold for a rand [then 50p] each at a Corporal Punishment gig. Fifty copies went in an hour at an anonymous hall in Johannesburg, and it seemed as if half the audience had bought a copy.

G and I were drunk, on gin and beer, and our fleeting fame. We had visions of moving to London, of working for the *NME* and writing books which would bring down apartheid or, at the very least, forge a link between James Phillips, Patti Smith and our strange white teenage selves. Reeling back to her flat, coins clinking in our pockets, we lingered over the two remaining copies of our fanzine before deciding we should start afresh. *Smoke & Ochre* would disappear and be replaced by something different. We had our first fight that night, as well. I was serious about moving to London, and working for the *NME*. And so I wanted to write grown-up record reviews.

Gillian was much more original. She argued that we should abandon all stylised imitations of overseas music newspapers. G said we should just write honestly about the country around us. She was right, and the truth stung. I said it was easy for her. She didn't have to go into the army.

'That's why you should write about it,' she said, sounding much older than eighteen. 'One day, no-one will remember how we all feel right now ...'

But how could I begin to explain how I felt at the bottom of Africa, in the long and confusing year of 1980? I was too young, and too frightened.

'I'm going home,' I said.

At two in the morning I shocked myself with a futile gesture, throwing my copy of *Smoke & Ochre* out of her open third-floor window. The pages fluttered and flared, looking white against the black sky. And, then much more slowly than a falling body, they scattered one by one. The separated pages made no sound as they floated down to the concrete pavement.

O N SATURDAY 30 MAY, 1981 I felt agitated in front of our television. Dad looked up from his work to see what was eating me up. I was worried about Errol Tobias. I could still remember how the newspaper had fluttered in my hands when, a few days earlier, I had read that Tobias would become the first 'non-white' to play rugby for South Africa.

An hour before the first Test against Ireland in Cape Town, I also switched on dad's radio. A snatch of *Forces Favourites* echoed around the room, drowning out the televised burble. I hadn't heard it for years and, for a few minutes, I was transfixed. Pat Kerr was still reading out messages to our boys on the border, as if she had never left the studio since the last time I heard her crooning to our troopies and their cherries [girlfriends]. I was soon in a bad mood again as, with a husky little chuckle, she introduced the next song: 'In The Navy' by The Village People.

My mother was still plugging away at the prospect of me joining the navy, which she considered less reactionary than the army. Dad's new plan, meanwhile, centred on his hope that I would allow him to use his government contacts to help me find a cushy job on the military newspaper, *Paratus*, after I had done my basic training. I said there was more chance of me joining The Village People.

There was another ritual exchange between me and dad before his wisdom intervened. Pointing out that it was Saturday afternoon and a historic day, he put away his work and suggested we have a beer. While dad got up to pour us a couple of cold ones I wondered what would happen if Tobias had an absolute stinker on his Test debut. Maybe, through sheer nerves, he'd drop every ball that came his way? Or maybe the white Springboks would refuse to pass to him, a dark-skinned Coloured man from Caledon.

'Let's hope old Errol does well,' dad said as we clinked glasses.

If we were that worried, how would Tobias himself find the strength to move one foot in front of the other? How would he convince all the racists that he deserved to wear a Springbok shirt? Could he be that cool? Could he be that brave? When the teams ran out at Newlands, the cameras zoomed in on Tobias. He was a shy man, and seemed shrunken as the enormity pressed down on him.

It was breathtaking in its intensity, at 3:28 on a Saturday afternoon in the autumn of 1981, to see a dark skin inside a Springbok shirt. South Africa wore white that day, not in honour of the past, or as a reminder to Tobias to remember his place, but to avoid clashing with the green of Ireland.

Tobias settled quickly, and we cheered his every move. We even jumped and shouted out with the commentator, '*Ja*, Errol, *Jaaaaaaaa*!' as his rock-solid display included a luminous break which opened up Newlands and sent Rob Louw over for a brilliant try. South Africa, with fourteen white men and one coloured, won 23-15, and Tobias stayed in the team for the second Test in Durban the following weekend. The Springboks won more narrowly, 12-10, and by then I had reverted to more typical misanthropy.

I asked dad some sneering questions: where would Errol Tobias wake the following Monday morning? He would not wake in a city hotel as an honorary white man. Tobias would be back in his coloured township. What would have really changed?

'Don't be so negative,' dad said. 'It's a start . . .'

Tobias was selected for that winter's tour of New Zealand – but his inclusion did not quell the furious protests that erupted when the Springboks reached the shores of their greatest rugby rival. We saw Tobias, again on television, finally wear the familiar green and gold Springbok shirt in the opening match against Poverty Bay on 22 July, 1981. Tobias shone that gloomy day, from the moment he scooped up a horrible pass and, without breaking stride, sliced through a gap and set up the first try of the tour. The Springboks' Afrikaans coach, Nelie Smith, smiled his crooked smile and said to the crowd of reporters: 'Not bad for tokenism, gentlemen?'

By mid-August the tour had soured for Tobias. He was consigned to the mid-week team but still forced to bear the most searing attention from demonstrators and supporters alike. He became more and more withdrawn, a sad symbol for a bleak tour.

Trouble had erupted in an early match. Before the players had even emerged, a large crowd in Hamilton pressed against a wire fence meant to keep them off the field. Those in front wore crash-helmets. They moved together like a multi-legged, helmet-headed insect, searching for an opening. Sometimes they hesitated, as if uncertain which sets of legs were taking the right turn. And then the crowd parted and divided themselves into separate sections about twenty-five yards apart. The helmet-heads in each group charged. The fence gave in without even a sigh.

The crowd jeered the demonstrators who formed a ring in the middle of the field. After five minutes, numerous units of New Zealand policemen trotted onto the pitch. 'We want rugby!' and 'Off! Off! Off!' chants came from the crowd. The police approached the anti-apartheid loop and rugby-mad Kiwis roared, and then groaned as the uniformed men stopped just short of the circle.

Eventually, the police began to forcibly remove each protester. After ten minutes they had led away just twenty-five people. Five minutes later, a van drove over the muddied grass and various policemen emerged with boxes of white arrest forms. The game was over.

'Unbelievably tragic,' a South African commentator said grimly, not knowing that the match had been abandoned because the authorities had received a threat that a terminally-ill man was prepared to crash a light aircraft into the main stand, as a protest against apartheid.

At each game from then on, helmeted protesters and baton-hammering riot squads smashed into each other. Helmets were dented, heads were cracked, noses were broken and faces were cut as New Zealanders fought pitched battles against each other over apartheid.

South Africa lost the first Test 14-9, with the struggle between policemen and demonstrators being even more riveting. There were only two Tests left and it seemed an absolute certainty that these would be the last matches the Springboks would ever play under apartheid. And, in August 1981, it felt as if apartheid had a hundred more years to run.

In the hours before the second Test, having just sold the last of our latest *Who Was That Masked Man?* fanzine at an Asylum Kids gig, Gillian told me she was moving in with a man she had been seeing for a few months. He was a dentist. I was fine as I had designs on another girl in my English III class. G and I would remain friends. We'd still work on our fanzine together, and we had stopped sleeping together as soon as she and the dentist had started going out. But G seemed strangely embarrassed, more by his profession than anything else.

'I can't believe it,' she kept saying. 'I'm fucking a dentist . . .'

I laughed, and felt like kissing her. But I remembered the dentist.

'It could've been different for us,' G said. 'But I've always known you're going to leave.'

I was determined to leave the country, and so I knew what she meant. I could have stayed that night but it would not have been right for G, the dentist or me.

So I kissed her on the cheek. I was on my way to watch the rugby, live from New Zealand, at three-thirty in the morning.

'You and the dentist,' she said. 'He's also watching.'

G hated rugby, and so I drove home from her small flat in Johannesburg to our huge house in Germiston.

In front of the television, after half-an-hour, South Africa were winning 18-3. I wanted to leap up, until I remembered that the Boks were the team of the Nationalists and the army. But to lead the All Blacks by fifteen points in Wellington was a feat of magic. I gave in and roared on the Springboks. In the end South Africa won 24-12, and the series was tied 1-1. There were, however, a thousand more injuries in the battles beyond the barbed wire.

O N 11 SEPTEMBER, 1981, the day before the final Test in New Zealand, it snowed in South Africa. It was the first time I had seen snow in my twenty years of life. Germiston was spookily hushed, and beautifully white, when we woke that morning. It was a terrible day, in some ways, because my one-armed Granddad Scott, my mother's father, was to be buried that afternoon. He was ninety-four years old, but we still felt the loss of the tubby little man.

I spent the morning in our garden, with the dogs, throwing snowballs in the air for them to try and catch with excitable snapping and barking. And then, just before noon, we left for church. It was hardest for my mother when, with the snow falling lightly on a spring afternoon, they lowered granddad's coffin into the freezing ground.

Later, it was easier, as we ate and drank and talk turned towards the following morning's last Test in Auckland. The violence of the tour had escalated in the preceding weeks. Over 1,500 people had already been arrested and 400 more soon followed.

I stayed in that Friday night. It felt right to be with my parents. By the time the house had been cast into silent darkness for four hours or more, I settled down in our study to watch the images being beamed back from New Zealand. In the grey Auckland sky, orange flares climbed up and a plane circled Eden Park. I thought of the dying Kamikazi pilot who had been ready to crash his aircraft into the main stand.

My cousin Kevin Scott had missed the snow, and our grand-dad's funeral. Kevin was back on the border. On the day that granddad died, my aunt Bobbie had managed to phone his base camp on the Angolan border. She spoke to a corporal who walked over to the soldiers and shouted, 'I'm looking for Trooper Kevin Scott . . .'

Kevin knew it would be bad news, and when his mother told him about granddad's death he quickly asked his commanding offi-cer if he might take compassionate leave to attend the funeral. The answer was a blunt no. And so, while we shivered in the snow, Kevin lay in the border sunshine, turning browner by the day as he thought of home and Granddad Scott.

In the early hours of that Saturday morning the Boks and the All Blacks tore into each other. Eden Park rocked and the plane flew lower and lower. And then it happened. After the teams had exchanged penalties, the first plane dropped its first bombs. Heavy bags of white flour fell to earth, faster than the accompanying leaflets against apartheid. If one of the bombs hit a player there was no telling what might happen.

A surreal match ground on until, with fifteen minutes left, the All Blacks led 19-18. And then, in the last minute, a drop goal made it 22-18. But the Springboks came back and from the kick-off they pulled off something like a miracle. Ray Mordt, their muscular wing, scored his third try which, in 1981, was worth four points. 22-22.

I jumped up in delirium, imagining G's dentist and white South Africans across the country doing the same thing in the dead of night. Naas Botha, who hardly ever missed a kick, looked up at the tall white posts as the plane turned back for one last attack. He wiped the black mud from his eye and stepped forward. Botha's kick sliced to the right. It looked as if the match, and the series, would be drawn.

But Clive Norling, the Welsh referee, refused to blow his whistle. The All Blacks ran at the Boks one last time. A tap penalty was conceded and the exhausted South Africans did not retreat quickly enough. The penalty was moved forward and, in the very last moments of the game, it was obviously kickable. I felt strangely heartsore.

Allan Hewson, the All Black full back, prepared himself. I hoped he'd miss, but I knew he wouldn't. The ball climbed and steepled, and then arced through the middle of the wide open poles. 25-22 to New Zealand, as the final whistle blew.

I stared at the barbed wire glinting around the muddied perimeter of the field. In front of it, Hewsen's thin arms were held high in a definitive gesture of triumph. The game was up, and not only for Springbok rugby but for my life at home.

The television became a blue blur as the pictures from New Zealand cut away to nothing. In the dark, I thought of the ten weeks I had left.

My parents had agreed that, as I was about to complete my degree in English and Politics, they would help me go overseas for the first time in my life. I imagined myself at concerts, seeing bands I had always read about and loved. I saw myself on the North Bank at Highbury, watching Arsenal, and walking down streets of a giant and seething city that might, one day, be my new home. The thought of leaving South Africa forever secretly terrified me. I knew I was not ready, and my only hope was that I would do well enough in my final English III exams in November to get into Honours the following year.

Slowly, I walked up the stairs of my old family home, just after five in the morning. I needed to steel myself for the tests ahead. I had to stay out of the army one more year.

A COUPLE OF MONTHS LATER, near the end of November 1981, Dad read out the names of the films he and mom wanted to see before Christmas: *The Postman Always Rings Twice*, *Raiders of the Lost Ark*, *Chariots of Fire* and Woody Allen's *Manhattan*. Mom was particularly keen on *Chariots of Fire* while dad was more intrigued by *The Postman Always Rings Twice*, and, I suspected, the sight of Jessica Lange being ravished by Jack Nicholson. That evening, however, rather than settling down at the plush new multiplex in Eastgate, a giant shopping complex in suburban Bedfordview, they would opt for the hard seats of the Market Theatre in downtown Johannesburg, where they had booked tickets to see Pieter-Dirk Uys's latest satire on life under apartheid: *Hell Is for Whites Only*.

The rest of white South Africa seemed agog at the prospect that, as *The Star* reported, 'Six Sexy Guys Head for the Sun'. The Village People were on their way to South Africa, intent on breaking the cultural boycott against apartheid, with all those buttock-clenching songs we hated at school discos – 'YMCA', 'Macho Man' and, yet again, 'In The Navy'.

I was heading north instead. On Friday 4 December, 1981, six days from then, I would fly to Luxembourg from where I'd take a bus to Brussels and then a train to Amsterdam before spending three weeks in London. Dad hoped a harsh European winter would persuade me to shelve my plans to leave South Africa for good.

My exams were over, but I would only learn my fate ten days before Christmas. I would have to phone my mother from London to discover whether I'd got the first or upper second I needed to be accepted into Honours. Instead of worrying about it, I'd decided I would go out with G one last time. The dentist was away for the weekend and that Saturday would be our final fling.

Late that night, in a darkened club in downtown Jo'burg, with the Asylum Kids playing so loud it felt as if our ears might bleed, I held Gillian close. I took a lingering look at my world as she leaned into me. We drank fast and eventually jumped around near the front of the stage, just a reeling boy and girl in a seething mosh pit.

When we left that sticky pit of a club, our ears ringing and our faces shining, we bumped into my friend, Pete, from Politics III. He was late, and looked distraught.

'Have you heard?' he asked.

'What?' we shouted back at him, forgetting that we no longer had to holler.

'You know Auret and Barbara?' he asked.

We didn't know them personally. But Auret van Heerden was the president of NUSAS, the National Union of South African Students, and Barbara Hogan had a formidable reputation as a student radical. We knew they had both been detained by the security police in September.

'They were just the first, china,' Peter said, grabbing my arm. 'More have gone . . .'

'Who?' Gillian said, suddenly looking straighter than I'd seen her all night.

'Neil Aggett and Liz Floyd . . . early yesterday morning.'

Pete's voice sounded husky. Again, I did not know either of them personally. Neil and Liz were seven years older than me and G. Pete had long revered them. They were both medical doctors and committed trade unionists. But, as he spoke, they were just Neil and Liz, a boy and a girl in deep trouble.

'They were together,' Pete said. 'Just like you *okes*. They were a couple ...'

I started to say that G had a new boyfriend, the dentist, but she pulled me tightly towards her and shivered as she heard Pete talk of them in the past tense.

They had been taken less than twenty-four hours earlier, Pete said, but who knew when either of them would get out?

'The country's fucked,' he said, his eyes glittering in the dark.

'C'mon,' he murmured. 'Let's go back inside ...'

I looked at G, and she leant over and kissed me. '*Ja*,' she said. 'Let's make a night of it ...'

And so, linking arms, the three of us turned away from the night outside and climbed the stairs back up to the noise and the bedlam. We wanted to escape.

'OK, boys,' G said. 'Let's get wasted ...'

PART III

THE DETAINEES
(1981–1982)

Neil Aggett

CHAPTER THIRTEEN

DETAINED

THEY HAD BEEN EERILY CALM as they sat on the old double bed. Facing each other, knee touching knee, their fingers laced around two mugs of tea, Neil Aggett and Liz Floyd felt a fleeting surge of power. Just before 3 a.m. on Friday, 27 November, 1981, as light rain fell across Johannesburg, they were locked in their own world. They ignored the sweating and swearing security policemen who tore the house apart. Every few minutes one of the bruisers yelled at them – '*Kyk hier!* (Look here!)' – in an effort to make the two doctors watch them wreak their destruction.

Liz and Neil appeared oblivious to the carnage as bookcases were overturned, shiny black records were flung from their sleeves, clothes were hurled on the floor and her underwear was examined or pocketed. To the bewildered fury of the invading policemen the young couple concentrated on themselves. They drank their last tea in freedom and looked intently at each other. Speaking softly, they might have been discussing their plans for the weekend. Nothing else, apart from each other, seemed to matter.

The men had come for them an hour earlier. It was a daunting moment the couple had anticipated for years, with the hammering on the door and the shouts of policemen at the dead of night sounding even louder than they had once imagined. Neil pulled on a T-shirt and his black jeans as he rose from their bed in a house he and his friend Brigitte King rented in Crown Mines. He looked back to check that Liz had also dressed quickly.

And then the Special Branch were in, with the noise and the bedlam enough to scare the life out of two ordinary people. Yet, miraculously, the opposite happened. An extraordinary composure brought Liz and Neil together. It was almost a relief after the years of being followed and threatened. So they shut out the surrounding madness and looming detention and, instead, savoured their last time together.

The security policemen ransacked the house for evidence. Even a photograph of Nelson Mandela, still in prison on Robben Island after seventeen years, would be enough to incriminate them on a charge of treason. But the police were after much more. They wanted detailed plans and lists of names linking Aggett and Floyd to the banned African National Congress or the South African Communist Party.

The men from the Branch had been questioning and torturing Liz and Neil's friends, Barbara Hogan and Auret van Heerden, for weeks at John Vorster Square in downtown Johannesburg, just a few miles from the Crown Mines house. They were sure they were now onto another pair of white terrorists. But the police needed proof of revolutionary plotting and communistic scheming buried inside Floyd's panties or Aggett's jazz records.

Outside, in the dark, the other corrugated iron houses in Crown Mines remained quiet. Tucked away among the blue gum trees and huddled mounds of the disused gold mines, the small neighbourhood stood apart from the rest of Johannesburg. There was no suburban comfort or pampered life here. It felt stark and gritty, especially when the wind blew dust from the mine dumps across this part of town. But, when it rained, the feathery grasses recently sewn into the mine dumps grew stronger. Eventually they would provide enough of a covering to hold down the dust from the dumps.

The longer the search went on the closer Neil and Liz came to being separated. They still did not show panic or dejection. Instead, they kept talking calmly.

Eventually the moment came. The policemen found nothing obviously incriminating, but the officer in charge instructed his men to tip all the political books and trade union pamphlets into a container. Something might turn up in a forensic examination at John Vorster Square, where the country's leading dissidents were detained for weeks or even years without access to lawyers or the rights of a judicial trial.

Almost two hours had passed since the house had been turned inside out. It was their turn now. Neil and Liz were parted roughly, without any chance of a final goodbye. They were each allowed to pack a small carrier bag of items and then led out into the cold morning air.

Neil was bundled into one car. Liz was pushed towards another vehicle.

They felt vulnerable in their separation. This was the start. This was what it meant to go into 'solitary', to be detained, to be tortured, to die slowly on the inside.

THE CRACKDOWN HAD BEGUN two months earlier. Barbara Hogan and Auret van Heerden were the first to be taken in late September 1981, as the security police instigated a systematic campaign to crush white opposition. The state had succeeded in quelling the black rebellion that had spread through the townships after the 1976 Soweto riots. Retribution had been swift and brutal. But the uneasy lull had been punctuated by the subsequent development of new cells of resistance. White student groups and the emerging black trade unions had started to organize themselves.

It was the third time Auret had been detained, and yet he surprised the fellow Afrikaners who arrived in force to arrest him at his home in Mendelsohn Avenue in the suburb of Glendower, east of Johannesburg. Pulling his house apart, in the ritual pre-detention swoop, they stepped back in shock when they discovered small mementos which linked them together.

'Jesus Christ, look here,' they shouted in Afrikaans when, instead of communist literature, they picked out Auret's clinking set of running medals which hung from satin ribbons. They could not believe that some of them had even run in the same punishing races as a long-haired left-wing radical like Auret. It was difficult for them to reconcile the evil he represented with the fact he was a passionate long-distance runner. How could a sportsman, and an Afrikaner *nog al* [as well], be opposed to apartheid? It made no sense.

Van Heerden's family were also confused. Auret's father, Dennis, encouraged him and his brother, Clive, who was also a student at Wits, to be critical of injustice. But Auret's mother was different. She and her own blood relatives were deeply conservative Afrikaners who felt wounded by his rebellion. They considered it an attack on his people and culture. The schism in the family, who lived in Bedfordview, an affluent suburb between Germiston and Johannesburg, widened.

Auret could not help himself. He knew what needed to be done. Ever since he had left Jeppe Boys High and arrived at Wits in 1974 he had been shaken from his complacency. He went to a mass rally on his first day at university and had been stunned when Charlie Nupen, the National Union of South African Students [NUSAS] president, made a blistering speech attacking 'John Vorster and his goons'. Auret was convinced that, in 1974, Nupen would be locked up for criticizing the prime minister and for daring to use a word like 'goons'. It looked to him as if Nupen did not care what the government might do to him. Auret was impressed by such courage.

He was even more amazed when, in his second year at Wits, his Industrial Sociology lecturer, Eddie Webster, stood in front of a packed lecture room and made a sincere apology. Webster explained that he was on trial for treason and due in court that morning at eleven, so he would need to cut short his lecture by a few minutes. From high up the steeply banked rows of seats, Auret looked down at Webster in wonder. The softly-spoken man in front of him knew that his life, and his freedom, were in jeopardy, and yet he still had the decency to think of a bunch of kids and to apologise for the way his treason trial affected their schedule.

Auret was already hooked on learning about political economies, and the study of work was of profound interest to him. They did not use their lectures to peddle rhetoric but, instead, Eddie and David Webster galvanized their students by explaining to them the workings of capitalist and totalitarian systems. Auret realized, with gathering indignation, that black workers were denied any rights in South African society. He began to meet regularly in the Wits cafeteria with his friends Barbara Hogan and Cedric de Beer as they tried to work out what they might do to help bring about change.

The three serious-minded students decided that they needed to join a political party to oppose the government. They knew the only legal option open to them, becoming members of the Progressive Party, which then had just one MP, the redoubtable Helen Suzman, would not be enough. And so they resolved to forge links with Nelson Mandela's ANC, even though the decision would leave them vulnerable to charges of treason.

There were enough security police spies in student circles to ensure that their detention followed almost automatically. Auret was detained for the first time in 1977, when the political clampdown was fierce in the wake of Winnie Mandela's banishment to a township on the edge of Brandfort in the Orange Free State. He was assaulted repeatedly by Afrikaner policemen led by Major Arthur Cronwright, who appeared determined to make him understand their anger.

'You've got it all,' Cronwright said to him in Afrikaans, 'and you stab us in the back like this?'

Auret could absorb the blows and the words, but he found it harder when he was left in solitary confinement for ten days and nights. 'It scared the shit out of me,' he said later. But at the end of it, when they finally released him in 1977, he felt stronger. 'OK,' Auret told himself, 'you can do this. You can survive it ...'

He was soon forced to make a further choice. His underground comrades told him that, since he had been 'blooded', they wanted him to take over the presidency of NUSAS. That very public role would almost certainly lead to further detention. Auret's girlfriend could no longer stand it. He had to choose between her and politics. Auret told her he was sorry; he had no choice. He broke up with her and began to prepare himself psychologically. Auret and Barbara Hogan researched torture by reading books on the subject, and, more helpfully, they spoke to former detainees who explained what had happened to them and how they had found ways of coping.

He felt ready. But this time, his third time, was different. Auret was detained on 24 September, 1981, under Section 22 of the Anti-Terrorism Act and taken to John Vorster Square. From there, he was shuttled between prisons in Pretoria, Sandton and Benoni before returning. Darkness engulfed him, and he was interrogated under the more serious Section 6 of the Act. He was still refused legal representation and, of course, detained without trial.

The shock was excruciating when they went to work on him. A

huge Afrikaner called Struwig, a violent man with a taste for inflicting pain, led the assault. They referred to Struwig as 'Captain', but Auret doubted he had the intellect to pass even the most basic officer exams. He had either become a captain for his exploits in the army or for his work as a brutal torturer. There was little art, or even any psychological dimension, to the crude hurt that Struwig administered. He was notorious for the way in which, a few years earlier, he had pulled out a black detainee's teeth, one by one, with pliers. Struwig needed to make his victim talk. It was only when the man's mouth had been reduced to a badly wounded pit, with holes lining his gums like graves robbed of their tombstones, that the words finally slipped out. The confession Captain Struwig extracted, alongside the bloodied rows of teeth, was deemed permissible in court.

Struwig was determined to force a similar admission from Auret. He wanted the young Afrikaner to admit that he had lost his way and become a communist working for the ANC. Why else would Auret have sold his soul to the black man? Struwig also wanted Auret to identify Barbara Hogan as a communist. And, finally, he wanted Auret to incriminate Neil Aggett and Liz Floyd.

Auret shook his head. None of them was a communist. They just did not believe in apartheid.

Struwig punched him again, in the face, as he yelled at Auret. Was he trying to be a joker?

Auret could feel the blood trickling from his mouth. He looked up at his torturer. Struwig was incensed. Why would a doctor like Aggett give up all the comfort and wealth of his career to work instead for a black trade union? Of course he was a communist. That sentence was delivered as another blow made Auret gasp and sag.

When he was able to breathe again, Auret said softly that Neil just wanted to help people. As a doctor he wanted to help the sick and the injured. Neil thought he could help black people more if he applied his education and skills in voluntary work for the trade unions. He remained a doctor and spent at least a third of his time working at a hospital. But he was more committed to helping black workers gain some rights. It had nothing to do with communism, Auret said, and everything to do with Neil's character.

Auret looked at his torturer. 'Some people have good souls,' he said. 'Neil has a good soul.'

Struwig hit him harder. 'You fucking liar,' he snarled. 'You're all fucking communists.'

Auret knew it was just the beginning. He could see how Struwig believed in his implacable logic. The battle between them would be terrible in its intimacy. Struwig looked as if he would never give up, and Auret dug deep into himself to summon the will to resist. He did not know how long he would last, or if he would die in the next few weeks and months, but the repulsive idea that he might betray Barbara or Neil or Liz or Clive, his brother, renewed his strength.

They worked on him in teams. He was made to stand for hour after hour until Struwig and his henchmen arrived for a new session. The torture would resume before, eventually, Struwig's crew was replaced by an apparently more reasonable selection of security policemen. These men, 'the good cops', would offer him a coffee, and a seat, while they lamented the crudity of Struwig's tactics. Auret liked them even less than the hard men.

It made his bruised skin crawl when university-educated men from the Security Branch, especially an English-speaking policeman like Lieutenant Stephan Whitehead, tried to ingratiate themselves with him. Whitehead saw himself as being superior to Struwig and another lump of fist-pumping concrete in a security officer called Laurence Prince. Rather than torturing him physically, like Struwig and Prince, Whitehead tried to fuck up his mind. In his creepy voice the lieutenant would tell Auret what Barbara had already revealed to them. Surely it made sense, Whitehead reasoned, that Auret should also tell them the truth. If he did, then Whitehead would be able to call off Struwig and Prince.

Auret felt more respect for Prince. He was nasty and thuggish but there were moments, too, when Prince stepped back and nodded a small tribute to Auret's courage. They were like two boxers then, in the ring, locked in a savage and unequal fight, and they shared the secret of the pain that they both knew Auret suffered. It was not enough to engender any compassion in Prince but at least he understood what he was doing to the twenty-six-year-old post-graduate student.

As his interrogation escalated, and he was taken to new extremes, Auret felt the benefits of all the long races he had run over the years. His body had grown used to pain, as a distance runner, and so his mind remained clear and resolute. He could withstand a lot more.

'*Ja*,' Prince murmured to Auret. 'You're good, *boet* [brother]. But, listen, you can't run in this place.'

Prince almost smiled. Then, as he left the room to be replaced by Struwig, a shutter of hardness slid across his face. 'OK,' he said. 'Now we get serious.'

LATER THAT NIGHT the Security Police assaulted Barbara Hogan in a darkened office. Prince did most of the dirty work. He hit the thirty-year-old master's student brutally, paying particular attention to the blows he landed on and around her ears. He told Barbara that he would burst her eardrums.

As she began to cry, Prince grinned. He said he found it 'a pleasure' to hurt communists.

In between the assaults they grilled Barbara relentlessly about the two doctors who appeared to form part of her circle – Neil Aggett and Elizabeth Floyd. They were curious about three particular facts of their lives together: Why did they follow such a stark lifestyle? Why did they show no commitment to making any money when, as doctors, they could live a much more lucrative life? What could she tell them about their relationship?

When Barbara praised her friends' selflessness, Warrant Office Deetlefts stepped forward and struck her hard in the face. She slid to the floor.

By the time she had pulled herself up she saw that Deetlefts had left the room. He soon returned with the severed cord of an electric kettle dangling from his hand.

Deetlefts plugged the cord into a wall socket and then fitted the frayed end to Barbara's handcuffs which were locked to the bare metal chair on which she sat. He sent Prince to fetch a wet cloth so that they could cover her face before they proceeded to shock her.

While they waited for Prince to return, the policeman gazed at his victim. 'This time, Barbara,' he promised, 'you'll be begging to talk.'

L IZ FLOYD SAT IN THE back seat, alongside a thickset policeman, while they raced through the dark. Two other men rode in the front, laughing and swearing, making her wonder if either of them had been amongst those who had phoned her repeatedly in the preceding months to tell her she needed 'a good fucking' or to claim that Neil was sleeping with Brigitte King, with whom he shared the house from which they had just been taken. Liz had long since grown weary of the grimily abusive, anonymous calls.

They were more sinister in their pursuit of Neil. Rather than harassing him over the phone they had often sent as many as five cars to tail him as he drove through Johannesburg on medical or union business. His hounding had intensified over the last eight weeks, ever since, on 22 September, Barbara Hogan had been detained. Auret van Heerden was taken a day later. His brother, Clive van Heerden, soon followed and their informal network began to crumble. Neil knew he was likely to be next, with Liz's own arrest seeming equally inevitable.

There had been other pressures. If it was a strategic decision to avoid discussing their political work in intricate detail, and so lessen the chances of betraying each other during interrogation, there had also been some tension between Liz and Neil. He was so immersed in his unpaid trade union duties, in organizing black workers in the food and canning industries, it sometimes seemed as if he did not fully acknowledge Liz's own political contributions. Had he forgotten that she had been politically active far longer than him?

There had also been painful mistakes. Two-and-a-half years earlier, in the middle of 1979, she had left Cape Town because she missed him so badly while he worked a thousand miles away, in Soweto. Arriving in Johannesburg she had been surprised by the depth of Neil's involvement in union work, and the distressing discovery that he had been sleeping with another young activist.

Neil's fling was already over but Liz, feeling let-down, had moved out of his house in a rundown Johannesburg suburb within a fortnight of her arrival. But the love between them could not be easily cast aside. Within another few months, in November 1979, they were together again. Over the next two years they had lived in the house he rented with Brigitte.

The last few months had been difficult. In mid-November, 1981, Liz stayed elsewhere for a couple of weeks in an effort to disperse the heat of police scrutiny. It felt as if they were being suffocated by the investigation and so she forced a confrontation with Neil. She knew how important it was that they expressed themselves fully so that nothing previously unsaid could be used to drive a wedge between them when they were seized. They were frank with each other and had reached a new level of understanding. Together again for the first night in weeks they fell asleep a few hours before they were invaded and then detained.

Neil and Liz had become an obsession for certain members of the security police. Owing to their profession, and romantic involvement, the doctors did not appear typically hard-bitten agitators, and their intelligence and freshness unsettled the security forces. The men tracking them were determined to discover what drove a young man and woman who, far from being interested in money or marriage, appeared ready to squander their medical prestige for some unknown aim.

The man in the front passenger seat turned around to look at her, as the streetlight cast a sheen across his face. 'I don't get it, Liz,' he said. 'A young woman like you, a bloody doctor, should be making babies and living in one of those fancy houses in the northern suburbs. I reckon you must get a kick out of being picked up by *okes* (guys) like us. Is that it, Liz? Do you like it?'

Liz Floyd turned her head away, as if she had not heard a word.

NEIL AGGETT HUNKERED DOWN in the back of the second car. Liz was mentally more resilient than him but the security police had developed a warped fascination for her. All the black detainees they knew had suffered at the hands of such men. Their torture had been grotesque. It was different for white detainees. The police went about their work a little more carefully when molesting people of the same skin colour. And so he felt strong. A crack of doubt opened up inside him only when he thought of Liz.

Their earliest years together, in Cape Town, belonged to another life. They were both nineteen when they met in 1973. Even though she was six months older than him, Neil was a year ahead of Liz at medical school. She had been a feisty presence in student politics while he was more a poet and a dreamer. His sensitivity made him stand out in a lecture hall crammed with thrusting young medical students. It was one of the reasons why a certain kind of woman always fell for him, because he was a thinker and a listener. Neil was content in his own company, but he had never been a loner or an outsider. He found it easy to be part of a team and to lose himself in sport.

Liz moved into his tiny cottage in 1974 and for a long while in Cape Town they needed only each other. She gave up politics because, in between the grind of med school, she was happy growing vegetables with Neil in their back garden or drifting down to the beach or sitting round the fire while they listened to Charlie Parker, Duke Ellington and Dollar Brand. He would read his sad and wistful poems then, the jottings he made in the back row of anatomy class.

In the police car he could even remember a poem he had actually called *Anatomy Class*. He would never become a great poet, even if that particular poem had been written when he was only eighteen. There was no time left for poetry. Even medicine had come to seem redundant against the grim backdrop he witnessed every day. He was a good doctor and he felt sure he could one day become a decent surgeon for he displayed a steadiness of nerve on wild nights in casualty. On an ordinary Friday night he was up to his arms in blood and gore at Baragwanath, the Soweto hospital which was overrun every week by stabbings and shootings. He was good at staunching and stitching, at staving off exhaustion and saving lives as a procession of wounded bodies was wheeled his way. It threatened to drive you to drink, but if you could cope with a Friday night at Bara you could cope with anything.

But what was the point of sending his patients back out into Soweto where the same desolate cycle awaited? What was the point when the reasons for the violence that split them open were found in apartheid? The people he treated were casualties of the very system which denied them education and work and electricity and housing, let alone a vote.

His despair with medicine had begun during his second stint of housemanship when he had moved to Johannesburg with the intention of becoming a community doctor. Neil worked for six months in Tembisa, an impoverished township fifteen miles east of the city, and felt bereft. Every illness he diagnosed in a child seemed to have been caused by poor diet or a lack of adequate sanitation or heating. Every fractured skull, lacerated face or severed limb seemed bound up in a political system distorted by one remorseless purpose, to control eighty-five per cent of the population for the comfort of the remaining fifteen per cent who happened to be white.

As he was a caring man, his patients began to tell him about their conditions of work and meagre payment. If they had been injured by an irate white manager or a piece of faulty machinery, Neil advised them on their compensation rights. When the men looked at him in confusion he steered them towards their union representatives, only to find that the labour movement had been shattered in previous decades.

Slowly, some unions began to rebuild themselves despite the chaos. Neil felt compelled to help. He soon became one of the premier union organizers in the Transvaal. No-one could pay him for his work and so he remained a doctor in Soweto. But such was his commitment to forming unions that, in order to meet the workload, he cut his hospital shifts from five to two nights a week.

His parents did not approve. They wanted Neil to follow a conventional path into medicine. His dad, Aubrey, was appalled as much by Neil's beard as his politics. Four years earlier, Aubrey Aggett had insisted that he would no longer pay for his son's medical fees as long as he sported a bushy black beard. Neil refused to shave it off. He thought it gave him a look of dashing gravitas and he was not about to bow down to his reactionary old man. The beard stayed and Neil earned himself a bursary from Anglo-American to pay for his last two years of medical school.

So, in the end, the bloody beard started it all. He had moved up to Jo'burg to earn some proper money so that he could pay off his student loan – and look where he had ended up?

Approaching John Vorster Square, Neil wondered how his aged parents would react to his detention. Would they be angry? He already knew the answer. Fear and love would cut off any anger. He felt sorry for what he was about to do to them.

His dad had transplanted the whole family from Kenya to South Africa in January 1964 because he could not abide the thought of living under a black government. Neil had been nine then and it had taken him a decade to absorb the political realities of the country he now called home. At the age of twenty-seven he knew that the mobilization of ordinary workers would be a more practical way of bringing about change than trying to stem the blood he saw every night in casualty.

The police car shuddered to a halt inside the bowels of John Vorster Square. He felt a lurch in his stomach as they opened the door and said just two words: *'Get out!'*

THEY HAD WARNED Auret van Heerden the night before his most harrowing spell of torture. 'Tomorrow,' they said, 'we'll start with the third degree. It's going to be terrible – and so you might as well get used to the idea that you will confess to us in the end. You might last a day, which will be very unlikely, but we will carry on into the night. We will work shifts. Intense shifts. You might last a second day. But that won't matter to us. We'll carry on. You might last a third day. But, even if you shock us all, we'll keep coming back.'

Auret looked away. He didn't want them to see even a passing tremor in his face.

Warrant Officer Johannus Visser did most of the beating. He had huge hands, hands that had become expert in administering suffering. His security police colleagues tried to lighten the fraught atmosphere. They made jokes about Visser's hands to Auret.

'Those aren't hands,' they said to Auret, pointing to Visser's hefty mitts. 'They're fucking *poote* [the paws or hooves of an animal].'

Auret couldn't join in the laughter. He was too caught up absorbing the trauma done to him.

On the second day, Visser used his giant *poote* to smash Auret to a swollen pulp. But Auret noticed how Visser brought some anti-inflammatories to help control the swelling. Auret made sure to memorize the name on the bottle, so he would have some evidence that he had been beaten so badly. But he doubted then that he would survive much longer.

Auret had endured two days and nights of continuous torture. He felt so bad he had begun to believe they would kill him. On the third morning, when Visser arrived for his latest shift, the sight of his victim affected him so much that the policeman struggled to stop himself from crying.

Visser insisted on massaging Auret. He used his *poote* to knead Auret's aching body tenderly. Auret could not shrug him off because he was too weary and battered, but his brain still registered the surreal nature of this intimate encounter. Visser tried to ease the pain Auret felt in his shoulders, and he allowed the young Afrikaner to slip into a chair as he worked on him.

The relationship that develops between the torturer and the tortured had already become apparent to Auret. When they shared a break, and allowed him some respite, the men who were so intent on breaking him would talk to Auret about their shared interests or, more bizarrely, some of their deeper secrets. They would talk to him about rugby or, in more complex moments, their private lives. There were occasions when a torturer would be on his own with

Auret and he would let slip a concern about his marital strife. Those moments strengthened Auret. Apart from extending his time away from pain, it bolstered him to know that his torturers had begun to respect him.

But then, of course, they reverted to cruelty. Visser used the same *poote* which had massaged Auret to make him cry out in agony less than half-an-hour later. The distressing bond between them thickened and tangled until it felt to Auret as if it might strangle him.

The leaders of the interrogation teams became increasingly frustrated with their failure to break Auret. Lieutenant Whitehead became more involved. He would read out the confessions they had apparently dug out of Barbara Hogan and Cedric de Beer. This spooked Auret because he heard details and previously hidden facts that could only have come from the mouths of his comrades.

Whitehead sneered into Auret's blood-spattered face. 'Of course,' he said, 'we tricked Barbara. She thought our spy in Lusaka [in Zambia] was a high-ranking ANC official. So when he asked her to send the names of all you people working with her she did exactly that. We've got it down in black and white. You might as well admit it. Barbara has . . .'

'But you tortured her,' Auret said. 'That confession won't hold up in court.'

Whitehead laughed. It was a short and vicious laugh. Was Auret really that naive?

They took their torture to darker extremes on the third night. Auret had endured seventy hours without sleep when they walked in with a hood. They pulled it roughly over his head and tightened it with such ferocity that he almost gagged as he inadvertently sucked the coarse cloth into his mouth. They poured water over the hood, making it even more difficult for him to breathe. He was meant to feel as if he was on the verge of suffocating. It was a technique of torture about which he had been warned by previous detainees. He had been expecting the hood.

But, out of nowhere, they shocked him. They had run an electric current from the wall socket and connected it to him – without Auret even noticing. He had been too busy concentrating on not panicking as he battled to breathe. The electricity hit him then.

It lit him up with such horrendous force that he could not stop screaming. As his body twitched with the current, his scream dragged the wet bag deeper into his mouth. The combination of electrocution and suffocation was like nothing he had ever suffered before.

The first shock ended and they allowed him to stop whimpering and trembling before they removed his hood. 'You can talk now,' they told him.

Auret shook his damp head, as water ran down the side of his twitching face. They re-hooded him. He dreaded still more water as it splashed down on his soaked and heavy hood.

They shocked him again. The voltage had been amplified, and the duration of the current lengthened, as his body went into convulsions.

Auret van Heerden, his mind working dimly above the excruciating pain, could imagine his demise. This, he thought, is death.

IN LATE DECEMBER, 1981, Liz Floyd was taken back to John Vorster Square for the first time since the night of her detention. She had spent a month in a prison cell in the small Afrikaans town of Bronkhorstspruit, forty miles north-east of Johannesburg. It was a depressing place to spend Christmas but at least they had not tortured her. She was mostly left alone, with her solitary confinement broken only by the arrival of her meals and two separate visits by a couple of senior security police captains, Naude and Olivier, from John Vorster Square.

They treated her relatively decently and gave her a sheaf of paper and a couple of pens so that she could write her life story. She was meant to start with her birth, in April 1954, and detail every incident of significance in her life, with particular attention being paid to her relationship with Neil Aggett, her friendship with Barbara Hogan and her work for the trade unions. It took her almost three weeks to complete her statement which she kept purposefully neutral.

Captain Naude, with surprising politeness, said it was not quite what they were expecting. She would have to make a more satisfactory attempt after Christmas.

On 27 December, exactly a month after her detention, she was transferred to Hillbrow Police Station in the hustling heart of Johannesburg. In an apparent softening, they allowed her mother to visit her that afternoon. Liz was permitted to receive one Christmas present, a pretty and free-flowing dress.

She wore her new dress the next morning when they came for her. Fear rippled through her when, in the back of the car, she was told that she was being taken to John Vorster Square. But, first, they made a short detour through Houghton and Parktown, two of the country's richest suburbs. As they drove through the relatively empty streets, with most wealthy Johannesburg families sunning themselves on vacation at the coast in Natal or the Cape, Liz caught the eye of a few passing drivers. What would they think if they knew a respectable young doctor was on her way to the most terrifying place in South Africa – the tenth floor of John Vorster Square?

They took her into the infamous concrete building and marched her to the lift. It was encased in a steel cage. From the inside she could see the wire mesh that covered the stairwell.

The first policeman explained that the mesh stopped detainees jumping to their death. They were going up to Timol Heights, the name the security police gave to the tenth floor, from where Ahmed Timol, an Indian detainee, had either leapt or been pushed to his death in 1971.

Liz's loose-fitting dress flowed around her, hiding her slender frame. It caught the eye of Stephan Whitehead, the ambitious young security policeman in charge of her interrogation.

Whitehead let out a low whistle as Liz was marched down a narrow corridor towards him. 'I like the dress,' he murmured. 'But, Liz, are you pregnant?'

She glared at him, a relatively short and plump twenty-four-year-old man in glasses, but Whitehead grinned mockingly. And then he got down to business.

They had given her a chance in Bronkhorstspruit and she had blown it. Her statement was a lot of rubbish. She had to start all over again and write the truth this time.

Liz stood her ground. She was a medical doctor engaged in perfectly legal work with the trade unions. Everything she and Neil did was out in the open because there was no point running an underground union. An effective labour organization had to be completely accessible to its workers. They had nothing to hide and she had made a complete statement. She could add one or two details, she said evenly, but they would do nothing to change the tenor of her account.

'You heard me,' Whitehead said tersely. 'Write it again.'

They left Liz to her rewrite, with only a policewoman watching over her, and the hours dragged. Later that afternoon, Whitehead was furious to see more of the same drivel from her pen. He thrust a photocopied article, from some unknown journal, onto her desk. Whitehead made her read it and then demanded that she include the inflammatory words, discussing the exploitation of the black proletariat and the need for mass revolution, and admit that she had written them.

Liz had never seen the piece before and pointed out that she would never use words like 'proletariat'. She would not include extracts in her statement and claim them as her own.

Whitehead moved towards her. She was a bright woman and so she had better listen to him. Liz knew what happened to people who messed around with the security police. She had better go back to her cell in Hillbrow and think carefully before they brought her back in the morning.

Liz raised her eyes contemptuously.

'Hey,' Whitehead hissed, grabbing her arm. He exerted enough pressure to make her wince. Slowly he loosened his grip and brushed aside a strand of her hair so he could whisper in her ear.

'I'm friendly with Neil,' he said, noting the pain in her eyes at the mention of his name. 'How come you're not friendly with me?'

WHEN THEY TOLD Auret it was over, after a hundred successive hours of torture, he thought it was just another trick. He was already half out of his mind, having not slept for five days and nights, and locked deep in pain. Auret just looked at them groggily, his eyes closing and his brain seemingly fried by the electric shocks he had absorbed.

'No, man,' the more extreme of his torturers, Prince, insisted. 'It really is over.'

Prince and his colleagues stretched out their hands to Auret, to tell him how much they respected him for everything he had withstood.

Auret shook their hands blankly, quivering with exhaustion, waiting for them to start laughing and to reach once more for the hood. But they meant it.

His torturers were awash with sentimentality. He had showed them what a tough Afrikaner he was, day after day, and in the end they had conceded defeat. They would get him another time, maybe, but they would let him sleep now.

There was even a garbled apology, for what they had been compelled to do, but Auret was too far gone to respond. He allowed himself to be led to his cell, where he fell into a dreamless sleep.

When he awoke, and the days passed, he realized that he had actually survived. And, as importantly, he had not broken. He not betrayed anyone. That solitary ambition, not to talk, had consumed him in the worst hours of his ordeal. He gave up the thought of not crying, or dying, but he had held onto what mattered most to him. Auret would not give them what they wanted.

They still came to visit him, or sometimes he was led up a few flights of stairs to see them again. But they always made sure he understood that he was free from torture – at least for a while longer. They had spent so much time together, and shared so many grisly secrets, it was almost as if they felt affection for Auret. They had put him under unbearable pressure but, like a diamond, he had glistened rather than broken. He would never tell them how close he had come to cracking. In the midst of his watery electrocution they had teased him with the hood. They had brought it close to his head, only to draw back with a soft one-word question: '*Enough?*'

Of course it was enough. How much more could he bear?

But every time he either said nothing or simply shook his head, before it was enclosed again in suffocating darkness. Auret tried to conjure up the faces of his friends, to remember why he could not betray them.

There had been moments when he felt as if he was flying. He was supercharged then, dancing with the electricity coursing through his veins. And afterwards he could smile at them with the most terrible smile when they said the word again: '*Enough?*'

'Hell, no,' Auret grinned.

They soon had him screaming again, but those were the moments which made them surrender before he did.

For most of the time he was being tortured, Auret had locked his emotions so deep inside himself that it felt as if he had sealed them up forever. He knew he could not show Whitehead and Struwig and Prince and the rest of them how close he was to giving up. And so the process of pushing his feelings down, of burying them, and then walling them up, had become so complete that he knew it would be years, maybe decades, before he would be free enough to allow those strangled emotions to come out of him again. Auret might have survived, but he had lost a chunk of himself in those hundred hours of torture.

He was consoled by the bland routine of his life. Every day he was taken from his cell to Lieutenant Pitout's office where he was given a chair and a desk so that he could read and write. The days passed by in a drowsy blur.

They were strange people, the torturers, because they seemed to think it was important that Auret liked them. Curiously, they had looked the happiest he had ever seen them when they invited him to share a couple of beers with them on Christmas Eve. It was as if they were inviting him to join their club. Auret could have refused, but he joined them because he did not hate them. And that seemed enough for him; to know that he had not been turned into a cowering animal by them. He could look them in the face, and remember how well he knew them. They had been through a hundred hours of hell together and, yes, he had won. And, for that reason, Auret could clink his bottle of beer against theirs when they said 'cheers'.

For three hours, during the early afternoon of that Christmas Eve, 1981, they had relaxed and drunk beer in Cronwright's office. All the big boys were there: Major Cronwright, Captain Swanepoel, Captain van Rensburg, Lieutenant Whitehead, a couple of colonels from the ninth floor. Only Whitehead persisted in bringing up 'work issues'. After a beer or two he came over and sat next to Auret.

'Listen,' Whitehead had said to Auret, 'there's just one thing. Don't you think Neil really is working for SACTU [the ANC-linked South African Congress of Trade Unions]?'

Auret laughed. Whitehead could not leave anything alone. But he was wrong. Auret went through it again, reiterating the fact that Neil was not a member of any underground movement and had no interest in helping SACTU. He told Whitehead that the security police had an over-inflated idea of SACTU's influence on the black trade unions. Most of the unions were anti-SACTU. Whitehead, sensing that Auret was telling the truth, looked bitterly disappointed.

NEIL AGGETT WAS HELD in Cell 209 in the basement of John Vorster Square. Across the passage from him, in 215, his friend, Auret van Heerden, had survived the worst of his torture. It had been bad, Auret said, and grim enough that he saw no point in rehashing every detail. But he had come through it. Neil would do the same when he was taken up to the tenth floor.

They considered themselves fortunate that a couple of times a day, at breakfast and dinner, when their cell doors were opened so that they could collect their food, they had a chance to talk. On good days, when the guards were a little more relaxed, they could sometimes spend an hour together. They had to ensure that they spoke softly but it provided crucial sustenance for them both, and gave Auret a chance to warn Neil of what lay ahead.

Lieutenant Whitehead was obsessed with them. Neil suspected it was partly because Whitehead needed to uncover some new subversive material to justify the three years spent tailing him. In all that time Whitehead had not been able to pin anything on Neil.

That was why he was so maddened by them; he could not allow himself to believe they were just doctors and committed trade unionists.

Auret liked the calm strength in Neil, but his interrogators would come at him with renewed purpose in the New Year. Neil needed to use some of the strategies Auret had employed. They went over the routine again: never be unduly provocative or try to humiliate the torturers with your more expansive education. Instead, try to forge a bond with them through common interests. It was important to get them talking about sport because it was a little harder for the torturer to go back to his most brutal work if you had previously shared some chit-chat about cricket or rugby.

Neil could talk cricket all day long. And he could handle Whitehead. He just hoped Liz was all right.

He tried to keep himself bright by telling Auret how much he loved her. Neil showed him the Christmas card their friend, Yvette Breytenbach, had sent. On the front Yvette had painted a picture of the house in Crown Mines from where he and Liz had been taken. She promised him she was looking after his two cats and the house was fine. He and Liz would return there soon.

And then Neil reached for the coloured scarf Yvette had knitted for him as a Christmas present.

'Isn't it beautiful?' Neil said to Auret.

'*Ja*,' Auret said quietly. 'It's very beautiful ...'

The two young detainees looked at each from across the passageway. Auret smiled then for the first time in weeks. It was a smile strong enough to make Neil grin back at him.

'Happy New Year,' the young doctor said to his friend and fellow detainee.

'Happy New Year,' Auret murmured in reply. 'Let's have a good one ...'

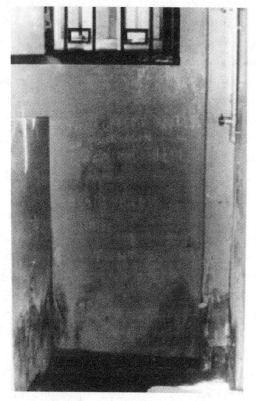

A stark image of a cell used for detention at
John Vorster Square police station

CHAPTER FOURTEEN

CELL 209

NEIL AGGETT AND AURET VAN HEERDEN were left alone for four days over the New Year weekend. From Thursday, the last day of the old year, until Sunday 3 January, they were only seen by a black warder who gave them their meals and allowed them a single shower. They were allowed to stand beneath the shooting jets of cold water on New Year's Day to celebrate the start of 1982.

The year began in earnest early on Monday morning, 4 January, with Neil taken up to the tenth floor even before breakfast was delivered to Auret.

IN ROOM 1012, Neil was surprised that he was brutalized by the policeman who had guarded him most closely. Warrant Officer van Schalkwyk had appeared a reserved and decent young Afrikaner – but, with Whitehead watching over him, he hit Neil repeatedly. They then made him strip naked. Neil had to do a draining series of exercises, from press-ups and sit-ups to squats and star-jumps, until the floor was covered in blood-flecked pools of sweat. Whenever he tired, van Schalkwyk would hit or kick him. After a long session beneath the fists and feet of van Schalkwyk, Neil was cut and bruised and walking with a limp.

Auret, returning from the showers just after four that Monday afternoon, was shocked by the sight of his friend. But he was soon heartened by Neil's humour.

'I kept trying to talk to them about cricket, like you told me,' Neil murmured. 'It didn't work.'

Neil, despite the bloodstains on his trousers, looked strong. 'It's good you're not freaked out,' Auret said.

'What can you do?' Neil shrugged. 'Liz and I will have a long holiday after all this is over ...'

They were taken back to their separate cells. Neil grinned at Auret and held his thumb aloft just before they closed him into the darkness. They would come for him again early the next morning.

L IZ FLOYD WAS DISTRESSED by the sound of a man scream-ing in pain in an office down the passage from where she was meant to write her statement on the tenth floor. It was a sound so inhuman she could not believe it came from Neil, even if Whitehead had taunted her by promising that he was about to see her boyfriend.

'Should I send him your love?' he asked.

Before she could stop herself, Liz nodded. 'Sure,' Whitehead said as he patted her arm. 'Me and Neil are real friendly.'

She had not seen Whitehead since; and the screaming echoed around her. Liz forced herself to listen more closely. She was sure it wasn't Neil.

'Who's screaming?' she asked the Afrikaans policewoman, Marietjie Snyman, sitting beside her, reading a glossy magazine called *Personality*.

Snyman shrugged. 'It could be anyone.'

Liz wrote a few more anodyne sentences. After another twenty minutes she looked up and, through the crack of the slightly opened door, saw a young black woman being led into the office across the corridor.

The woman began to sob hysterically. 'Are they assaulting her?' Liz asked Snyman.

'Doctor,' the policewoman sneered, 'don't worry. They mostly use psychological methods on you people.'

The psychology between Liz and Whitehead turned venomous that afternoon. 'Neil's talking about you,' Whitehead revealed. 'He's pouring his heart out.'

Liz would not allow herself to ask him about the screaming man. Instead, she thrust her statement into the policeman's hands.

Whitehead skimmed through it, his face darkening.

'This is the same rubbish!' he said. 'Where is the article you wrote?'

'I never wrote any article.'

'You're lying!' Whitehead yelled. 'I want a proper document from you.'

'I'm tired of you and your fucking document,' Liz snapped.

'If you swear at me I'll hit you,' Whitehead warned.

'If you hit me,' Liz said quietly, 'I'll hit you back.'

Whitehead shook his head and gestured to Warrant Officer Prince, who had dealt so effectively with Barbara Hogan.

Prince looked hard at Liz. 'We won't have you on our conscience,' he said. Moving quickly, Prince backed her into a corner. 'You're a lady,' he said chillingly. 'We want to treat you like a lady.'

By mid-January the security police no longer took either Neil or Liz up to the tenth floor. They were allowed to languish in their different cells – Neil in the basement of John Vorster Square and Liz at Hillbrow Police Station.

Neil felt he had been through the worst. He and Auret had also received little hints that they would both be released at some point in February. It was almost certain he would be banned and placed under house arrest, so preventing him from continuing with his union work, but as long as he could be back with Liz nothing else would matter as much as it once did.

Whitehead, however, was far from finished. He resumed his war of attrition against Neil with renewed vigour. The few privileges which Neil had been granted, such as the odd food parcel and his surgery textbooks, were withdrawn. Auret was still allowed to study every day in an office on the tenth floor and he was no longer questioned or harmed by anyone. But life had changed for Neil.

One morning he was taken back up to the tenth floor. Whitehead threw Neil's rewritten statement onto the cement floor. 'You are going to do this again,' he said.

Neil picked up the scattered papers. 'No,' Whitehead said softly. 'Not now. I am going to come and fetch you late one night and I am going to take you out of your cell and I'm going to bring you back here. And then we are going to give you an incredibly rough time.'

When he got back to Cell 209 Neil repeated those exact words to Auret. Judging from the way his friend looked away, jerking his head back as if a memory flashed through him, Neil could only imagine what Whitehead meant when he whispered that strangely quaint threat of giving him 'an incredibly rough time'.

O N FRIDAY 29 JANUARY, 1982, Cell 209 was empty when Auret went for his shower. He knew what it meant. They had taken Neil in the early hours of that morning.

Auret was back up on the tenth floor at 9 a.m. He was shown into Lieutenant Pitout's office, next door to the room where black members of the security police gathered to drink their morning tea and coffee out of tin cups. The white tea-room was further down the corridor.

Pitout's office was directly opposite Room 1012. The door was shut and Auret could hear only muffled sounds from inside. A black policeman leaned over to close the door to Auret's small room. But the young Afrikaner's mind locked on Neil, and memories of his own torture.

T HEY STARTED BY making Neil stand in Room 1012. The hours dragged as he tried to keep the blood circulating in his feet by wiggling his toes and shifting his weight from one leg to another. A black policeman, Sergeant Chauke, was instructed to hit Neil if he made any attempt to sit down or talk.

Around four o'clock that afternoon, when Whitehead and van Schalkwyk entered the room, Neil confirmed he had nothing further to add to his original statement. Whitehead accused him of being a communist and working underground for the ANC. 'No,' Neil murmured, 'I'm just a doctor who works for the trade unions.'

'Liar,' Whitehead said quietly. The word was a cue for van Schalkwyk to knock Neil down.

Whitehead watched him get up and, then, he asked Neil to confirm that his girlfriend, Elizabeth Floyd, was a Marxist who supported the ANC and the South African Communist Party.

'No,' Neil said as he wiped the blood from his mouth, 'she's just a doctor.'

'Liar,' Whitehead muttered as van Schalkwyk hit him more punishingly.

Whitehead moved onto Barbara Hogan. Did Hogan recruit actively for the ANC?

'No,' Neil said.

'Liar,' Whitehead repeated as van Schalkwyk, breathing hard amid his exertions, went back to work.

They made Neil stand up again. He would stand all weekend. If he did not start to tell the truth he would still be standing on Monday morning, in three days' time. They could go on for four or five days. They would enjoy it if he could break the hundred-hour barrier of torture. But what good would it do? He would still break down and sob out the truth they wanted. Why ruin himself for nothing? He could suffer unspeakably and then talk. Or he could just talk and everything would be fine. He could be back in his bed in his cell in an hour if he just saw sense.

'OK,' Whitehead said. 'Let's start again. Let's talk ...'

CELL 209 REMAINED EMPTY all Friday. When Neil had not returned by the time they closed the passage for the night Auret began to worry. He knew they would torture Neil until the next morning, without allowing him any rest. Sleep did not come easily to Auret as he strained to hear any sound from the opposite cell. The silence remained unbroken.

Again and again, he went over the conversation he had overheard in Lieutenant Pitout's office that afternoon. Captain Swanepoel had strode in to instruct Pitout that he would need to be on duty that Sunday, from six in the morning until six that evening. Auret knew that over the past weeks of interrogation Swanepoel had repeatedly asked Neil for medical advice. Swanepoel was concerned about his own health and he had no qualms about consulting Neil as a doctor, even though, in-between receiving his snippets of reassurance, he directed the young medic's torture.

Pitout protested that he had a family engagement late on Sunday morning, after church, and it would not be convenient to accept an extra shift.

Swanepoel was emphatic. As long as the business in Room 1012 remained unresolved, Pitout needed to report for work on Sunday.

Pitout shrugged, and looked at the shut door behind which they worked on Neil Aggett. '*Kyk* [look],' he said, '*ek glo nie hy sal so lank uithou nie* . . .[I don't believe he'll hold out that long . . .]'

Room 1012, Tenth Floor, John Vorster Square, Johannesburg, 29 January, 1982

DEEP INTO THE NIGHT of his long standing they brought in a stark metal chair. It had begun to brown with rust.

Captain Naude, whom Neil had always considered to be in over-all charge of his investigation, walked into the room just before midnight.

'Neil, please,' he said kindly, 'sit down.'

Naude looked at the haggard young doctor. He said they were getting close with the statement. It would help them bring it to an end if Neil added a few more details.

Neil refused. He would write only the truth.

Naude patted him on the leg, in apparent sympathy. The problem, he said, was that Lieutenant Whitehead remained distinctly unsatisfied. And Whitehead was frighteningly ambitious, the son of a police brigadier who had set his heart on a big promotion within the security police. He was not a man to cross, Naude warned, with apparent sincerity.

Neil closed his eyes. He felt exhausted.

'Wakey, wakey, doctor,' Whitehead yelled on his return. 'I want you to meet a friend of mine.'

Whitehead gestured to the smiling policeman standing next to him, Warrant Officer Deetlefts.

'Hello, doctor,' Deetlefts said pleasantly. 'Please stay in your chair.'

Deetlefts walked over to Neil. He reached into his pocket and drew out a long coil. It was the severed chord to a kettle. 'I wish I could offer you a cup of tea, doctor,' Deetlefts said, 'but Lieutenant Whitehead wants us to have a little chat first.'

Neil shook his head, the horror of understanding sweeping through him.

Deetlefts reached into his other pocket and pulled out a pair of steel handcuffs. He cuffed Neil to the metal arm of the chair and turned to plug the cord into the closest socket.

Whitehead moved closer to Neil after the black policeman, Chauke, handed him a white towelling hood. Neil felt its wet and suffocating heaviness as Whitehead covered his face and head. It worked as both a blindfold and a mask. Whitehead tied the hood so tightly around him that it was difficult for Neil to breathe.

The first shock, when it came, made him scream compulsively. It lit up his body in a flaring sheet of pain. As he screamed, the bag was sucked deep into his mouth. It became impossible to breathe. Neil did not know if they planned to electrocute or suffocate him to death when, suddenly, they turned off the power.

His body was still juddering as they dragged the bag off his head. Tiny drops of moisture clung to his beard.

They asked him some more questions and then covered and wet his head again. It was worse the second time, and then the third as well, because, as with Auret, they lengthened the period of each electrocution. He tried to stop himself from screaming, so that he might be able to breathe inside the bag, but he was helpless as his body shuddered with the current surging through him.

'Your kettle isn't working,' Whitehead eventually complained to Deetlefts.

Masked and gasping for air, Neil wondered if they were about to stop. But then someone bent down and removed his shoes and socks. They attached electrodes to the soles of Neil's feet while someone else poured more water over the bag.

The electrodes sent a far more powerful current shooting up through the bottom of his feet. His whole body was consumed by a crazed dance. But, still, when they removed the bag and allowed the life to return to his dazed eyes, Neil would not give them the answers they wanted.

They covered his head again and attached more electrodes to his wrists, his forearms, the nape of his neck and the base of his spine.

When they turned on the power it went beyond pain. The force knocked him off the chair. He lay in a pool of water, after-shocks pulsing through his body, as they turned off the switch. He was sure he was dying; and he wanted it to end.

They pulled him up and forced him down into the chair again. Then, slowly, the bag was raised.

'OK, doctor,' Whitehead said as he stared into the hollow face of a shocked man, 'let's talk ...'

NEIL HAD STILL NOT returned to his cell when, at ten the following morning, they took Auret up to Pitout's office. They moved him quickly past Room 1012 and shut the office door.

Across the corridor, Neil Aggett began to write the second statement of his detention. He was watched closely by a white security policewoman who had just started her shift.

The doctor wrote down the words that Whitehead advised him to use at the very top of the page:

1.

I support the Marxist ideology and therefore I am a communist. I am also an idealist.

2.

My father was a farmer in Nanyuki, Kenya, and I had one elder brother, Michael, and one elder sister, Jill.

Neil had only just begun to write and, already, at that mention of his family, his eyes filled with tears. A couple of drops, either from his eyes or his damp hair, smudged the ink. He asked for a clean sheet of paper.

The young policewoman sighed, and passed him another new sheaf so that he could begin again.

NEIL HUDSON AGGETT
Born on 6th October at Nanyuki, Kenya
Youngest son of J.A.E. Aggett residing at:
    PO Box 136,
    Somerset West

1.

I support the Marxist ideology and therefore I am a communist.

2.

My father was a farmer in Nanyuki, Kenya, and I had one elder brother, Michael, and one elder sister, Jill. I went to school when I was six at the Nanyuki Primary School, where I was a boarder until the age of ten. In January 1964, my family and I left Kenya by ship and

arrived in Durban. My father sold his farm and invested his money in
South Africa.

Neil had not slept for three days and nights and he was close to the
point of collapse – but he had to keep writing. Images of his family
swam slowly through his clogged mind.

IN JANUARY 1964, just weeks after Jomo Kenyatta formed
Kenya's first post-colonial government, Aubrey Aggett and his
wife, Joyce, and two of their children, Jill and Neil, had sailed to
South Africa with the aim of beginning a new life in a safe white
world. Their eldest son, Michael, had already spent a year at
boarding school in South Africa. Aubrey had read the signs. The
Mau Mau rebellion against British rule had plunged Kenya into
a State of Emergency in the 1950s. Kenyatta's subsequent rise,
and emergence as Kenya's first president, filled Aubrey with trep-
idation. He could not bear the thought of his family growing
up under black majority rule and so he had sold his farm and
emigrated.

In September 1966, the stabbing of Prime Minister Hendrik
Verwoerd in parliament troubled Aubrey Aggett. He had moved his
family from Kenya with the precise intention of escaping violent
political upheaval. But political assassination had reached South
Africa, the country he considered the last refuge of civilization in
a vast and unsettling continent.

Neil, who was a month short of his thirteenth birthday when
Verwoerd was murdered, remained largely oblivious to the political consequences. Home for a week's holiday from boarding
school, he pottered around his parents' new home in Somerset
West, a thirty-minute drive from Cape Town. 'I have begun setting
up a new sort of "lab" in the basement,' he wrote in his diary, 'and

it is quite good. I caught a lizard but it got away again. But I've set a rat-trap and I'm going to shoot a bird. I will also look for some frogs in the marsh.'

When he lived in Kenya, in the market town of Nanyuki, Neil had grown up as an African farmer's son. In the Rift Valley he had learnt to fire a shotgun by the time he was seven.

His hunting skills, however, had declined since arriving in suburban South Africa. 'No luck catching anything,' he wrote the next day. 'Even the rat keeps getting away. He keeps stealing the cheese and leaving the trap – but I think I've fixed him now! I beat dad by seven at billiards, but I lost by 15 at Scrabble. Mom has finished knitting dad his jersey and it looks good – in fact excellent.'

His first lonely years as a boarder, in a new country, had been eased by the binding power of sport. At Kingswood School in Grahamstown, tennis and cricket and hockey helped Neil become close to boys like Dave Pitman, Andrew Rein and Neil Collett. There was something beautiful in slipping on his whites, whether they were the flannels, cotton shirt and sleeveless pullover of his cricket gear or his pristine Fred Perry tennis kit. And then there was the distinctive sound each sport made. He liked the rhythmic pop and thump of tennis as a small fuzzy yellow ball went back and forth across the net during a long rally.

But Neil thought there was nothing sweeter than the sound of a red cricket ball being clipped across the green outfield by a flashing blade of willow. If the shot was timed perfectly, and the ball was driven or hooked over the boundary rope, he liked to see the different ways in which an umpire might signal a four. It was even more exciting when he made the umpire lift both arms in the air, with a grin, to confirm he had just hit a booming shot clear over the rope for six.

His father urged him to work hard so that he might get into medical school. The idea of becoming a doctor intrigued him, but not for the same reasons as his father. His dad was most concerned with him finding a reliable income, and a respectable position, but Neil knew he would be happiest working in a field where he could help other people. They began to bicker and argue.

By 1973, Aubrey and Neil Aggett were engaged in a pitched battle. Neil, a third-year medical student in Cape Town, could not believe that they were at war over hair, and the ever increasing length of his curly black locks and beard. His father was distraught at the emergence of a hippy in the family. Had Neil forgotten, as an aspiring doctor, how much appearances mattered?

Neil shrugged as his father raged. He believed a person was defined best by the thoughts and the ideals he carried deep within himself. Anyway, most of the Nationalist politicians ruining the country with apartheid favoured short-back-and-sides and closely-shaved faces of bile and thunder. Neil was happy to underline his difference from them. Back and forth they went, with Neil embracing the accusation that he wanted black majority rule as a hopeful sign that perhaps his father was beginning to understand him. That tart little remark incensed Aubrey still further. He would turn off the money-tap that had been keeping Neil in clover and refuse to pay for any of his son's medical school fees, or living expenses as a student, until he shaved and cut his hair. Neil shrugged. He was not about to change himself for the sake of convention.

N EIL WAS DRAGGED BACK to the present, and John Vorster Square, by a hard slap on his desk. 'You're not writing,' the policewoman yelled at him.

Neil wrote all morning, page after page, the words flowing as if he was writing about another person. And, more often than not, he wrote honestly:

'While I was working at Tembisa I became aware that the problems of my patients were not only medical problems; but were basically social problems due to them not getting enough wages, unemployment and the poor conditions in the townships. This meant that sometimes I would stitch up a patient, only to have him return the following week due to alcoholism, unemployment, or extreme poverty, with another assault wound. Also, I was working in a neurosurgery ward where I saw many people, particularly paraplegics, who had been injured at work. Often these patients did not get their compensation or, if they did, they got very little ... it became clear that the workers needed proper job security and they could only get this if they were members of a union.

'I felt that if I worked in a trade union I could at least contribute towards seeing these things gradually changed. I felt that it was important that people should learn about their rights, learn to have self-respect and therefore get rid of injustices themselves. I felt that if people learnt this in all spheres of life, life would gradually become better in South Africa.'

Neil tried to be less specific when instructed to write about his personal friends and colleagues. 'In about mid-1979,' he wrote, 'Liz Floyd came to stay with me in Joburg. We had personal problems and I felt it would be good to get away for a while. So I telephoned a friend of mine, Dr Mtshembla, who was working at Umtata Hospital, and asked him if any locum job was available. After about six weeks at the hospital, I returned to Johannesburg. Occasionally, Liz Floyd would mention the problems they were having in Industrial Health but generally we agreed not to discuss our work too much with each other, as we had our own problems and were very busy.

'I was invited to a meeting by Gavin Anderson at which Barbara Hogan, Cedric de Beer, Sipho Kubeka, Valley Moosa and Auret van Heerden were present. The meeting was a general political discussion about "Total Strategy". The discussion centred on what the government was trying to do to prevent any change in the country. We discussed how the government was facing economic and political problems, and the response to this was to turn the minds of the population onto a war-like footing to counter the threats inside the country.'

By the time he reached page 22 of his confession he knew that he had to at least allude to the crux of their obsession with him. He wrote down his deliberately neutered views of the ANC, the South African Congress of Trade Unions, the South African Communist Party and the White Left. 'I am not a member of the ANC. They seem to be more active outside South Africa than within it, and not very active in the areas that affect people's daily lives. Furthermore, if there is no democratic control over the leadership of the ANC, their policies may not correspond to what is wanted by the South African people.

'I have read about SACTU but when it went underground a basic contradiction arose. It is impossible to have an underground trade union. A trade union must be open, legal and run democratically. For this reason I believe SACTU is taking a wrong path, although it has a good history.

'I know nothing about the South African Communist Party apart from what I have read. I have heard that they are close to Moscow and this does not stand in their favour. What the workers and the people need are open democratic organizations in which they can participate.

'As a trade unionist I had neither the time nor the inclination to become involved in the circles of the white left. I used to be friendly with Gavin Anderson and Dave Dyson and met some other young people in a vegetable garden; but I never discussed labour or politics with them.'

Neil signed his statement at the end of page 23, and they called

Whitehead. The lieutenant was happy with the opening page but he was furious by the time he had skim-read his way to the end.

'This is rubbish,' he shouted. 'There's not enough here ...'

Neil shook his head. He had nothing more to add.

'OK,' Whitehead grunted. 'We're not going to fuck around any-more.'

He yelled out for Prince, and for Struwig. 'Take him back to the room,' he said, pointing to the bowed figure of Neil Aggett.

AURET KNEW NEIL HAD returned to his cell at some point that Sunday, 31 January, but he could not make any contact with his friend. Neil did not answer any of his whispered calls or low whistles.

When the prison guard arrived with their respective trays of food at lunchtime Neil did not appear at the barred gate.

The same guard returned that evening and placed Neil's supper tray next to his untouched lunch.

'What's the matter with Neil?' Auret asked the guard.

'Nothing,' the guard said evasively. 'He's just sleeping.'

NEIL WAS GONE from his cell early the next morning, on the first day of a new month, Monday 1 February. Auret could not concentrate in Lieutenant Pitout's office opposite Room 1012. 'Is Neil OK?' he asked Pitout.

'*Ja*,' Pitout nodded. 'He's just writing his statement now.'

AURET FINALLY SAW HIM AGAIN that Monday evening. But Neil drew back into the shadows of his cell. When Auret beckoned him to come closer, Neil hesitated. And then he moved slowly to the middle of the cell and, pointing up towards the tenth floor, indicated that Whitehead knew that they talked. He held a shaking finger to his lips to plead for silence.

'How do they know?' Auret whispered.

Neil pointed towards the guard at the end of the passage, and gestured again for silence.

Auret nodded but he could not help himself. He had to know what had happened over that long and terrible weekend.

'How are you?' he murmured.

Neil shook his head, his eyes welling up through the bars. And then, holding his hands up in front of his face, he curled his fingers shut into tight little fists. He made it appear as if he were holding a stick. And then, with a muffled cry, he snapped his hands downwards, as if breaking that imaginary stick.

At the same time he whispered the words which would haunt Auret van Heerden for years: 'I've broken . . .'

Auret had never seen anyone look so dejected. 'What did they do to you?' he asked.

When Neil did not answer, Auret pressed a fist against his own head. 'Did they beat you up?'

Neil nodded. But he also thrashed his hands wildly around his rolling head, to indicate that they had given him electric shocks.

Auret looked away, remembering how they had covered his own head with a bag, and then attached electrodes to his body.

Neil now held up three fingers, to show him how many days they had kept him awake.

'What did you tell them?' Auret said softly.

'I admitted I had SACTU links,' he replied. 'They forced me to admit I am a communist.'

Neil had now forgotten the guard at the end of the passage. He told Auret, despairingly, that they had made him talk about Barbara and Liz. Neil held onto the bars and began to cry.

He looked up at Auret, tears rolling down his face, and said, simply: 'They must not ask me any more questions.'

THE NEXT DAY slipped past and Auret did not see Neil, even if he could hear his friend moving around the back of his cell. Early the following morning, Wednesday 3 February, Auret was told that the whole security team would end their day at noon so they could attend a staff *braai* [barbeque] at the local rugby club.

'We all need a break,' Pitout said. 'We're going to let our hair down and have a good time.'

LATE THAT AFTERNOON, when the lone black guard walked down the corridor with their evening meal, Neil scurried across his cell. As soon as the guard had opened their doors, and left their food, Neil began to talk. He was agitated by the fact that Whitehead had returned him to his cell before lunch. It seemed a certain sign to Neil that they had finished working on him. But there was no relief in his words.

He believed that they would go after Barbara now, harder than ever before. Neil was worried most of all about Liz. What if they had already started to torture her?

Auret tried to calm Neil, explaining that the security team had left early for the rugby club *braai*.

Neil did not hear him. He started to cry again, fearing that he had betrayed Liz and Barbara.

The commotion roused the guard and they were forced to retreat to their cells. They could communicate only through sign language.

Auret, concerned about his own future, pointed at himself. Had Neil written about him?

Neil shook his head. He pointed directly at Auret and lifted his thumb in the familiar gesture of reassurance. Auret was going to be OK. Neil had not betrayed him.

WHEN THEY PASSED each other the next morning, on Thursday 4 February, with Neil on his way back from the showers, Auret greeted him warmly.

'Howzit, Neil!' he said.

Neil looked up, but showed no sign that he even recognized Auret. He shuffled past. When Auret tried to touch him, Neil kept walking.

BACK IN HIS CELL, Neil called the guard. He wanted to lodge a complaint with Officer McPherson, the man in charge of their cells.

When McPherson heard that Neil hoped to make a statement about his torture on the tenth floor he agreed to send down an officer to take some notes. McPherson was a man who liked to approach his business with a modicum of decency. He promised that he would make a copy of the statement before he handed it Magistrate Wessels who visited the detainees once a month.

A young Afrikaans policewoman, a sergeant who did not work for the Security Branch, met Neil in his cell. She was shocked by his appearance and agreed to take down his statement.

'I was arrested on 27 November, 1981, by a Captain Crouse of the Security Police,' he began slowly. 'I am detained under Section 6 at John Vorster Square cells ...'

As the details of his torture unfurled the young policewoman shook while writing down his words:

'Van Schalkwyk went to wash the blood off himself. When I was next assaulted by him he grabbed me by the scrotum and squeezed my testicles.

I was kept awake from 28 to 30 January 1982. During the night of 28 January Lieutenant Whitehead and another security sergeant whose name I don't know, and another black male, also a policeman, were present when Lieutenant Whitehead blindfolded me with a towel. They made me sit down and handcuffed me behind my back. I was shocked through the handcuffs ...'

After he had finished, and sworn an oath that he had told the truth, he thanked the policewoman. She reached out to take his hand. Could she do anything else for him?

He suddenly trusted her. If she saw Liz Floyd, his girlfriend, could she pass on a message?

The woman nodded. And then the previously hunched and broken figure of Dr Neil Aggett smiled for the first time in more than a week.

'Tell Liz,' he said softly, 'I want to marry her ...'

Tenth Floor, John Vorster Square, Johannesburg, 4 February, 1982

LIZ FLOYD WAS TAKEN back to the tenth floor for the first time in almost a month. They treated her differently now, handcuffing her and pushing her hard in the back.

Three men waited for her in the old room at John Vorster Square – Captain Olivier, Lieutenant Whitehead and Warrant Officer Carr. Whitehead took charge. He told Liz how they had grilled her boyfriend over the past week. The contrast between Neil's statement and hers was huge.

When Liz shook her head, Olivier ambled over. He put one foot on her chair, and opened his arms wide apart. 'If you take Neil's statement here,' he said, waving his left hand, 'it's this far from your statement.' He lifted his right hand to show the distance from his left. It was time that she closed that difference between her lies and Neil's truth. Otherwise, he said, Liz was in real trouble. 'The difference between them,' he said, looking carefully at his separated hands, 'is enough to get you a five-year sentence for withholding information.'

'You're bluffing,' she snorted.

Whitehead told her to stand. 'You'll stand here until Monday,' he warned as he left the room.

Carr, a heavily overweight man with a reddish face, rocked in his chair. 'This is how it started with Neil,' he said. 'They made him stand for two days.'

Liz maintained her silence for the next forty-five minutes when, looking over at Carr, she asked if she could sit down. She suffered from arthritis.

Carr, unexpectedly, relented, only to be disturbed by the return of Whitehead.

He kicked away Liz's chair and made her stand again. She was shaken further when they began to discuss a particular union meeting which she and Neil had attended. They told her that Neil said she had taken a line which was in direct support of SACTU. She was more upset when they also said that Neil regretted that he had ever studied medicine in Cape Town.

Liz knew how much Neil valued his medical training, but it was not a claim she could imagine the security men inventing. What could they have done to Neil to make him say such a thing?

Carr was now screaming in her face, demanding that she start telling them the truth.

Liz held her nerve. She had already made her statement. Whitehead reached for the handcuffs and dangled them in front of her face.

'You're coming back tomorrow,' he said, 'and we're going to cuff you to a metal chair. And we're going to talk properly then.'

The men left the room. Liz knew she had to stay strong, whatever they had in mind for her.

An Afrikaans policewoman she had never met before walked her to the lift. Before she handed Liz over to the two guards who would take her back to Hillbrow for the night, the young sergeant paused. She said quietly to Liz that she had seen Neil only a few hours before. He wanted to pass on a message to her.

Liz looked up in surprise, her face taut with tension.

'It's all right,' the policewoman said. 'He wants you to know that he would like to marry you.'

Those words jolted through her. Liz was shocked, and she did not know what to say. She simply stared, in surprise and wonder, at the young policewoman who nodded her confirmation. It was true, Liz suddenly knew, and she smiled. 'Thank you,' she said.

And then, before she could say anything else, two new security policemen arrived to take her away for the night. Liz Floyd walked with her head held high, as if she could stand anything now.

IN PARLIAMENT late that afternoon, in the shadow of Table Mountain in Cape Town, Helen Suzman, the only member of the opposition Progressive Party who dared question the state policy of detention without trial, stood up once more. She deplored the recent and largely unreported spate of detentions that had swept across the country. Suzman, a middle-aged Jewish woman from Johannesburg, demanded the release of all those who had been seized.

Louis le Grange, the Minister of Law and Order, rose from the front bench with a small smile. 'As usual,' he said, in Afrikaans, 'our honourable friend Mrs Suzman is getting hysterical. I can tell her to stop worrying. I have spoken directly to my commanding officer at John Vorster Square and he assures me that the investigations we have been carrying out are very close to a positive conclusion. It is quite possible that they will be charged soon with carrying out subversive activity against the national interest. Other linked investigations have been concluded satisfactorily and the resulting charges will be announced soon.'

Suzman lamented the 'utter lack of real justice' in South Africa. She argued that any charge laid against a detainee would need to be closely scrutinized. Her lonely urging became even more passionate as, above the heckling, she voiced fears for the safety of those still being interrogated at John Vorster Square.

'Mrs Suzman,' Minister le Grange sneered, 'my men are complete professionals. And, remember, we haven't had a bad incident in detention for years. We are in complete control of the situation.'

AT 7:30 THAT EVENING, while Liz prepared herself for her looming ordeal, Auret lay on his narrow bed in Cell 208. He pressed a small radio to the side of his head so that he could listen to a current affairs programme, *Deadline Thursday Night*. It was difficult for him to focus on the radio because his mind was consumed by thoughts of Neil.

Auret could not shake from his head the image of Neil as a zombie-like figure. He had looked so bad that Auret decided to see Major Cronwright in the morning and urge that Neil be transferred to hospital as a suicide risk.

Having decided on a course of action, Auret began to doze. He was woken when he saw that Officer Agenbag had pulled back the slats to check on him. Auret waved to him, reassured that they would also look in on Neil in Cell 209. He fell into a deep sleep then.

IN THE EARLY HOURS of the following morning, Friday February 4, 1982, Auret van Heerden sat upright in his bed. The noise from the corridor outside chilled him. There was a terrible commotion as agitated officers shouted at each other in Afrikaans.

Auret listened closely, concentrating on each word until, at last, he understood. Neil Aggett had been found hanging from the bars of Cell 209. He was still dangling, limp and lifeless, at the end of a long, coloured scarf wrapped tight around his neck.

I T WAS THE SAME scarf Neil had received as a Christmas gift just over five weeks before. On the floor next to his body they found the prison-library novel he had started reading early in the New Year – Nikos Kazantzakis's *Zorba the Greek*. The book was opened to page 246, where a young man kills himself after he has been rejected by the woman, a widow, he loved:

'Every minute death was dying and being reborn, just like life. For thousands of years the young girls and boys have danced beneath the tender foliage of the trees in spring – beneath the poplars, firs, oaks, planes and slender palms – and they will go on dancing for thousands more years, their faces consumed with desire. Faces change, crumble, return to earth; but others rise to take their place. There is only one dancer, but he has a thousand masks. He is always twenty. He is immortal.'

But, in Cell 209, a young doctor of twenty-seven was dead. Neil Aggett believed, tragically, he had betrayed Liz Floyd and Barbara Hogan, who had already been charged with treason.

L IZ WAS STARTLED the following morning when, rather than being taken to see Lieutenant Whitehead at John Vorster Square, she was ushered into an office at Hillbrow Police Station.

Her parents moved quickly to embrace her; but relief choked

inside her. She knew something terrible must have happened and so she pulled back. 'Neil?' she asked.

Her mother nodded and, gently, she told Liz that Neil was dead.

They allowed her to see his body at John Vorster Square and then Liz, distraught with grief, was transferred to Johannesburg General Hospital.

PART IV

MR ELECTRICITY
(1982–1987)

Neil Aggett: the only white South African
ever to die in detention

CHAPTER FIFTEEN

SLEEPWALKING

A WEEK BEFORE CHRISTMAS, in December 1981, less than a
month since the detention of Neil Aggett and Liz Floyd, the
soft crunch of my black boots on the white snow made the only
sound on a deserted suburban street in north London. I walked
slowly towards the red telephone booth on the corner. The snow had
begun falling on 11 December, and the oppressive sky made it easy
to believe the forecasts. London expected its heaviest winter snow-
fall in history. It did not look like a day for good news from home.

Just a few minutes from then, I would hear if my delinquent life
of reading books, listening to records, chasing girls and moaning
about the injustices of apartheid could continue. But if I didn't
squeeze into English Honours I would be condemned to a choice
between giving in to the army or leaving South Africa forever.

After three weeks away I was broke and almost ready for home.
How would I feel after three years or, possibly, three decades?

Amsterdam, Brussels and London had drifted past in a flurry of
sweaty gigs, subtitled movies and long train journeys. I missed

home, but I loved being away from the cloistered politics of South Africa.

Small moments touched me the most. In the London underground one freezing night, standing on a creaking wooden escalator as it descended into the depths of Holborn tube station, I felt the difference. A sign on the escalator asked commuters to stand on the right of the mechanical staircase, so that people could pass on the left. It made a polite contrast with the signage we saw every day in South Africa. In London, none of the staircases and trains and buses and benches was colour-coded.

I reached the bottom of the Holborn escalator and raced towards a train that was just about to resume its journey along the dark blue Piccadilly line. The tube doors were in the midst of closing as I hurtled between them. I slumped down in a seat and, as I looked up, tried to hide my surprise at an unfamiliar sight.

A young black girl was kissing a white boy. She caught me staring and broke away from her kiss. I looked down in embarrassment.

'It's OK, sweetheart,' she said in a husky London accent, 'It's just a kiss . . .'

I wanted to explain that, where I lived, she would not be able to sit on the same train as us. Where I lived, she and her white boyfriend would be locked up in jail for doing something so innocent. But I just blushed instead, and buried my head in the *NME*.

A few weeks later, stepping inside the icy phone booth, I fed ten 50p coins into the metal slot. I pushed the thirteen digits slowly and deliberately, and with each click in my ear I came closer to learning my fate.

Mom answered on the second ring, her achingly familiar voice sounding strong and clear. She cut to the heart of it.

'It's OK,' she said, her happiness bouncing across the six-thousand-mile distance between us. 'You made it . . . you've got another year . . .'

A WEEK AFTER RETURNING HOME, my reprieve seemed more poignant than thrilling. On 12 January, 1982, two days before he succumbed to national service, I went to see my best friend, Hilton Tanchum. He looked haunted that late Monday afternoon as we sat on the grass of the garden in Frank Street where we had played so many games of cricket and football through the sunlit days of our childhood. Hilton had another couple of years left to complete his degree and he could easily have delayed the inevitable. But he could no longer stand the waiting.

'I just want to get it over with,' he said.

He had two nights left before, early on a Wednesday morning, he and thousands of other army recruits would gather on a patch of bare ground near our university. They would then board a military train to Potchefstroom, his designated camp for basic training. He was about to enter a world we had discussed with dread and loathing ever since, seven years earlier, we were dragooned into army uniforms at high school.

We had been each other's closest confidant since long before then, from when we were still small boys. And in our later years only Hilton, and my family, knew how the army scarred me.

He asked me about London, and listened quietly when I told him that I could live there. I might have had no money, and no prospects of a job in a teeming city where I knew no-one, but I could adjust to the change. I could cope with the rainy greyness and the loneliness. I had Arsenal and gigs and movies to sustain me. All I needed was to find some money to pay for it all, as well as to leave enough to rent a bedsit and buy a little food every day.

Hilton said he was less brave than me. There was no such choice for him because, so he claimed, he did not have the emotional resources to leave the country. But I thought he was the courageous one. I was full of big talk of conscientious objection and political exile, but that meant nothing when set against the moment he entered the army for two years.

It was not the time for grand speeches. Hilton did not feel brave or noble. He was simply miserable and terrified. I stretched out my hand to him, and offered him luck. I did not know what else to say as he headed towards the South African army.

IN THE SUFFOCATING HEAT of early 1982, while my oldest friend was in the army and security policemen tortured young detainees to their death, I listened less to my usual fare of American and British music and more to shuddering *mbaqanga*, a rough and ready township blues, and to gospel-infused Zulu soul. Mahlathini, a throaty growler known as the Lion of Soweto, and the honeyed voices of the Soul Brothers thumped from my speakers in the suburbs.

Maria, our usually shy black maid who had replaced Maggie, would break away from dusting the stairs or cleaning the bathroom to rush into my bedroom for an impromptu shimmy. Her long wooden feather duster served as a dancing partner while she shook her booty with an abandon that made me laugh. 'Shew, Donny,' she'd sigh, '"Ngidlala Ukuhlupheka" by the Soul Brothers!'

I could not even pronounce 'Ngidlala Ukuhlupheka' and so I just grinned at Maria and her feather duster. She sang along to the music in a way I could never manage for I knew only a handful of Zulu words while Maria spoke four different black South African languages, as well as English and Afrikaans. When I pointed out my envy of her linguistic skills she just said, '*Aikona* [No way], Donny, *moenie* [don't] make me *lag* [laugh],' apparently unaware that she had just blurred three languages by including Zulu, Afrikaans and English in a single sentence.

It was a black trait to use various languages in the same

conversation. Eighty per cent of South Africans spoke a mix of nine different black languages which supposedly superior whites like me had never tried to learn. I could speak only English, and rudimentary Afrikaans, which made it one-and-a-half languages in contrast to Maria's half-dozen.

But, in white South Africa, 'our natives' were still considered vastly inferior to famous black Americans. Despite the depth of their politicization, and vocal opposition to racism, Muhammad Ali and Arthur Ashe were immensely popular. Ali was considered as hilarious as he was brilliant, while Ashe was praised condescendingly for his tennis-playing 'dignity'. Bill Cosby, meanwhile, was loved because his TV show was one of the few American imports to reach our screens. That evening, being a Friday, promised the usual re-run of *The Cosby Show*.

I was more interested in the Soul Brothers. Their album was cranked up so loud I did not hear the phone ring just before lunchtime. Maria answered. 'OK, Pete,' she said, 'he's coming now.'

My university friend Pete sounded uncharacteristically grim. 'Have you heard?' he asked.

'What?' I said innocently.

'They found Neil Aggett hanged in his cell this morning ...'

Pete had broken the news of Neil Aggett and Liz Floyd's detention to me and Gillian seventy days earlier, the weekend before I flew to Europe. 'Fuck them,' he said, meaning the security police. 'Neil was a good *oke* [guy] ...'

I had never met Neil Aggett. I did not even know what he looked like before his bearded face appeared on posters demanding his release. And so I did not share Pete's personal grief or rage. I was just shaken that a white man had died in detention.

As soon as I put down the phone I told Maria what had happened. Her hand flew to her mouth in horror. 'Shame,' she said, her eyes widening.

It was a peculiarly South African word, 'shame', which was muttered repeatedly every day. You could tell someone you'd just burnt your toast or fallen in love with an unattainable girl or been diagnosed with cancer and that same ritualistic word would be offered: 'Shame'. It normally drove me mad but, with the news of Neil Aggett's death, it seemed the best word to use. The whole country was shamed.

Maria retreated to her room in the backyard when my mom came home. She must have thought we needed to be alone, a white mother and her son, suddenly confronted with a new reality of apartheid: it could extinguish the life of a compassionate white doctor.

'His poor parents,' my mother said.

Jess, my mother, is a small woman, with tiny feet and a big bosom, but I've always thought of her as incredibly strong. It does not matter that she cries easily. Her tears are evidence not of weakness, but a depth of feeling. She was crying then, her bags of supermarket shopping strewn around the kitchen floor. Her head sank down onto my chest and I could just make out her words: 'I couldn't bear it,' she said, 'if that happened to you ...'

Mom brought herself under control. She said that she now knew it was better for me to leave the country. It would shatter her to see me go but if I was alive and well in London she and dad would eventually find a way to be happy again. I helped her unpack the shopping and, as she'd forgotten to buy cheese for the toasted sandwiches she'd planned for lunch, I offered to walk across to the Greek-owned corner shop. She patted me on the arm, and gave me a R5 note, which I waved away. I would pay, as if a block of cheddar might soften her misery.

Life seemed normal outside. The Friday afternoon air was thick with the scent of freshly-mown lawn. Wilson, our gardener, waved from beneath the shade of the fir trees which stood like steepling sentries at the front of our big white house. I waved back. Wilson was twenty-seven, the exact age of Neil Aggett. He had once told me that he would've loved to have been a doctor rather than a gardener.

I called out to Wilson. Did he want a pint of milk, which he often liked to drink after mowing the lawn, or a packet of cigarettes? Wilson brought two fingers to his lips, and took an imaginary puff, smiling as he shouted, 'Twenty Luckys – I pay you back!'

In the Cachet Road shop the Greek owner, Charles, did his usual irritating trick of clicking his tongue against his teeth as he tried to dislodge a wedge of the salami he had chewed on for lunch. It was like nothing had changed in the world outside. I bought Wilson his packet of Lucky Strikes, a hunk of cheese for mom and the afternoon edition of *The Star* for all of us. Charles slapped down my change on the counter and worked on that rogue chunk of salami with his curling tongue.

Neil Aggett's death was splashed across the front page: **Detained Man Hanged in Cell.** As I walked home I read the lead story: 'Dr Neil Aggett (27), Transvaal secretary of the African Food and Canning Workers' Union, held under the Terrorism Act, was found dead in his cell at Security Police headquarters early this morning. Police said he hanged himself. He became the 46th South African to die in detention since 1963 – but the first white person to die in this way.'

Wilson wandered down to the garden gate to await my return. He ruffled the cocked ears of our border collie, Ginny. Wilson then lifted his hand high so that she leapt and twirled in an effort to touch him with her cold shiny nose. He laughed as Ginny yapped in excitement.

'What's up, my *bra* [brother]?' he asked.

I showed him the newspaper. He held it in his cracked hands, reading slowly while I leaned over the garden gate to pat my dog.

'He was a doctor?' Wilson eventually asked.

After explaining that Neil Aggett had worked part-time as a

doctor in Soweto while devoting the rest of his life to the black trade unions, I read out loud a paragraph from the paper: 'A colleague at Baragwanath Hospital said yesterday that Dr Aggett was a highly competent doctor who had "the most amazing rapport with his patients" – with whom he would speak in "bad Zulu".'

Wilson whistled at the revelation that the white doctor had at least attempted to speak Zulu. And then he shook his head. 'How can they kill a doctor?'

IN THE *Rand Daily Mail* the following morning, Neil's family and friends 'were all bewildered by suggestions that he committed suicide. A union colleague, Mr David Lewis, believed, "He was probably the sanest of the lot of us. He had incredible inner resources." His sister, Mrs Jill Berger, said, "Neil was very quiet and gentle but a very strong person and very mature. He thought through things very carefully and he was a very committed man prepared to make great sacrifices – as he showed when he gave up full-time medicine for the trade unions."'

The Star voiced different white reactions in a banner headline – **Cell Death: Anxious SA Fears World Reaction**. 'The death in detention of trade unionist Dr Neil Aggett has brought shocked reaction from South Africa's business and labour leaders. They are appalled by the death and fear international repercussions.'

Dad was usually intent on accentuating the positive, believing that South Africa was not the evil country I denounced. 'There are good and bad people everywhere,' he always said. But, looking weary and thoughtful, he said we were in crisis.

PARENTS OF OTHER young detainees were distraught at the thought that their children were also being tortured. The

Detainees' Parents Support Committee petitioned Louis le Grange, the Minister of Law and Order, to allow them 'emergency visiting rights'. It was a measure of the intense international pressure that le Grange allowed brief family visits to all white and Indian detainees who had been seized around the same time as Neil Aggett. He declined to extend the same 'privilege' to black families.

On 7 February, 1982, the *Sunday Times* reported that the detainees were 'handcuffed, but waving defiant salutes to friends and family who had gathered to visit them yesterday at John Vorster Square. Some family members had not seen the detainees in months but they were forbidden to mention Dr Aggett's death or ask about conditions in detention. Only personal family matters could be discussed and two Security Branch men were always present.

'Mrs Hilary Hogan, mother of the detained activist, Barbara Hogan, who has been in detention since last year, said her daughter "told us that she had undergone an operation to have a lump removed from her breast. It was the first we knew of it." When Mr and Mrs Hogan prepared to leave, their daughter burst into tears.'

South Africa's largest newspaper made Liz Floyd a mere appendage in their dramatic story. Glossing over the fact that she had been denied permission to attend the funeral of the man with whom she had lived for most of the previous seven years, the *Sunday Times* opted for a breathless headline: **Drama of Aggett's Girl**. 'Liz Floyd, fellow detainee and lover of Dr Neil Aggett, the trade unionist who died in the cells at John Vorster Square on Friday, was admitted to the psychiatric unit of the Johannesburg Hospital after she was told of his death. She is being held under police guard in a private ward. Police have permitted her parents to visit her.'

Exactly five weeks since I had weaved through a heaving

Trafalgar Square on New Year's Eve, that same old London landmark was engulfed by a volatile demonstration. The South African embassy was surrounded by hundreds of demonstrators. In an accompanying photograph, Frank Dobson, the bearded Labour Party MP, held a poster which read **THATCHER: Why So Silent?**

Chanting had swept across Trafalgar Square as the protesters shouted, in sing-song sloganeering, 'Smash Apartheid Now ... Smash Apartheid Now ...'

The noise and placard-waving were stilled only by the arrival of Helen Livingstone, Liz Floyd's elder sister, who worked as an architect in London. She told the crowd that 'my parents requested that Liz be moved into hospital because they were afraid of the dangers of her being in solitary confinement after hearing the tragic news about Neil. My parents say that Liz is hanging on ...'

In the photograph of her standing in Trafalgar Square, Helen looked helpless.

A silent vigil for Neil Aggett was organized in Johannesburg, and my friend Pete was among the fifty Wits University students who stood quietly on the side of the busy road along Jan Smuts Avenue during rush hour on Monday 8 February. Standing fifty metres apart from each other they held burning torches in honour of their dead friend. They made no attempt to hide their faces as security policemen, driving past in the slow-moving traffic, made a great show of photographing each member of the vigil, some of whom also held up posters which read **46 Deaths in Detention: You Should Not Be Silent.**

I was in one of the cars that Pete had organized to drive up and down Jan Smuts, hooting at every protester we passed. It gave us a thrill, especially when the police started trailing our car, but it soon felt more like a student prank. Rather than inspiring a mass protest of honking horns, our isolated parps sounded ridiculous and, after ten minutes, we were forced off the road by a couple of glowering policemen who warned us to not to make an unnecessary disturbance.

West Park Cemetery, Johannesburg, 11 February, 1982

A MASSED CROWD ROLLED towards Neil Aggett's burial that cloudless Thursday afternoon. Three thousand black mourners led the procession from his funeral at St Mary's Central Cathedral. Carrying his coffin high they were tracked throughout their long journey to the graveside by photographers and cameramen riding on the back of motorbikes in order to keep just ahead of the cortege, so that the extraordinary images could be screened around the world that night.

As they ran with his coffin the voices of young black people rose up in song: '*Aggett, wethu Somlandela noba siyaboshwa!* [We shall follow our Aggett even in detention and death!]' and '*Ayesaba amagwala ayadidizela!* [The cowards are afraid and confused!]'

They carried posters bearing the inscription *Lived For His Country – Died In Detention*, and chanted and danced the *Toyi-Toyi*, the black dance of the struggle against apartheid, as they lowered his coffin into the ground. Aubrey and Joyce Aggett, Neil's parents and former supporters of apartheid, were embraced by mourners as red earth was shovelled over the casket.

Two hundred thousand black workers across South Africa had gone on strike for thirty minutes to honour the memory of Neil Aggett at the exact time of his funeral.

'It might be strange to say at such a time of deep tragedy,' Archbishop Desmond Tutu said years later, 'but those scenes warmed the cockles of our hearts – even those of us who were crying at the doctor's grave. Young black comrades from the townships showed a commitment that went beyond sloganeering to genuine non-racialism. Here was a white doctor, now dead, and here were tens of thousands of young black people who had come out in these huge numbers to do this salute for him, in the form of the *Toyi-Toyi*. Even in those dark days you felt there was this tremendous light that it was going to be all right, that, through Neil Aggett, you could understand that people really didn't want to look at skin colour any more. They just wanted to know if you were for or against the struggle to defeat apartheid.'

IN DIRECT REACTION to the international outcry, and the threat to apartheid, the government announced increased call-ups for all white South African men. Beyond the statutory two years of military service the nine additional army camps faced by ordinary conscripts would be lengthened, with rumours suggesting they could be extended from three to six months each.

Defence Force Is To Get More Fighting Men announced *The Star* on Friday 12 February, 1982, as they reported a speech made by Constand Viljoen, the Chief of the Defence Force, just hours after the funeral. General Viljoen warned that some young South African women, and previously exempt white men, would be co-opted into military duty.

Heather was twenty-three. Her husband, Ross, had lived in South Africa with his British parents for over twenty years and he was part of what Viljoen described as 'that shadowy group who have not done their military duty despite enjoying all the privileges and securities that South Africa provides them'. If it seemed unlikely my sister would be summoned, Ross would soon be vulnerable to conscription.

Ross and Heather were emphatic that they would also leave the country rather than be co-opted by the army. My parents faced losing both their children.

Dad asked me to think of the affect on my mother. But I was merciless and mentioned coolly that I was thinking of moving to San Francisco.

'London is bad enough,' dad said, despairingly. 'Why San Francisco?'

The answer was simple. Aggett's death had sparked such a furore that the city of San Francisco had put forward a resolution to 'accept up to 1500 South African refugees who have left their country to avoid military service over the next three years. We would like to extend a hand of friendship and support to those who are forced into exile as a result of their refusal to take part in the military forces which are waging war against black people on behalf of apartheid.'

Dad read the cutting: **US Call To Welcome SA Draft Resisters**. He looked like a man about to have both his children torn away from him.

I suddenly wanted to console him, but I was too young and ill-equipped. 'I'm sorry, dad,' I said, turning away quickly at the thought of our parting.

THE FOLLOWING MONTH the South African government authorized the bombing of the London office of the African National Congress. Instigated by Louis le Grange, the Minister of Law and Order, and sanctioned by Prime Minister P.W. Botha, three security policemen, led by Eugene de Kock, obtained false passports and flew to London, where they collected explosives shipped two weeks earlier to a safe address.

In the early hours of Friday 12 March, 1982, having scaled the back fence to the ANC's office in Patten Street, de Kock and his men then broke into the building and packed the dynamite behind a discarded chair. The explosion, which occurred just after 9 a.m.

in London, was meant to coincide with the arrival of the ANC's leader in exile, Oliver Tambo, who had replaced Nelson Mandela after his close friend had been sentenced to life imprisonment in 1964. At the last minute, Tambo and his colleagues decided to head directly for Trafalgar Square where they would address a rally expected to draw 20,000 people to protest against the death of Neil Aggett.

A caretaker, the only person in the building at the time of the explosion, was injured. The South African government had failed in their attempt to assassinate leading members of the ANC. But de Kock and his men were awarded the Police Star for Excellent Service when they slipped back into South Africa a day later.

THAT SAME SATURDAY, 13 March, 1982, marked the first time I had seen Hilton Tanchum since he had disappeared into the army. He looked like a ghost. After two months in uniform he was thin and exhausted. We laughed when we saw each other; how else could we react to all he'd been through during basic training? We knew each other so well that, arriving early for his belated twenty-first birthday party that evening, he did not have to pretend to be anything other than himself. Hilton gave me a stark insight into life in the South African army for a boy like him.

He seemed more like his old self when he described the absurd welcome he had received from the army on his first morning. Watched by his parents, and thousands of other mothers and fathers who had taken their sons to the parade ground where they would sign up for conscription, Hilton and the recruits were addressed by a barking sergeant. The man in uniform hollered that they should snap to attention and pick up their suitcases.

Each boy had a heavy case with him, and there was a great scuffling noise as they picked up their belongings in readiness for departure. Once they all held their suitcases, and silence had descended, another order rang out from the belligerent sergeant.

'Put your suitcase down!' the army man yelled.

They followed his instruction and placed their cases on the dusty ground next to them. Soon, all was quiet again.

'Pick up your suitcases!' the sergeant shouted.

The boys picked up their suitcases. 'Put them down!' they were commanded.

Some parents tittered at an apparently hysterical army game. The inevitable shout rose up into the thin Highveld air. 'Pick them up!'

On and on it went: 'Put them down ... pick them up ... put them down ... pick them up!'

The boys did not dare join in the laughter. Hilton, meanwhile, felt like weeping at the idiocy. This is it, he thought, this is how it's going to be for two years. And the worst of it, for him, was the power they wielded over him. It was like he was about to go into prison that morning, on behalf of a political system he reviled.

His powerlessness was made obvious on his third day in the army, which just happened to be the day he turned twenty-one. It felt like the worst day of his life. That morning, having barely slept on his first two nights, he and his platoon were told to pack up everything and prepare to be transferred to an Artillery unit in Potchefstroom. All day, as the January sun beat down on them, he and his fellow soldiers ran up and down, carrying their *trommels* [a large metal tank in which they kept their possessions], as they were shunted from one area to another.

The ordinary corporals and sergeants in the infantry were like demure old grannies compared to the Artillery bombardiers. The Artillery crew were amongst the roughest in the army. They would destroy any shirkers, especially if they found out that Hilton's platoon included a number of Jewish boys like him.

At the end of a miserable afternoon, they were told that a mistake had been made. They were going back to their infantry corps. Hilton's relief at escaping the Artillery was tempered by the order that he had to immediately pack up everything again, hoist it into his *trommel*, and march back to the very camp where his day had started.

It was only the beginning. Wherever they went they had to run or, at the very least, march with a quick-step. 'Hurry up and wait,' they were told over and over, rushing from one mindless duty to the next where they would hang around before being abused again. Sleeplessness added to the strain. Beyond being woken every day at 4 a.m., there was corrosive anxiety.

Each soldier had a thin mattress, about 10cm in depth, and a canvas cloth called a *pisvel* [piss-cover] that had to be sewn over the foam. The mattress was placed on top of the steel frame of a bunk bed and the *pisvel* and the single sheet had to form a perfect square with an exact right angle at each corner. If there was even the slightest deviation, or a semblance of a crease, hell would break out during inspection. The soldier would be humiliated and the whole tent of conscripts could be punished.

Many of the infantrymen made their beds the night before and, terrified of inspection, slept on the floor. But they were also subjected to night raids and anyone found on the floor would be kicked by the P.F. [Permanent Force] hulks for 'illegal activity'. Hilton was more concerned about not waking up in time at 4 a.m. Anyone caught sleeping had a bucket of freezing water poured over him. He slept so lightly, despite his utter fatigue, that he sat up with a jolt every fifteen or twenty minutes.

It still did not prevent him from failing an early inspection, as his sheets were ripped from his bed and ground into the mud by a screaming corporal. The effort it took to then wash out the dirty stains from the sheets, and dry them, before the next inspection became a new ordeal, especially for a white South African boy who had never done any washing or ironing before.

One night, when all was quiet, a group of balaclava-wearing soldiers stole into Hilton's tent, which he shared with five other infantrymen. They had all been classified as G3 conscripts which meant that they were either not in peak physical condition or were, as in Hilton's case, wearers of contact lenses. It seemed as if some of the older G1 K1 group, the soldiers who had been passed fit to do everything, had decided to dole out some punishment to the G3 shirkers.

Hilton, being closest to the flap of the tent, was their random victim. They had no idea who he was and, in the dark, they were simply intent on hurting anyone in a G3 tent. Before he could squirm away they lassoed him with ropes. Hilton's arms were pinned and they began to pull him across the stony ground and out of the tent. As he had already been awake, fretting about his inspection, he was more alert than they had expected. He found the strength, out of desperate fear, to fight back. Hilton managed to lift a hand between his body and the ropes and, as they tried to pull him, he pushed with all his might. The ropes loosened and he pushed even harder. He somehow managed to lift the ropes above his chest and head. He was free.

His attackers disappeared as quickly as they had come, their silence as sinister as their balaclavas. Shivering and shaking, Hilton knew he would not sleep the rest of that night.

Four tents along from theirs, the balaclava gang found someone else. A boy, who had either been fast asleep or simply lacked the suddenly demonic strength of Hilton, was lassoed and dragged from his bed. They pulled him along the ground until his screaming became so loud the corporals came running. Most of the skin was ripped from the back of the roped boy. He was taken to hospital. Hilton knew how lucky he had been.

There were more appalling incidents. A boy in the next tent felt so hopeless he attempted to kill himself early on in basic training. The soldiers in his tent found him lying on his back after he had swallowed a few bottles of sleeping pills, and they ran to a commanding officer. Hilton caught sight of the suicidal boy, who looked grey and close to his death. But his fate infuriated the short lieutenant who burst into the tent. Looking contemptuously at the soldier on the ground, he knelt down. The lieutenant grabbed the boy by his shirt collar and shook him as if he was a rag-doll. The soldier's head lolled from side to side and his eyes rolled back in their sockets.

'If you ever do that again,' the lieutenant hissed at him, 'I'll fucking kill you myself.'

The squat lieutenant walked out of the tent in disgust, leaving the infantrymen to pick up the conscript and take him to the army hospital.

The boy survived and, after a week, he was back in the tent next to Hilton. There were rumours of a further suicide six weeks later when it was said that a young soldier had gone into the shower block and shot himself with a newly issued rifle. But it was military policy to investigate a particular camp only once there had been an unacceptable number of suicide attempts. Hilton was told that each camp was allowed five such incidents before they became answerable for the way they treated their soldiers.

One particular sergeant relished the abuse he meted out to the conscripts. Hilton found himself brooding in uncharacteristically murderous fashion. He decided that if he had the power to make him die he would have no compunction in bringing a sudden end to the sergeant's life. Hilton imagined two buttons in front of him. Pressing the green one would spare the sergeant, while pushing down on the red would kill him instantly. He felt certain that, given the choice, he would reach for the red button.

Hilton began sleepwalking in his turmoil. The first incident occurred when, in his sleep, he rose up like a troubled ghost and, slowly, packed his suitcase. He closed his case with a click, waking a boy called David Leibovitz in an adjoining bunk. Hilton walked out and, realizing that something was amiss, David followed him. Hilton strode purposefully away and would have walked into the barbed wire fence surrounding the camp had David not intercepted him.

'What you are doing?' David asked.

'I'm going home,' Hilton said in a voice so distant it was obvious he was sleeping, even if his eyes were wide open.

He went sleepwalking again weeks later, and was nearly attacked with a mallet when a shocked soldier found a zombie looming over him. It was Hilton Tanchum, trying to find a way out of the darkness.

Hilton's unease intensified still further when each soldier was issued with a semi-automatic rifle. He realized that he might be expected to kill someone with his rifle. The shock of holding a gun, which he soon had to learn how to strip down and reassemble, was profound.

He also hated the songs they were meant to sing – 'My gun is my wife, this is what I shoot with ...' – and was so hopeless at putting his rifle together that soldiers like David took mercy on him and helped before an angry officer discovered how ineffectual he had been.

The stories tumbled out of Hilton on his first weekend pass home, as did his revelation that when his dad had picked him up the previous afternoon he had fallen asleep in the car even before they reached the camp gates. It was the first time in two months he'd been able to close his eyes peacefully.

Yet, at home, Hilton said he felt so spooked he had been unable to walk to the shops at the bottom of the road. He needed to pick up some more drinks for his low-key party. But the army had made him so paranoid he feared he would be watched by everyone.

I persuaded him that, walking with me, a fighting machine in my own head if nowhere else, he could feel secure. We trudged down Frank Street, with Hilton laughing as I spoke about how many beers I planned to drink that night and how I was hoping to get off with one of his sister's friends. Lowering the tone helped and he began to relax in the late Saturday afternoon sunshine.

That evening I was true to my word. I drank plenty of beer and I was caught on camera eyeing up a girl called Verity, ogling her with a drunken eye as I tried to entertain her with my increasingly slurred witticisms. I was out of luck with the girls but at least my old friend was amused. It was almost as if Hilton had forgotten that, the following afternoon, he would have to pull on his heavy brown uniform, pack his bag and return to the army camp he hated.

The Grand Hall, University of the Witwatersrand, Johannesburg, 26 March, 1982

ON A FRIDAY deep into my first term of English Honours, my seminar on the great American novels of William Faulkner was abandoned. I loved Faulkner, especially *The Sound and the Fury*, but a far more momentous event was about to unfold. The news had broken early that morning.

Liz Floyd and six other detainees were about to be released. They would travel together to Wits, the most multiracial campus in the country. Three of the detainees – Clive van Heerden, Keith Coleman and Debbie Elkon – were still students at the university. The four remaining prisoners – Nicholas Haysom, Morris Smithers, Colin Purkey and Liz Floyd – all had close ties with Wits. And so the Great Hall seemed the best place for a public reunion.

The hall normally held a thousand people. By lunchtime, double that number had crammed into the seats and aisles and along the edge of the balcony. It felt as if the whole place was rocking on its foundations. There was jubilation in the air, a feeling that a small victory had been won with the release of the seven. As they entered the hall together, slipping through a side door near the stage, it seemed as if the roof might lift and expose us all to the bright blue sky above.

Liz Floyd, near the back of the procession, smiled shyly as the sound of black students dancing the *Toyi-Toyi* and crying out *Amandla! Awhetu!* [Power to the People] engulfed her.

I did not raise my fist in the air, like many around me, because I felt more like an observer than an activist. I was not one of 'the people' so disenfranchised by apartheid, and yet I felt proud as I looked up at the seven young detainees. They lifted their hands in celebration and waved. Each of them spoke and the hall was at its most hushed when Liz Floyd stepped forward to take her turn at the microphone. She was the least polemical of them all and I thought she looked tired as she blinked at the huge crowd staring up at her.

'Although I am very happy and relieved that my friends and I have been released this morning,' she said, 'this is a bitter-sweet day. Being here has brought back our sadness over Neil's death.'

The young doctor gathered herself and then, speaking to all of us as if we were just a single person, a friend she'd not seen for a long time, Liz said, "You know, it's been a long and difficult time. Neil and I were together for seven years, and I've had so many emotions to face.'

Liz, speaking with growing authority, stressed that she had been 'strengthened by news of the massive response there has been to Neil's death both in and outside South Africa. Neil expected to be banned on his release from detention. He did not expect to die. He always said that if he was banned, and could no longer continue his union work, he would become a surgeon in Soweto. And so, while I continue my own union work now, I will return as a doctor to Soweto.'

After the applause had subsided, and she looked up at us again, Liz Floyd spoke just a few more sentences. 'It is more important than ever to say how much we all believe in the creation of a free and democratic South Africa. It was the cause for which Neil Aggett gave his life. He would have been very proud if he could see us all today – united in this very same cause.'

People were crying as she retreated into the shadows of the hall; and then the singing started. Two thousand people stood and sang the banned anthem of Nelson Mandela's African National Congress, *Nkosi Sikelel' iAfrika* [God Bless Africa]. The singing of more freedom songs and the rhythmic chanting of black students echoed around the hall: *'Mandela, Aggett, wethu Somlandela noba siya-boshwa!* [We shall follow our Mandela and Aggett even in detention and death!]'

I looked up at the stage and saw that, amid the defiance and pain, Liz Floyd was embraced by her friend, Yvette Breytenbach, a young activist. As the two women held each other, while the singing and the chanting soared above them, freedom had never looked more haunting.

A CROSS TOWN, that same afternoon, three other white detainees were brought to the Johannesburg Regional Court. Handcuffed and surrounded by security policemen, Barbara Hogan, Alan Fine and Cedric Mayson had all been found guilty of treason under Section 2 of the Terrorism Act.

The following morning, alongside a giant photograph of Liz and Yvette, the *Rand Daily Mail* reported that 'Miss Hogan, Mr Fine and Mr Mayson smiled and waved at relatives and friends who packed the public gallery. All three looked pale but were obviously delighted at seeing friends and family after their long isolation in solitary confinement.

'Mr Mayson's wife, Penny, and their three children were ordered out of the court by an orderly – who said the children were under age. Mrs Mayson tried to reason with him but the orderly was adamant and threatened to call the magistrate. Dr Hendrik Koornhof, brother of Dr Piet Koornhof, Minister of Information, intervened. "For God's sake, it's their father!" he said to the orderly. "Please cool it and let them stay." The orderly then left them. Dr Koornhof's daughter, Hanchenn, seized by security police on the same night as Dr Neil Aggett, remains in detention.'

When the sentence of 'life imprisonment' was eventually handed down to each of the three defendants, the court fell silent. Attention focused on the Mayson children and on Barbara Hogan, the first South African woman to be found guilty of treason against the state. The evidence against her had been obtained during interrogation at John Vorster Square in early November, three weeks before the detention of Neil Aggett. He had not betrayed her after all.

Auret van Heerden at a memorial service for his friend
and fellow detainee, Neil Aggett

Chapter Sixteen

SHOCK TREATMENT

Aᴼᵀᴇʀ ᴛʜᴇ ᴅᴇᴀᴛʜ of their son, Aubrey and Joyce Aggett received letters of sympathy from some famous names in the struggle against apartheid. It no longer mattered that the people writing to them were classified as 'non-white'. Victoria Mxenge, the lawyer and wife of Steve Biko, the Black Consciousness leader who had died in detention in 1977, had written first to the couple:

Dear Friends

The news of Neil's death in detention was shocking to say the least. I am singularly ill-equipped to comfort you but rest assured that I share your grief and sorrow. Neil was a man of deep compassion and a firm believer in justice for all people. Small wonder that he took the cause for the underdog with such passion and tenacity. We all admired and revered your late son. He was a gentle and humane person, and the epitome of a patriot. He was the kind of man whose death makes

the rest of us feel that in some way we have lost part of ourselves. I
hope the knowledge that others care will comfort you.

Yours faithfully
Victoria Mxenge

A letter from Hawa Timol, mother of Ahmed, who in 1971 had plunged to his death from the tenth floor of John Vorster Square, was also heartfelt. Mrs Timol, a Muslim from an Indian township outside Roodepoort, west of Johannesburg, wrote her message on blue-lined paper torn out of a plain exercise book:

Dear Mr and Mrs Aggett and Family

My deepest sympathy at the loss of your son Neil. I can imagine how
you must be feeling because I felt the same when I lost my son – also in
detention and also at the same age. Please be brave. God is great and
may He rest the soul of your son in peace.

Yours truly
Hawa Timol

Bolstered by such support, the Aggetts hoped that Kobie Coetsee, the Minister of Justice, meant what he said in announcing that a full inquest would be held into Neil's death. Coetsee promised that, 'No stone will be left unturned to ensure that the true course of events is revealed.'

Aubrey and Joyce appointed George Bizos as their lawyer. Bizos had helped represent Nelson Mandela at his treason trial in 1964 and the Biko family during the 1978 inquest into his death. Aubrey's staunch support of the Nationalist government had evaporated. He and his wife were also reeling from the fact that their home outside Cape Town had been broken into on 15 March by the Security Branch. They had flown to Pretoria to discuss the inquest and, as their telephone calls were monitored, the security police knew their exact plans.

Lieutenant Stephan Whitehead, having been involved in the interrogation of both Neil and Liz, was instructed to break into the Aggetts' house in an attempt to find 'evidence' which could fabricate a case against the dead detainee, and suggest that he had been a suicide risk for years. Whitehead knew the entire system of detention without trial could be undermined if he failed.

He was accompanied by another security policeman, Paul Erasmus, who carried out the attempted burglary. But Erasmus was interrupted by the Aggetts' coloured maid, Sarah Isaacs. He drew his gun and made her sit down while he kept hunting for anything that could be used against Neil.

Sarah's husband, Isak, ran to William Anderson, a white neighbour. Challenged by Anderson, Erasmus introduced himself as a private detective and claimed that the Aggetts wanted him to carry out research for a book about Neil that would be written by an overseas journalist. Anderson was unconvinced and said that he had already phoned the police. He had no idea he was facing a policeman from the Security Branch, especially as Erasmus then fled.

Whitehead tried to cover the tracks of their bungled mission. He drove to the Somerset West police station where his Security Branch badge was enough for him to take command. Whitehead said it was imperative that he personally visited the Aggetts' neighbour. He would pose as an ordinary detective and placate the man.

Yet Whitehead did not succeed. Anderson remained deeply suspicious and told the Aggetts everything that he and Sarah Isaacs had witnessed.

Aubrey Aggett and his legal advisers drew up an affidavit. He signed the six-page document in front of a Commissioner of Oaths, his eye lingering over item 15 which would be repeated during the inquest:

> *'I verily believe that one of my late son's interrogators before his death in detention was a certain Lieutenant Stephan Peter Whitehead who is attached to the South African Security Police. This knowledge causes me grave disquiet. This is particularly so in light of the failure of the local police to adequately explain to me or to my legal representatives the murky circumstances surrounding the appearance of Lieutenant Whitehead at my home.'*

The inquest began in Pretoria on 14 April, 1982. Aubrey and Joyce were shocked again when their dead son was compared to 'an interested party at an automobile accident'. Pieter J. Schabort, the lawyer defending the security police, conjured up that surreal comparison when arguing that an affidavit Neil had signed fourteen hours before he died was not permissible evidence. An affidavit offered by a witness to a traffic accident would not be allowed in a civil case unless that particular 'interested party' was subject to cross-examination. As Dr Aggett was no longer available for questioning, the police lawyer said, with a queasy smile, his signed statement detailing his extensive torture had to be ruled as inadmissible.

Aubrey and Joyce sat at the front of the crowded court. They leant forward when Bizos, an avuncular Greek South African, voiced his incredulity. Schabort's attempt to remove Neil Aggett's affidavit was nonsensical. Even if it could be proved that the young doctor had indeed hanged himself, his sworn evidence contained legitimate proof that his suicide had been induced by the security policy. And inducement of suicide, Bizos reminded the court, was still a crime under South African law.

Bizos argued that, when the time came for him to challenge the testimony of the chief medical officer who had performed the autopsy, he needed to establish whether the abrasions and bruises on Dr Aggett's body were consistent with the assaults he had described. Even the magistrate, the reactionary Pieter Kotze, agreed with Bizos and ruled in favour of the Aggett family.

The security police lawyer called for an immediate recess and, on their return, Schabort announced that he would appeal to a higher court. After a single morning in his court, the magistrate confirmed that the inquest would be adjourned until the police appeal had been heard. The charade had begun, and the distress of an old couple, Aubrey and Joyce Aggett, was obvious.

AMID OUR PAINFUL CONFUSION, Jess McRae found courage. She became bold. In fact, my mother felt fearless as she and dad drove towards our old hometown of Witbank. The country had begun to wear her down, and so many feelings conflicted inside her. But it was time to act.

We had entered a decisive stage in our family war. My parents, having wavered in the immediate aftermath of Aggett's death, were again certain I should accept conscription. We read that Neil had been on the run for years. He was a conscientious objector who had used various methods to avoid his call-up. But he had been saved from the military police, and six years in jail, only because the security branch said Aggett belonged to them.

My parents were determined that I should submit to a happier fate. They suspected that, working together, they would make me succumb.

A return to our old battleground, however, hardened me. I could match my parents' certainty because I was young and reckless. I could say, easily and carelessly, that it didn't matter if I went to jail or died. I was ready for anything, except the army. And so our war escalated.

Approaching Witbank, it was hard for Jess to shake the contrasting memories of our happy lives from twenty years earlier. She could not stop herself thinking how much sweeter and more innocent our Witbank days had been. Her children had been small and adorable, and her husband a young and dynamic engineer who had more free time for us then than he did two decades later. In Witbank, Jess had lived a life with little of the anguish that now defined both South Africa and our family.

Yet, turning east, towards Hendrina Power Station, she remembered that, even then, darkness had framed our world. Mom had needed dad to stop her plunging headlong into trouble.

Their blinkered comfort had been disrupted by Ian Thompson, a young Presbyterian minister in Witbank who made my mother look in a new way at the country around her. Thompson was called 'a bloody radical'. But, to Jess McRae, he seemed especially humane. He did much of his pastoral care in factories with white and black workers. They were segregated from each other but Thompson believed the men should be treated equally, irrespective of their colour. He was a real firebrand in Witbank in the 1960s.

Reverend Thompson was outraged that a local factory supplied a bus to transport its white workers from their neighbourhoods, and back, while refusing the same service to any of their black employees. Every day the white bus, which would often be half-empty, drove past the black workers trudging to the factory. Thompson encouraged the black men to catch the white bus. But the natives knew enough not to even attempt to board it. They had no option but to walk to work. And so Thompson himself refused to catch the white bus again. He made a point of walking to the factory alongside the black workers.

He cut a defiant figure, one who also spent many hours in the townships, or locations as we called them then, helping destitute families. His stories from the pulpit affected my mother deeply and, sensing her compassion, Thompson asked if she would help him set up a feeding scheme in the largest Witbank location.

Jess was enthused and galvanized, and was only stopped from pouring herself into Thompson's scheme by dad. He shared her empathy but, being dad, he was also more practical. How could Jess put herself, and our family, at risk? The police would place her under intense scrutiny, while there were everyday dangers of being attacked in the location.

Dad persuaded mom to think sensibly and to put me and Heather, and our whole family, ahead of her noble ideals. And so, reluctantly, she turned down Thompson's request.

Twenty years later, and seeing parallels between the idealism of Ian Thompson and Neil Aggett, Jess wondered if she'd made the right choice. That question might have reeled through her head when she and dad took to the stage at Hendrina Power Station. She didn't know it then but she was about to make a dramatic human gesture.

My parents had attended so many Eskom awards functions that the evenings blurred. As the boss's wife, Jess was expected to present certificates and trophies, many of which related to Ian's drive to reduce the risks of working with electricity. Most power stations sailed past the 'Million Man-Hour' mark without a single accident.

Hendrina was renowned for its safety record. It was, however, a power station set in a fiercely conservative corner of the south-eastern Transvaal. Apartheid was enshrined, and many at Hendrina were uncomfortable with Ian McRae's policy of instigating multi-racial evenings. He believed that white and black workers should celebrate success together. The two racial groups sat apart but mom liked looking out at a sea of black and white faces.

A wave of white managers, engineers and maintenance men appeared on stage, beaming with pride, as Jess congratulated them and handed out their prizes. But, near the end, the names of two women in the administrative department were announced. The first, a young and pretty Afrikaans woman, swapped handshakes with my mother, who also pecked her on the cheek.

A middle-aged black woman was called to the stage. It jarred with many that a native should be allowed to climb the same steps as the white workers of Eskom.

Jess didn't care. She smiled at the woman and stretched out her hand. The black lady accepted her handshake and bowed her head. Jess had not planned anything but, in that small moment, her instinct took over. She congratulated the woman and then, as she had done with the Afrikaans girl, Jess leaned closer to her.

The surrounding silence thickened as people watched her. Jess McRae, the wife of Eskom's head of generation, did something unthinkable then. She kissed a black woman. Jess did little more than brush her lips against a black cheek but gasps echoed around the hall.

The black woman smiled at my mother, but she looked shaken by the reaction of the audience. She walked quietly back to her seat.

Later, as the scandalised people of Hendrina disappeared into the night, shaking their heads, Jess was cornered by an Eskom executive who had also travelled down from Johannesburg. The man was in a junior position to Ian, but he still had sufficient authority to question her.

'Hell, Jess,' he said, 'why do you have to put on such a show?'

'What do you mean?' Jess replied.

'Kissing that girl,' the man said derisively. He looked at Jess, forgetting all the dinners he and his wife had shared with her and Ian. His next question was withering: 'What are you trying to prove?'

'I just think we should treat everyone the same,' Jess said.

The man shook his head. 'Jessie!' he exclaimed in exasperation. 'She's just a native.'

UNAWARE OF THE uproar my mother had caused, I concentrated on the fact that, where Neil Aggett's parents had changed, it seemed as if Ian and Jess McRae had become intransigent. I mistook my parents' ambition to stop me leaving the country as evidence of their reactionary beliefs.

Escaping South Africa was the obvious solution and I offered the same old ridiculously hopeful answers to their pressing questions. Where would I go? London. Mom sighed. An expensive city like London? Yes. How would I survive? I would find work. What sort of work? I would become a writer. A writer? Dad looked too furious to laugh. Without any experience of life, or even writing, I must be joking. I was deadly serious. Who did I know in London? No-one. Did I understand how difficult it was to make a life in London? I shrugged. Had I not read any of the articles dad had pointed out before, detailing the spiralling unemployment figures in Britain?

Dad always ended up shouting in frustration. I had to go into the army. The alternative was ludicrous.

My sister was my ally. Heather and Ross had bought a flat across the road from Germiston Lake. I would retreat there when the fighting at home became too intense to bear. As much as I liked to appear impregnable to my parents, I could be less certain with Heather. I could show her all my doubts, while knowing she would not tell me to give up or even shut up.

On the weekend my parents returned from Hendrina I partied hard. Falling a few times on the paved driveway, I made it to the front door. I managed to turn my key in the lock and reached the downstairs toilet, where I threw up violently. The familiarity, as much as the drink, was sickening.

Even my sister was shocked by the gaunt sight of me the following afternoon. Having hardly slept, and feeling deathly, gloom had taken hold of me. It was the worst hangover of my life, but everyone else suspected something worse.

It was not an affliction that would haunt me in later life, but I looked to be wasting away. I had begun to wear braces with my jeans. I said it was in homage to the Nutty Boys of Madness, as I loved their melancholic ska-infused pop from London. But my clothes really were falling off me.

Heather said later that I had slipped into a psychological state of 'learned helplessness'. I certainly looked helpless as I curled up in bed. Rejecting my mother's suggestion that she go downstairs to make us all a cup of tea, Heather insisted I stand up. I would make the tea. It would help lift me out of my distressing torpor. Zombie-like, I said I couldn't even make a cup of tea.

'Right,' Heather said, 'leave the tea to me and you go outside with Ross.'

She asked her husband to walk me round the garden, as if that might help shake the demons. Heather then made some tea and sat my parents down. She told them that I was on the brink of a break-down. It was then that the possibility of my seeing a psychiatrist was first broached. My mother felt it might help me to speak to someone outside our fevered family.

I must have been feeling ill because, to everyone's surprise, I agreed.

We were at our lowest then, in 1982. I was twenty-one and hardly spoke to my father. He might not have known it but I still loved him. Yet it had become impossible to say those words out loud. I was sure they would signify weakness and encourage my parents to make me go into the army.

And so I said yes. I would speak to a doctor about the family dilemma we had already exhausted.

My mother spoke of the night, years before, when I had turned again to my father in White River. It was a story that, in our family, had been retold many times. One day, she promised, I would come back to them, just like I had done then, as a small boy crying out for his dad.

SIXTEEN YEARS BEFORE I had to cut open my face, and bleed on the white pillows, before I spoke to dad again. At Jatinga Hills, on the outskirts of White River, the big gash on my left cheek ended the long silence. One Saturday night, in the winter of 1966, we were in the bush during a break from Witbank. We were in the Lowveld, near Blyde River Canyon and God's Window. My sister and I shared a thatched rondavel surrounded by squawking peacocks and chattering monkeys at Jatinga's small holiday resort. Heather was nearly eight years old. I had just turned five.

A couple of hours earlier my mother had put us to bed. Mom had kissed us and told us to sleep tight as, outside, the black crickets rubbed their legs together in a mysterious song. Hazy with tiredness in my blue shortie pyjamas, I closed my eyes. I knew mom and dad had moved across the dark stretch of lawn separating our hut from the hotel lounge. They were having a drink with their friends, the Masons, a tiny woman called Mimi and her moustached husband, Alec.

For six months I had spoken only rarely to dad. He was swamped by his job and it seemed as if he had less time for us at home. I must have set about punishing him. It reached a point where I would not allow him to feed or dress me, or play with me, and I would cry until my mother picked me up. There were days when dad wondered if I would ever accept him again.

Everything changed that night at Jatinga Hills. I woke up

suddenly, feeling thirsty in the heavy heat. Somewhere above my head a mosquito buzzed persistently. Heather switched on the light and looked groggily at me as I croaked for water like a boy lost in the desert. She slid out of bed and padded across the cool cement floor. At the sink she filled a plastic cup. I drank quickly and flung myself back towards sleep, only to feel a slicing pain as my cheekbone slammed into the metal bedstead. When I eventually reached up to touch the flap of skin, feeling a gluey wetness on my cheek, I couldn't help it. I cried out for dad.

Heather, seeing my gashed face, was too frightened to race across the lawn to find my parents. Instead, she tried to clean me up with her cream flannel. It was soon tinged with crimson streaks. When that damp cloth could not stem the blood she used all the towels in the rondavel. I lay there, whimpering for dad, while Heather ran to the sink and back. The mosquito made a black speck on the white wall opposite. It looked ready to bomb my bloodied cheek.

Then, from out of nowhere, dad stepped through the doorway. He had come to check on us. Heather rushed over, words tumbling from her. By the time dad took the towel and pressed it down gently on my wound, he knew exactly what had happened.

I could feel the pressure of his fingers on my face. I was no longer crying as I looked up at him. I began talking to him, asking if I was going to die.

Dad smiled, his blue eyes crinkling. There was no need to worry. They just needed to take me to a doctor to clean up the cut before he covered it with a large plaster. I would look like a pirate.

He squeezed my hand. I squeezed back, cradled by his warmth and size. 'You're going to be fine, chum,' he promised.

Dad lifted the towel from my cheek. The air felt cool on the opened skin. My eyes were fixed on his as he examined the damage. 'It's looking better already,' he decided, before pressing the towel down once more when the red trickle resumed. Dad kept talking, his words soothing both me and Heather. Nodding earnestly, she ran barefoot across the grass to mom.

Ten minutes earlier, had the blood not come, I would have spoken only to mom. And when she reached me I was happy to be taken in her arms, to hear her voice, to see her concern matched by the certainty that she and dad would make me better. But after clinging to mom a while, I broke away. I held out my arms to dad, calling for him, sealing the end of my mute pact.

He wrapped me in a blanket and scooped me up in his arms. Dad walked out into the Lowveld night and towards our car, the grey Holden. I stretched out across the back seat, shivering under the blanket and with my head propped up on a pillow mom had placed on her lap. Heather rode up front next to dad. I closed my eyes as we headed towards White River. I was soon swept away by the familiar hum of the Holden, and the jostle of our hilly journey down a dirt road.

Crocodile River Valley lay in the darkness below. Dad always told us that, in the moonlight, you could see the crocs gliding through the inky water, their scaly backs shining like silvery logs drifting downriver. Their crooked yellow teeth, jutting out of their closed mouths, usually scared me. But, with the blood drying on my face and my head resting on mom, I felt safe as dad drove us towards Witrivier, as White River was known in Afrikaans.

Inside the hospital they wheeled me into a white room. I held dad tightly, and he kept chatting softly to me. A doctor and a nurse stood at the far end of the table onto which I had been lifted from a metal trolley. The man eventually walked towards us, tugging at his gloves. He looked unhappy at having been stuck with me and the Saturday night shift.

The doctor picked out some shiny instruments spread in front of him. I looked away. '*Hou hom vas* [Hold him tight],' the doc told dad, as if he knew I was about to squirm.

'I've got you,' dad whispered as he turned my face towards him.

The left side was exposed to the Afrikaans man in the white coat. He made me jump as he quietly stuck a needle into the area around the cut.

'That's to stop it hurting,' dad said.

The anaesthetic deadened my face. But, on the inside, I no longer cared about anything but being with dad. The needle went in and out of my skin and sealed shut the wound as if it was also closing the hole between us. Once the stitches were in, and they cut the black thread, they lifted me off the table and I nestled into him. Mom rubbed my head and smiled down at me while Heather looked up with big round eyes. Dad carried me to the car, and I closed my eyes. I didn't stir once as the Holden sped through the night from White River back to Jatinga Hills.

When I woke early the next morning, my face feeling puffy and sore as I opened my eyes, I saw the new white pillow was unmarked by blood. I ran my finger along the metal bar that had cut my face open. It was cold and hard but, in the blue light of an African dawn, it looked strangely beautiful. I knew why. It had brought me back to my dad.

IN 1982, AGED TWENTY-ONE, I saw three psychiatrists in Johannesburg. Each of them asked about my relationship with dad. It was hard not to trace a finger along the scar still visible above my left cheek when I told them about the end of our war in White River. I liked feeling the slight indentation the stitches made in my skin. It was soothing to remember that we had come through that silence. But I tried to explain the subsequent difference. Our new battleground was shaped by ideology. It seemed as if dad was willing to set aside his misgivings about apartheid to keep progressing in his work and ensure our family stayed together. In contrast, I was willing to allow our family to break apart rather than go into the army.

The first two doctors were both men and I did not last more than a session with either of them. They could not understand why I was making 'an issue', as the second man said, over a national duty. I needed to listen to my parents. I should be guided by them and do what was right for the country and my family. Such prescriptive reactions went down badly, especially with my mother who said I needed to be listened to, rather than lectured at again. It was yet more evidence of her innate generosity, and that of my father, when they decided I needed a sympathetic hearing.

I was far happier in the company of a woman. She was a clinical psychiatrist who appeared warm and intelligent. Even the fact that she worked in a room with four walls painted deep blue, a colour that seemed almost amusingly wrong for her line of work, made me like her. It was as if she was saying: 'I know you're feeling blue, but relax. Even walls get blue ...'

I understood my turbulent emotions. I also knew I was in control of any depressive tendencies because, in my second session with the woman, my fantasy life returned. She was attractive rather than beautiful but I was willing to become her twenty-one-year-old sex toy. I was yearning to meet a middle-aged woman who could, in my post-graduate years, become my Mrs Robinson.

But, rather than encouraging me to stretch out on her couch, she asked me which writers I liked to read most. I was then locked into a deep and romantic crush on Kafka. I also loved Beckett.

'Interesting,' she purred, and I probably got excited at that point. 'Why Kafka?'

I had always loved *Metamorphosis*, Kafka's story of Gregor Samsa, the travelling salesman who discovers he has been turned into an insect. I surprised myself by quoting the opening line aloud to a clinical psychiatrist who was meant to be assessing my mental well-being. She looked at me curiously as I said the words:

As Gregor Samsa awoke one morning from uneasy dreams he found himself transformed in his bed into a gigantic insect.

This time, rather than murmuring 'Interesting', she said 'I see ...' in a voice that suggested a few doubts about my sanity. She asked what I liked about this rather strange story.

In an effort to please her, and make *Metamorphosis* at least seem relevant, I said it was a story about a family.

'Mmm-hmmm?' she said, arching an eyebrow.

I wittered on about the Samsa family's reaction to Gregor's meta-morphosis. While his parents are repulsed by the change, with his mother weeping and his father throwing apples at him, Gregor's sister, Grete, is sympathetic to her big beetle of a brother. She brings him food, and moves furniture out of his room so that he can have space to climb the walls and ceiling. I explained the poignancy of the end, as Grete wearies of Gregor when he fright-ens away the impoverished family's new tenants. She says the real Gregor, her human brother, would never have allowed his changed presence to cause such pain. Gregor, feeling love for his family, retreats to his room and, after waiting for the sun to rise on a new day, finally slips away into death, so freeing his family.

The psychiatrist looked quizzical, but I rambled on to tell her about *In the Penal Colony*. My favourite Kafka story, about an elab-orate machine of torture and execution that carved the sentence of a condemned prisoner onto his skin, had haunted me even before Ian Curtis used it as his template for a Joy Division song called *Colony*. And of course it resonated with peculiar power in South Africa, I said, a country where detainees were tortured to death.

'Perhaps,' the doctor said as she looked at her watch. Would I mind, she asked, if she met with individual members of my family for one-to-one sessions?

Clearly, my homage to Kafka had not quite made a middle-aged doctor want to sleep with me. She would not even ask me about my deepest fantasies, let alone give sumptuous flesh to them. And so she might as well talk to my family.

I was less sanguine after my sister's meeting with her. Heather looked anxious when I visited her and Ross's Germiston Lake flat. In their session, Heather said, the doctor had told her that I was obviously troubled. If she did not start receiving more balanced responses from me then it would be difficult for her to resist the earlier psychiatrists' recommendations that I be given ECT.

I looked at Heather blankly. 'ECT?'

My big sister was always the scientist in our family and so she spelt out the meaning of those shocking initials: Electro-Convulsive Therapy. The doctors, Heather said, believed they might have to shock sense into me. It was one possible treatment for a white boy who refused to serve in the South African army. Heather, who was twenty-four, seethed at the thought.

We had just seen *Frances*, a film about the Hollywood actress Frances Farmer, played by Jessica Lange, who, in the 1940s, had been confined to a mental institution, against her will, and given shock treatment. I must have shuddered because Heather told me how she had argued strongly against such harrowing treatment. But the doctor insisted that, unless I showed real improvement, she would have little option but to discuss ECT with my parents.

Heather made it seem as if mom and dad might even consider such treatment – if it meant my mind could be straightened to the point where I went into the army. A brief flash of terror ran through my imagination as I pictured the heavy, wet bags and electrical shocks given to Neil Aggett, Auret van Heerden and thousands of other South African detainees.

I didn't believe my parents would ever allow electrodes to be pinned to the side of my head. My dad, a connoisseur of electricity, would have resisted the jolting shortcut of burning a chunk of my brain to pacify me. And my mother would not stand such an idea.

Heather was less certain. 'You've got to be careful,' she warned.

At our next meeting in the blue-walled room I was much more alert and precise with my language. I spoke calmly to the woman. I told her why I didn't want to go into the army and, in turn, she showed me that she was thoughtful and compassionate.

'I agree with you,' she said at the end of my careful explanation. And, as I smiled at her in relief, she said another more loaded phrase: 'Catch 22.'

I hesitated, not sure I should go down another literary alley. 'Have you read it?' she asked of Joseph Heller's novel.

I nodded and, less flamboyantly than a week before, explained that in English Honours it had been one of my first-term American literature set books. I knew all about John Yossarian and the 'Catch-22' he faced as a US Air Force bombardier in World War II. The doctor, in her blue room, must have been sufficiently reassured to reach for the book herself and read a key passage to me:

'There was only one catch and that was Catch-22, which specified that a concern for one's safety in the face of dangers that were real and immediate was the process of a rational mind. Orr was crazy and could be grounded. All he had to do was ask; and as soon as he did, he would no longer be crazy and would have to fly more missions. Orr would be crazy to fly more missions and sane if he didn't, but if he were sane he had to fly them. If he flew them he was crazy and didn't have to; but if he didn't want to he was sane and had to. Yossarian was moved very deeply by the absolute simplicity of this clause of Catch-22 and let out a respectful whistle.'

I wanted to whistle in surprise myself but I was still so worried about shock treatment that I remained silent. Closing the book, she advised me that I should avoid the army as long as possible, by studying further, so that I might buy myself the necessary time to make a mature decision with regard to my future.

'You're going to be all right,' she said.

'What changed your mind?' I eventually asked her.

'Your sister ... ' the doctor said quietly. 'She spoke very convincingly about you ...'

Heather had saved me. My parents were relieved, and, again, my sister helped them understand that my sanity had been endorsed rather than questioned. I knew, then, I would never be shocked to the core of my brain. My family believed too much in me, and in the positive power of electricity.

THE MEN IN THE security police who used electricity as a means of torture were still obsessed with Liz Floyd. Major Arthur Cronwright, in particular, wanted to crush her. The trouble she and her dead boyfriend had caused them at John Vorster Square meant that Liz had become Cronwright's 'pet hate'. Paul Erasmus used that phrase to describe the reason why Cronwright had undertaken an increasingly personal vendetta against her.

Erasmus might have failed hopelessly when instructed to burgle Aubrey and Joyce Aggett's house, but he led a sustained campaign of harassment against Liz. Cronwright knew Erasmus had a flair for making sexually abusive telephone calls and set him to work. Erasmus would phone Liz at disconcertingly random times of the day and night, then allow his calls to lapse for a week or even a month before, suddenly, resuming his telephonic stalking.

Cronwright often told Erasmus that he wanted Liz Floyd to be killed. 'You should assassinate her,' Cronwright shouted and Erasmus downplayed that apparent order by claiming that, '*Ja*, I'll look into it.' Erasmus had no intention of killing Liz, because he thought Cronwright was half-crazy and he knew that the death of another white detainee, especially the girlfriend of the now internationally famous Neil Aggett, would cause the Branch more harm.

Erasmus, however, enjoyed taunting Liz psychologically. He would sometimes visit her, just to say a sinister hello, or suddenly appear in the same street, stopping Liz in her tracks as he asked the same old terrible question: 'Hey, Liz, I just wondered about Neil – is he still hanging around?'

The way Erasmus said 'hanging' sent his colleagues at John Vorster Square into convulsions of laughter. As a conscripted soldier in the army, Erasmus had fought on the border, and he had seen enough carnage perpetrated by black terrorists in Ovamboland, in the north of South-West Africa, to believe that opponents of apartheid had to be destroyed. They were fighting a war, Erasmus believed, and Floyd belonged to the enemy.

Even as the months passed since her release from solitary confinement, Liz was still unable to carry out certain everyday functions with simple efficiency. On a bad day a task as mindless as brushing her teeth could take up to half an hour. She also could not easily remember basic facts like her own home telephone number. Everything seemed fleeting and elusive, as if her detention and Neil's death had unmoored her.

But she was more able to accept Neil's suicide than many of their old comrades. Liz understood that detention was akin to a kind of death. On the day she had first been locked up in a cell Liz had thought to herself that, if she was driven to the point of wanting to take her own life, she would use the bars on the windows as a place of hanging. She said, when interviewed by Joseph Lelyveld in the *New York Times*, that detention was 'just a continuous suicide story'.

But she also recalled how, the night before he died, when preparing herself for the start of her own torture, she had tried to communicate with Neil, using the highly unscientific method of mental telepathy to tell him he had not betrayed her. It didn't work but, as she told Lelyveld, 'I remember sitting down that night and saying to myself, because I wanted to say it to Neil: "Look, Neil, I understand. I know." I kept on saying, "It's OK, Neil, it's OK." I was trying to talk to him, just to say, "Anything you said about me you would've said under pressure and that's all right."'

Liz told Lelyveld that, 'my first thought was that he had killed himself for me, to save me from what he had just gone through. But what's so distressing is that he just got it wrong, you know. I would rather have been tortured and come out of it and found Neil alive – rather than go through any of this.'

Most haunting of all, Liz said, she could no longer even remember what Neil had looked like. As hard as she tried to summon up a picture of him in her head, she could no longer see him. It was difficult to know when, if ever, she would be able to remember his face.

D AD KEPT BREAKING new ground at Eskom. He spent long and exhausting days travelling to remote power stations as he tried to convince white management that they should increase opportunities for their black staff. His hardest struggle was with managers who abhorred the idea of helping black workers develop new technical and engineering skills. Yet dad was a determined diplomat and he won over most of his opponents, so that every power station across South Africa adopted a new code to promote the rise of black workers.

It was a strategy which would have won the approval of Neil Aggett, but I was too wrapped up in my own life to acknowledge my father's almost revolutionary commitment. When he tried to tell me about his work I listened for a while, nodded or grunted, and then made another withering jibe about seventy per cent of the population still being without electricity.

I also fell upon newspaper coverage of an American report which suggested South Africa would soon produce nuclear weapons. This looked like evidence that my father and Eskom were still doing much to prop up apartheid. *The Star* revealed that a study of the military situation in Southern Africa, prompted by the Pentagon in Washington, had concluded that P.W. Botha and his government would be prepared to use a nuclear weapon 'in order to protect the status quo of the apartheid system and to protect the interests of the Afrikaner people and its ruling elite'.

The report had been published by the Stanford Research Institute's Strategic Studies Center and its authors were Kenneth L. Adelman, America's deputy ambassador to the United Nations, and Albion W. White, a retired US army general. Adelman and White, in an article headlined **SA Could Use Nuclear Weaponry 'Very Soon'**, concluded that: 'Afrikaners tend to adopt a more dismal, apocalyptical view of the world than most other people. The personalities of top South African officials are still dogmatic and exceedingly security minded. A nuclear device could be used if they perceived Afrikanerdom or apartheid to be truly threatened by hostile forces.'

My father was responsible for the country's sole nuclear power station, at Koeberg outside Cape Town, and I could imagine that the government would soon ask him and his leading engineers to assist in the creation of a 'nuclear deterrent'. Of course he laughed, pointing out the difference between nuclear power and nuclear warfare. Dad dismissed the prospect that the government would focus on nuclear weapons as the next step in resisting 'The Total Onslaught'.

'Have some faith,' he said.

A S THE LONGEST DROUGHT in living memory stretched across South Africa, the waiting continued. The outcome of the inquest into the death of Neil Aggett was expected to be announced shortly before Christmas in 1982. The clash between George Bizos, the Aggetts' lawyer, and Stephan Whitehead, the policeman who had shaped the interrogation of Neil and Liz, was a compelling spectacle.

Whitehead was emphatic that his investigation had been carried out in 'a civilized routine' and whenever Bizos trapped him in a glaring contradiction the magistrate intervened. Pieter Kotze was meant to be impartial, but he ruled so often in favour of the security police that Bizos could barely contain his contempt. The attorney still refused to give up and, during the testimonies of Liz Floyd and Auret van Heerden, he revealed the severity of detention without trial.

On a clammy December morning, Bizos demanded the court should find Major Arthur Cronwright and Lieutenant Stephan Whitehead responsible for the death of Neil Aggett. He insisted that nothing less than a charge of culpable homicide could be considered appropriate. 'I trust that, finally,' he said, 'we will see justice prevail in a country that needs to break free from terror and prejudice. This should be a landmark ruling. I trust the court will place itself firmly on the side of truth and justice and find these men guilty of inducing the suicide of Dr Neil Aggett.'

The magistrate had studied the conflicting evidence for the past few weeks, and the longer he took the more hope grew that perhaps he would discover a sense of justice.

My own sense of optimism had, just as it did every December, become clouded again. The same old question rose up as I waited to hear whether or not I would be granted another extension from the army to continue my studies. I had drifted happily through English Honours and had already been offered a position as a master's student, as soon as I could dream up a suitable topic. But if my latest request to defer my call-up was denied I would have just weeks left to prepare for a new life six thousand miles away.

Eventually a slim brown envelope, bearing the dreaded insignia of the South African Defence Force, was brought to our front door by our usual postman.

'Army blues again, hey?' he quipped.

I had been summoned for national service on four previous occasions and, each time, I had managed to defer my call-up for another year. Usually, only medical students were able to take a fifth year of study as deferment. And so I tore open the envelope clumsily. The crucial words were printed in italics in the middle of a long letter reminding me of my military duty:

Military Conscription Deferred To 01 July 1984

I stared at the words in disbelief. I had been given eighteen more months. It sounded like sweet eternity. I had never been given more than a year before, and so the only explanation was that my request for deferment must have been granted by a very bookish or a very drunk commanding officer. *Eighteen more months!* I felt as if I had been given another chance to live again.

THE FOLLOWING WEEKEND, on 18 and 19 December, 1982, Eskom's nuclear plant at Koeberg was rocked by four separate and powerful explosions. As the man directly responsible for

Koeberg, my father flew to Cape Town to consult with his engineers and inspect the damage. I heard him on the radio, and saw him on television, as he confirmed that no-one had been injured and that there was no danger of any radioactive leakage. He declined to comment on speculation that the blasts had been carried out by the banned African National Congress. I admired his restraint.

The *Rand Daily Mail* reported the following morning, on Monday 20 December, that, 'the ANC have claimed responsibility for the attack on Koeberg nuclear power station. In a statement issued in Dar es Salaam, Tanzania, the ANC said the sabotage was carried out by *Umkhonto we Sizwe*, the organization's military wing. It was in direct response to the SADF raid against the ANC in Lesotho last week. Thirty ANC members killed by the SADF were buried in Maseru yesterday.

'At the funeral Oliver Tambo, the exiled leader of the ANC, paid tribute to Dr Neil Aggett, who died in detention earlier this year. Mr Tambo said that Dr Aggett's work with the black trade unions would never be forgotten. He also warned that world attention would be fixed on the outcome of the inquest into his death which will be announced later today.'

It had been the most tortuous inquest in South African legal history. Fifty-two witnesses had been cross-examined with their testimonies filling 3,254 pages. Hundreds of reporters squeezed their way into court to hear Magistrate Kotze's ruling. Television cameras had already filmed the arrival of Liz Floyd and the Aggett family. Major Cronwright and Lieutenant Whitehead made their way into court through a back entrance, so avoiding the international media.

It took Magistrate Kotze six long hours to sum up the testimony of both sides, and just under a minute to announce his decision.

'In the inquest into the death of Neil Hudson Aggett, I conclude that he

gave full consent to his being interrogated by Lieutenant Stephan Peter Whitehead and his colleagues. I find, furthermore, that in considering the unassisted suicide of Dr Aggett, absolutely no blame can be attached to any member of the South African Security Police. If any moral blame must be apportioned then it should be in the direction of Mr Auret van Heerden, Dr Aggett's fellow detainee, who failed to alert the authorities to his fears that his friend had become suddenly suicidal on the evening of 4 February 1982. But there are no obvious legal guidelines to a prisoner's level of responsibility and so that must remain an issue for Mr van Heerden's conscience. In contrast, the conscience of the Security Police can be clear. I find them not guilty of any of the charges laid against them in this court.'

The world's press – from *The Times* in London to *Le Monde* in Paris to the *New York Times* – was united in outrage. They reported the angry comments made by the Aggetts, Liz Floyd and Auret van Heerden soon after court adjourned. Van Heerden described the ruling, and the allegation that he was morally responsible for Neil's death, as 'obscene'. Joyce Aggett said, 'everyone told us we were crazy to try and fight the government – and maybe they were right. This ruling is just very wrong. It breaks my heart.'

Her husband said simply that, 'the loss of Neil, and the deeply disappointing outcome of this inquest, has changed me as a man. I can now see, quite clearly, which side is right and which is wrong. It is time white South Africans woke up to the realities of this country.'

Liz Floyd described Magistrate Kotze's closing comments as 'utterly cynical and morally bankrupt'. Addressing foreign and local newspapermen, she spoke calmly: 'I know that Neil was tortured and assaulted in detention. He saw no relief from those conditions and he expected the pressure to increase. He got to the stage where he was totally desperate and, driven to the brink by Lieutenant Whitehead and the security police, he saw suicide as the only way out.'

She was asked by a journalist if her own pain would lessen, now that the inquest was over. 'No,' Liz said, 'this has just made it worse. It will take me a very long time to get over Neil.'

The Minister of Justice, Kobie Coetsee, expressed his 'complete satisfaction' with the verdict. 'I don't understand all these complaints,' he shrugged. 'The case was heard in open court and all the facts were thoroughly aired. We can safely say that justice took its course.'

Josh Sepheto (left) and the Soweto posse, 1983

CHAPTER SEVENTEEN

THE LAST
COMPILATION TAPE

AT THE END OF A LONG Sunday afternoon, early in January, 1983, I found Dave Kaplan hunched over a pile of records on his bedroom floor, slipping shiny black vinyl discs in and out of their sleeves as he studied the length of specific songs. I knew instantly that Dave was in the midst of making another compilation tape. He needed just one more song to complete a perfect collection. Timing was everything because, like me, Dave distrusted compilation tapes which cut off the last song. The best home-made mixes always ended with just a few seconds left at the end of the second side of music. So he waved at me as he examined the timings of another album and calculated which song would fill up the remaining space on his TDK C-90 cassette.

He eventually nodded in satisfaction, and turned to me. I saw how fragile he looked, and I knew the reason. Dave was on the brink. Early the following morning he was meant to begin two years of national service at Voortrekkerhoogte, the large army camp just outside Pretoria. Thousands of other young white South African men would journey across the country to their respective military bases where they had been summoned.

Dave Kaplan, however, was different. He had chosen a more harrowing course. Dave had told me that, when his name was shouted out by a sergeant, he would step forward and announce just as loudly that he refused to serve in the South African Defence Force. In the ensuing silence he would take a deep breath and then confirm he was a conscientious objector on the grounds of his opposition to apartheid.

He was not one for grandstanding speeches, being a wry and witty soul, but this would be a moment of utter gravity. Dave wanted to ensure his reasons would be heard clearly by all the bewildered conscripts, because he had spoken often during drunken reveries of his sweetest fantasy. In his imagination he described how other young soldiers would then step forward to say that they too declined to wear an army uniform. One dissenting rebel would lead to two and three and then dozens of conscientious objectors falling in a line behind the soon-to-be-famous Dave Kaplan.

When we got especially drunk Dave would joke that he'd make the front page of the *New York Times*, as news spread across the world that he had galvanized a mass protest amongst white South African conscripts. The whole military system would disintegrate as dissent spread and, eventually, apartheid itself imploded. Dave Kaplan would be awarded the Nobel Peace Prize, Jean-Luc Godard would make a film of his life which might be a surprising international blockbuster, Nelson Mandela would be released and I'd eventually get to write the book about how a charming Jewish boy changed the world with one small step and defiant shake of his head.

But we were not drunk then, on a fading Sunday afternoon with his suitcase packed for prison. We knew that no-one else would follow his lead. Instead, once the court-martial had been heard, Dave would be jailed for six years. There were no mitigating circumstances or grounds for appeal.

Six years sounded like an eternity.

Dave looked frightened. And so I told him about two boys I knew who had decided on different routes out of the army. Mano Gougoumis, the dark-skinned Greek kid from Germiston, was on his way to America. Having torn up the first conscription papers he had received at the age of fifteen, Mano had always vowed that he would never serve in the army. His only disquiet in leaving South Africa centred on the loss his father would endure.

Mano could sometimes despair of the fact that his dad supported the Nationalist government and apartheid. But as the day of his leaving approached he thought more of how his father had spent twenty years building a restaurant business that Mano and his young brothers were meant to help run before assuming control on his retirement. But, with Mano having encouraged his brothers to follow him to America, there would soon be no Gougoumis family left in South Africa. Mano would head for northern California as liberal politicians and lawyers in San Francisco, Berkley and Oakland were willing to assist draft-dodging white South Africans applying for the chance to remain in America.

Even if Dave didn't like England, why didn't he follow Mano to America? He loved American music and movies more than anyone I knew. It would be hard but, surely, better than jail?

One day, Dave said, he would love to take a long holiday in America. But he had no desire to flee to a country he had never visited before.

I knew Dave had loved Amsterdam on his solitary European trip.

He raved about Dutch girls, and the dope, and no other country was more sympathetic to our plight than the Netherlands. Another tape-swapping friend, Ian Kerkhof, had just written to me from Durban, to explain he had settled on Amsterdam as his choice of asylum. We were all going slowly mad and so we might as well opt for a tolerant and welcoming city. Ian had been assured that his political asylum would be a formality, even for a boy like him who had no money for lawyers.

Dave eventually shook his head. 'No,' he said. 'I couldn't do it.'

'Why not?' I asked.

'I don't want to leave Africa,' he said softly.

Dave was white and Jewish. He came from an affluent suburban family, and he loved European and American culture. But, essentially, he remained an African.

'I belong here,' he said.

I envied Dave. I also believed that I belonged in South Africa, but the intensity of that feeling was nowhere near as deep in me as in him. I was not courageous enough, or even ready, to give up six years of my life for the country. I lacked the same bolstering conviction as Dave and, unlike him, I could imagine a life for myself in another world. It might be a more muted and downbeat life, without the danger and intensity of Johannesburg, but for me it would be better than prison.

Dave reminded me that we were both twenty-two. He would be out by the time he was twenty-eight. One day he would get to see the end of apartheid and all his anguish would be consigned to the past. It sounded simple, but it was heart-wrenching.

His parents, Dave said, suffered more than him. He had thought he might buckle when that morning, over a painful breakfast, his dad had offered one last alternative. They would drive north, in the direction of Pretoria. But they would keep going, past the camp turnoff and the Voortrekker Monument, moving beyond the city and all the way through the *platteland* of the far northern Transvaal. Dave's dad had looked at the map, and worked out the distance between Johannesburg and Harare. It was a little over 1,100 kilometres between their home and the Zimbabwean capital. They could be across the border before nightfall. And once they were inside Zimbabwe they could plot a new life for him in a different African country.

Dave had discussed with me previously the option of moving to Zambia or Tanzania, and joining the ANC, but he could not commit himself to any form of armed struggle. He could never imagine himself as a revolutionary soldier, and he suspected that the political structure of the ANC would not be as pristine as some hoped. Anyway, he said, he would always be a far better teacher or writer than a politician or exiled dissident.

He had still wavered that morning. The thought of being helped out of the country by his dad seemed more enticing than the loneliness of prison. But, in the end, he had to do what he felt was best. His parents had both cried when he said it was too late for him to change. He had to step forward and declare himself a conscientious objector.

I asked Dave what songs he had taped for his beautiful girlfriend, Kay. Dave looked up at me, and laughed as he told me that his Jewish parents had actually invited Kay over for Shabbat on the previous Friday evening.

'Wow,' I said, suitably stunned. Kay was a blonde-haired, blue-eyed gentile, 'a Catholic babe' as Dave called her, and her romantic involvement with their son distressed his mom and dad.

'Yeah,' Dave joked, 'it took the army to bring us together ...'

Kay supported his decision, even if Dave said she was too young and gorgeous to be expected to wait for his release in 1988, seventy-two months from then.

'I broke up with her last night,' he said disconsolately, before making another forlorn attempt at a quip. 'My mom almost smiled when I told her ...'

It was not quite over between Dave and Kay. He had made her this one last compilation tape which he hoped she would always play, even after she fell for someone else.

'Maybe it'll be my movie soundtrack,' he said.

Aretha Franklin's 'I Say A Little Prayer' started the compilation. 'I'm Jewish,' he shrugged, 'she's Catholic ...'

I still remember some of the other songs Dave taped for Kay – old standbys like Ella Fitzgerald's 'Miss Otis Regrets', The Velvet Underground's 'Femme Fatale', Miles Davis's 'All Blues', Joy Division's 'Atmosphere', Abdullah Ibrahim's 'Mannenberg' and, of course, Bobby Bland's 'Cry, Cry, Cry'. It was a beautiful if downbeat farewell.

I watched Dave lift the stylus from its cradle and place it in the groove of his last chosen track. As the familiar crackle of vinyl cut through our silence, he pressed down the Record button on his adjoining tape deck.

Eventually, when he was done, Dave returned the cassette to the plastic container he would slip through the letter box of Kay's flat in Orange Grove later that night.

He looked up at me and nodded. 'Let's go for a beer ...'

SEVEN HOURS LATER, just before one o'clock that Monday morning, Dave Kaplan's father sat on the edge of his bed in a darkened room. There had been no sleep in the old family home all night.

After Dave and I had parted in nearby Norwood, where we'd had a couple of beers in a muted bar, I had shaken him by the hand. I had never said goodbye to anyone about to voluntarily give himself up for a six-year jail sentence. My farewell had been abject. But what could I say?

I heard later that Dave made the short drive to Orange Grove where, giving into temptation, he knocked on Kay's door so he could hand over his last compilation tape to her. The hour they shared marked him so deeply that, when he came home, he broke down with his parents. They talked for a few hours before they led him to his bed where, as if he was a child again, his father helped him out of his clothes. Dave slipped between the cool sheets and tried to close his eyes.

For another hour or two the house was quiet and dark. And then Dave heard his heartbroken parents rise from their bed in the room next door. His mother, trying to tread across the creaking floorboards as gently as she could, went downstairs to the kitchen. Dave could hear her rustling around, opening drawers, lifting out cutlery and snapping shut the lids of Tupperware containers as she made everyday noises at the dead of night.

His dad locked himself away in the bathroom. Dave knew he would be shaving because he could hear the rush of hot running water being turned on and off. His father never went anywhere, even if it was pitch-black outside, without a closely-shaved face. And once that ritual had been completed, Dave listened as his dad emptied his bladder in the adjoining toilet before, after a long pause, he turned on the shower. If nothing else, his dad would be clean for the day ahead.

When the shower shut off, the sounds of his mother in the kitchen returned. Dave could hear the hiss of the kettle and the ping of the microwave as she made tea and defrosted some bread rolls that they could eat in the car. He lay in the room that had been his own for twenty years, and wondered if he'd ever return. Listening to his parents engaged in routine chores threatened to overwhelm him. But he held on. He was calm when his dad entered his room and sat on his bed.

'Did you sleep?' his dad asked.

'No,' Dave admitted.

'But you're ready?'

'Yes.'

'OK,' his dad murmured, bending down to kiss him on the top of his head. 'You should get up now . . .'

Dave waited until his father left the room. And then, for the last time, he snapped on his bedside lamp, which was made to look like a set of wickets and a glowing white cricket ball. He looked up at the ceiling, his eye following the familiar cracks in the plaster. His gaze then swept across the hundreds of books and records filed in alphabetical order around the perimeter of his room.

His mother had packed his suitcase. It stood waiting for him in the hall downstairs. In the kitchen, it looked as if she had made enough food to last a week. Their old family picnic hamper was crammed with sandwiches, biscuits, cakes, fruit and cartons of juice. His mom had even remembered to pop in some biltong, which both he and his dad had always loved, as if it was a symbol of the white South African life he was about to reject.

'Everything I love, mom,' Dave said as he looked down at her.

'You're going to be all right,' his mother said, handing him a bowl of cereal.

Carrying his cereal, Dave slid open the glass doors that led out onto the patio where they'd had so many family meals through all the summers of his life. In the garden, just before one-thirty in the morning, the silence was punctuated by the metallic chirp of the Parktown Prawns. In the northern suburbs of Johannesburg, where Dave's family lived, a King Cricket, or *Libanasidus vittatus* to give it the Latin name his dad insisted on using, was always called a Parktown Prawn.

They were scary beasts, with hard-backed shells, spiky legs and big orange antennae on their heads. Three inches long and as tough and mean as scaly-backed crocodiles, and as prehistoric looking, a Parktown Prawn seemed indestructible. No ordinary slipper or rolled-up newspaper could stop the King Cricket. Even a shot of Doom, the killer insect spray, just infuriated the Parktown Prawn. When threatened, the insect had been known to leap at its human assailant or to empty a smelly black effluvium from its bowels as a warning.

Dave's dad liked picking them up, as if they were friends of his, and scaring screaming visitors as he approached them with his chosen Prawn. While his guests shrieked with hysterical laughter, old man Kaplan pointed out the cricket's distinctive features and mused on the fact that the Parktown Prawn was only really found in pampered suburbia, preferring the damp, leafy seclusion of lush gardens surrounding elegant old houses like the one in which they lived.

There were no Soweto Prawns because the townships were too dry for the King Cricket. Of course they made people almost jump out of their white skins on hot summer evenings, when the windows were open and a Parktown Prawn leapt onto a sofa or even someone's bed, but Dave's dad cherished them. He said they did a fantastic job keeping the Kaplan garden free of snails, old plants and any rotting fruit which fell from the overhanging trees.

It was hard to know when Dave might next see a Parktown Prawn. He did not know exactly where he would end up but he knew it would be stark and barren, and not quite *Libanasidus vittatus* territory. The rest of the garden seemed deathly quiet and, in the cool night, Dave shivered when he heard his dad's voice from the edge of the patio.

'We'd better get going . . . ,'

Dave rose from the bench and followed his father inside. In the brief time he had spent in the garden, eating his last bowl of cereal, his mother had changed out of her dressing gown and nightie. She had slipped on a dress, combed her hair and added some lipstick.

His mother held him tight. And then she told Dave that she loved him. She rose up on her toes so that she could reach his face. She kissed him on both cheeks and, for once, Dave did not use his sleeve to wipe away the trace of her lipstick.

'I'll see you soon,' she said.

His dad had placed his suitcase in the boot and he hovered at the door, anxious to get moving. He hugged his wife and then ushered his son towards the passenger seat.

Dave could hardly believe what was happening to him. He felt empty, as if he was watching someone else wave goodbye to his mother. He held his hand up in a silent salute and, looking over his shoulder, saw how motionless his mother stood as she watched the car roll down to the bottom of the drive and then glide quietly through the security gates.

They headed north, towards Pretoria. The smooth black tar of the N1 highway flashed beneath them. There was no need to talk, and neither of them had any words left. As they neared Pretoria the silhouette of the Voortrekker Monument rose up. It looked almost ghostly in the moonlight.

Dave's dad pressed down harder on the accelerator.

Mike Kaplan did not even turn to glance at his son as they raced on into the night. As they had agreed only hours earlier, they flew past Voortrekkerhoogte and moved deep into the darkness ahead, towards Zimbabwe, a thousand kilometres, and another world, away.

DAVE KAPLAN'S ESCAPE into an African exile was shrouded in secrecy for years. It would be more than two decades before I heard everything that happened on that last night, in the turbulent hours when, having spoken to Kay and his parents, he changed his mind. They convinced him he could do more on the outside, teaching in Africa, in countries stretching from Zimbabwe to Kenya to Senegal, than by giving up six years of his life in prison. He was unable to return to South Africa for almost ten years and, when he finally got back, Kay was married and the mother of twins.

He and his old girlfriend had remained in contact, mainly via handwritten airmail letters, or through small gifts that his parents passed back and forth between them when they visited Dave twice a year in the African outposts where he lived and worked. Even though he no longer had the equipment to make her compilation tapes, he still sent her cassettes crammed with African music that he bought in the streets and markets.

'Dave's Tapes' remained essential listening even as Kay's life changed and she met and fell in love with another man. And sometimes, when the house was quiet, and she had a little time alone, Kay played the last compilation tape her old boyfriend had made all those years of Sundays ago.

IN THE DAYS FOLLOWING Dave's disappearance, in mid-January 1983, my own life was transformed. The idea of a dramatic change came to me just before I kissed the girl I had sat alongside the previous year in our English Honours seminars on Jane Austen. Her name was Julia and she came from London, which was enough to make her seem impossibly worldly to me. On the Wednesday night after Dave Kaplan's last compilation tape, Julia and I had gone out for a drink. She was about to leave the country in less tumultuous circumstances.

After an eventful few years in South Africa, Julia was going home to England. I said I would soon meet her in London, promising I was impulsive enough to just pack my bags and get the hell out of

South Africa for good. She laughed, and asked why I didn't go to Soweto instead.

It was a painfully acute question for a moaning young white South African like me. *Soweto?* I must have looked disturbed by such a revolutionary thought. The security police, surely, would pick me up soon after I entered the white country's definitive no-go area?

But, the week before, a relaxed Julia had phoned a school in Diepkloof, an apparently radical hothouse called Bopasenatla High, and asked if they had any spare teaching posts. Beguiled by her crisp intelligence and cool English voice, the black headmaster had offered her a job on the spot. Julia had accepted before, mulling over her options more carefully, deciding she would be better off going back to London. Why didn't I call Bop High myself and take her place?

To secure a spot on the English MA course that had earned me my eighteen-month exemption from the army, I had decided on my chosen subject with some reluctance. The prospect of a master's thesis on the Jazz Age novels of F. Scott Fitzgerald was hardly thrilling, but it was the most obvious topic I could dream up in the few days I had to confirm my deferment. The prospect of doing nothing but reading and writing about Fitzgerald, devoid of money, seemed depressing. And without the need to attend lectures, I was at last free to earn some cash in a proper job.

Soweto suddenly reared up as my own alternative universe. It seemed remote and dangerous, but full of intriguing possibilities. I liked the idea of going somewhere new and illicit, of drinking in a shebeen where they played township jazz or American rap. I imagined losing myself in a world where a beautiful black girl might seduce me. We would triumphantly ignore the Immorality Act that turned any sexual act between people of different races into a criminal offence. You could go to jail for a long time if you slept with a black woman, but Dave K and I had always said what a way to go, baby, what a blow to apartheid, doing the dirty with a township honey who rapped along to our favourite song of 1982, 'The Message' by Grandmaster Flash and the Furious Five. 'Don't push me,' the Brooklyn posse warned, "cuz I'm close to the edge . . .'

I thanked Julia when she kissed me. 'What for?' she laughed.

'For that kiss,' I said, 'and for telling me about Soweto . . .'

I kissed her again and made up my mind. I was on my way to a new world.

THE FOLLOWING MORNING I called Bopasenatla High. They must have been less impressed by my South African accent, and wary of potential Security Branch spies because, rather than instantly giving me Julia's job, I was invited to meet the principal in central Johannesburg later that week.

I felt nervous, but Abel Maseko quickly deduced that I was far too soft and green to be working undercover for the police. Mr Maseko probably even guessed that my motives were more selfish than subversive. Yet he patted me kindly on the arm and said I would be very welcome at his school. I would become the first white teacher he had ever employed and he was sure we'd all benefit from our shared adventure. He explained that, as a state school, we were compelled to follow the government syllabus.

Mr Maseko might have preferred it if I could have taught Ralph Ellison's seminal *Invisible Man* or a great African novel like *Things Fall Apart* by Chinua Achebe, but he understood the importance of Shakespeare and Hardy and Keats and Yeats and George Eliot, whom I was expected to teach instead. I had studied them all. I was ready for my new life in Soweto.

'Wonderful,' Mr Maseko enthused. 'Why don't you start tomorrow morning?'

Germiston, South Africa,
14 January, 1983

I WORE A CRISP WHITE SHIRT, a skinny black tie and black trousers to breakfast that Friday morning. The shirt and trousers had been freshly pressed by Maria, our sweetly smiling middle-aged black maid who could not quite believe that the young master was about to drive into the mysterious and violent black township of Soweto to begin his first job in the outside world. Maria rarely called me 'the young master' any longer. She usually called me 'Donny', as if I belonged to the Osmonds. I liked Maria and so I usually let that one ride. What was the point of badgering her about my certainty that, as a self-proclaimed existentialist, I was about as far removed from a group of beaming and singing Mormons as you could get in sunny South Africa?

'Shew, madam,' Maria chuckled in surprise, 'doesn't Donny look smart?'

My mother was less impressed. She had lived through my post-punk years, and my belief that wearing a skinny tie was a revolutionary act and a sure-fire way of catching the eye of any girl who might have heard of the French new wave or liked English ska groups like The Specials or The Beat. To my mother, I looked less smart than desperately lost. She did not know a single white person who had ever visited Soweto, even though it was a mere twenty miles away.

'He will be all right, won't he, Maria?' my mother asked anxiously as she straightened my tie.

'Yes, madam,' Maria replied politely. She did not tell my mother, as she had revealed to me a few days earlier, that she had never visited Soweto herself because it scared her half to death.

Soweto had long been called 'The Murder Capital of the World', but in recent years the death rate had escalated still further. The

Rand Daily Mail had just reported that six people were murdered a day in Soweto, a killing every four hours. Feeling queasy, I brushed away my mother's fussing. I was no longer sure I had the stomach for either breakfast or the day ahead in a township crammed with a million black people brutalized by apartheid. I could imagine their murderous reaction when I arrived alone to teach some Shakespearean sonnets and Thomas Hardy's *Tess of the d'Urbervilles*.

At the age of twenty-one, I did not feel like a profound teacher. I had not taught a single lesson in my life. And why would I not become one of the six people murdered in Soweto that day?

I could babble about my opposition to apartheid but militant students would soon learn I lived with my family in a big white house in the suburbs, with maids and a gardener, two black women and an elderly man my otherwise well-meaning parents referred to as 'the girls' and 'the boy'.

My parents gave Maria thousands of Rand every year, on top of her basic wage, to pay for her children's education. But why couldn't she use our cups, spoons or plates? It was a pointless argument. I just ended up getting mad with the two people who loved me most in the world. Still, these were not the kind of guilty secrets to be voiced in Soweto. My students might even know that my father worked for Eskom, the state-owned Electricity Supply Commission, because he was frequently on radio and television and in the newspapers.

Eskom was one of the world's leading power utilities. Yet, as I reminded dad indignantly, it neglected to supply electricity to the majority of its own people. Perhaps the children of Soweto would set me ablaze amid the fires used to warm and light some of their un-electrified houses.

I knew the seriousness of the day ahead when, rather than reading the *Mail* over breakfast, dad pushed his newspaper aside as soon as I sat down. We had been at battle for years, dad and I, but over our hushed breakfast table we looked at each other. After I had eaten, and we had spoken, the moment was almost upon us. I would soon leave home for Soweto.

Dad did something strange then. He put out his hand and, switching to Zulu, a language neither of us spoke, he said '*Hamba kachle*' ['Go well' or, more precisely in this case, 'Be careful'].

MY BRIGHT YELLOW Ford Escort did not look much like a hearse from the outside. It still had a cheerfully battered mid-1970s feel to it, especially on those summery days when James Brown and Al Green could be heard whooping through the open windows. Yet, on that overcast Friday morning, all was quiet and solemn as the old car crawled through the heavy traffic at a funereal pace towards Diepkloof in Soweto.

Beyond the abandoned gold mine dumps of Johannesburg, the M2 highway split into two at its south-western edge. The three lanes to my right were all crammed with white drivers heading towards the city centre and the northern suburbs. But, in the inside lane, the road cleared as soon I curved to the left in the direction of the township. No other white person, it seemed, was crazy enough to drive this way.

In the distance Soweto remained hidden in the dense smog that shrouded it every morning. But I could sense its presence in the concealed dip of a valley. As I closed in on that ghostly low cloud, fear filled the car.

I could have turned around at the next turnoff, because no-one was forcing me to drive into Soweto. I could have just gone home and pretended that the whole miserable experience had never happened. But I thought of Dave Kaplan, and I knew I would never forgive myself if I veered off the barren road to Diepkloof. So my hands gripped the steering wheel a little tighter, and the dented Escort rolled on into the unknown.

THEY SURROUNDED ME QUICKLY, three black teachers called Shorty, Moses and Joshua, and formed a barrier against the thousands of eyes that fixed on me as soon as I parked my car inside the dusty grounds of Bopasenatla High School in Diepkloof.

'Welcome to Ghost Town,' Shorty cracked, rubbing his bald head and cackling in disbelief at my arrival. 'We didn't think you'd make it. Call me Shorty, brother.'

Alongside him a very tall, very thin black man with a straggly beard stretched out his hand. 'I'm Joshua,' he said with a face-splitting smile to soothe my obvious anxiety.

'Don,' said the third member of my welcoming committee with exaggerated reverence, 'my name is Moses.'

He was a short, round, brown ball of a man and I thought he was going to cry as he looked up at me with glazed eyes. 'My man,' Moses said softly, 'don't look so worried. You're safe here.'

Mr Maseko, the kindly headmaster soon joined us, parting the crowded playground with understated authority. He thanked me for coming to Soweto, and revealed that a special assembly would begin in fifteen minutes so that I could be presented to the whole school.

I felt embarrassed by the prospect of having to face a thousand black students, most of whom were already staring at me. But whenever I looked directly at anyone, their gaze remained coolly neutral as if they were holding their fire for the moment. Everyone knew that, since the riots of 1976, power in the township resided with the angry mass of black students.

There was, thankfully, no stage on which I could be paraded. The school assembly, in the absence of a hall, was held outside. I stood to the side, sticking closely to Josh, Moses and Shorty, and was relieved that attention was drawn away from me by Mr Maseko as he led the school in prayer. My eyes stayed open, fixed on the sheen of dust that already covered my black shoes. Maria had polished them early that morning, when I was still in bed.

Near the end of his prayer, Mr Maseko gave thanks for the addition of a new teacher to Bopasenatla. The Lord was asked to walk with me, to guide me and let me know how welcome I was amongst his people. As the echoing chant of 'Amen' rolled across the schoolyard, pale sunlight filtered through the smog.

Mr Maseko lifted his hands to the sunshine. 'Already,' he beamed, 'it feels a little brighter this morning.' He gestured in my direction and called out my name.

In the sudden silence he encouraged me with a beckoning flutter of his fingers. And then he held up his hand as if to underline the significance of the moment.

'We all know the great white doctors at Bara,' he said gravely, as he pointed in the direction of Baragwanath Hospital which was less than a mile from the school gates. A rippling murmur spread through the students. Neil Aggett had worked at the township hospital for years before his detention.

Mr Maseko spread out his hand towards me. 'We now have our first white teacher...'

It was hard to comprehend he was talking about me, and I felt even more stricken when hundreds of girlish voices trilled in unison. I heard the sound of a traditional black South African celebration, as the young women of Bopasenatla High ululated a wordless chant, while the boys stamped their feet in a drumming accompaniment.

'They're welcoming you, my brother,' Shorty whooped above the noise as he slapped my back and brought his own feet down in a dusty war dance. 'They're welcoming you...'

TEN MINUTES LATER, with my first English lesson of the day put on temporary hold, Shorty, Joshua and Moses extended that welcome by leading me out of the school gates and down a rutted road to an anonymous house on the left, little more than two hundred metres from the school.

I must have still looked dazed for my trio of wise men had decided I was in need of a shot at the closest shebeen. I looked at my watch and saw it was not even 8:30 a.m.

'Don't worry, bra,' Shorty winked, 'this is a twenty-four-hour establishment ...'

Moses and Josh were keen to stress that drinking amongst teachers usually did not begin so early in the day, but this was a special occasion that demanded a swift salute.

The shebeen was an ordinary and very small house, and the initial shock of the old lady who lived there was replaced by an exclamation of delight when she heard I was a new recruit.

She brought an unopened bottle of brandy into her living room and, surrounded by photographs of great American jazz giants and boxers, from Duke Ellington and Charlie Parker to Sugar Ray Robinson and Muhammad Ali, we took our seats.

'Just a quick one,' Moses reassured me. 'A toast and then off to work we go.'

'Man,' Shorty complained, 'we gotta have a couple of slices of toast ...'

He poured a large slug of brandy into each glass and waved away the accompanying cans of Coke.

'Welcome,' he said to me, before knocking back his drink in one.

The rest of us touched glasses and followed Shorty with a more sedate series of sips, which still made my eyes water as the neat brandy burned my throat. But a warm glow soon spread inside me and I could not help grinning when Shorty gave us our second 'slice of toast ...'

Moses gestured for silence. 'I met him, you know...' he said, looking meaningfully at me.

'Who?' I asked

'Dr Neil,' Moses said quietly. 'One of the union guys brought him here after an all-night shift ... me and Shorty met him.'

'*Wragtig!* [Truly!]' Shorty exclaimed in a burst of Afrikaans. 'He sat right here in this room.'

Moses lifted his glass and led our last toast of the morning. 'Dr Neil ...'

We chinked glasses one more time and, with my head swimming, I echoed the others. 'Dr Neil,' I murmured as I tried to imagine how Neil Aggett might have looked, talking to Moses and Shorty, not long before the police came and took him away forever.

As his son parties in Soweto, Ian McRae moves towards
becoming the new chief executive of Eskom and
the man eventually known as Mr Electricty

Chapter Eighteen

SOWETO DAYS

SOUTH AFRICA, in its tough and unsparing way, remained a surprising country. Bitterness and intransigence were embedded into apartheid. Yet tolerance and forgiveness flowered in the most unexpected places. In a courthouse canteen it could be seen every day at a corner table when recess was taken and polystyrene cups of weak coffee and lukewarm tea were drunk by a group of Afrikaners. They shared a terrible secret which had become a matter of legal scrutiny.

At the Pretoria Supreme Court, Auret van Heerden had issued a claim for damages of R65,000 [then £32,500] against ten security policemen who had tortured him in November 1981. Major Arthur Cronwright headed a list of the accused which included the two men who had administered the worst suffering: Warrant Officer Laurence Prince and Captain Andries Struwig. Auret detailed the sustained brutality he had endured, documenting the electric shocks, suffocation with a wet bag, strangulation by towel, sleep deprivation and excessive standing as well as the fact that he had been punched and kneed in the face. He also itemised the beatings done to the soles of his feet with a *sjambok* [whip], the violent assault on his testicles and the fact that his fingers had been stamped on until just before the point of breaking.

Auret felt compelled to seek judicial recognition of his torture, and a form of recompense, for two reasons. He wanted to highlight, in a public domain, the security police's routine inhumanity towards its detainees and, as importantly, refute the wild allegation that moral responsibility for Neil Aggett's death lay with him.

Yet Auret bore no malice towards his torturers. It felt natural that, during breaks from court, he should sit with the security police. People who had heard how badly he'd been tortured by these same men were bewildered. But Auret knew how fallible and haunted they were on the inside.

He understood the unsettling relationship that can develop between a victim and his torturer. When you share such horrendous intimacy, Auret told me years later, you look deep into each other's souls. They had spent thirteen weeks delving into each other's secret selves and so there was no need for artifice or politeness when they met again.

Auret found it easy to be magnanimous over tea and coffee. He was suing the security police in the Pretoria Supreme Court with a formidable legal 'team from hell' led by Sidney Kentridge. His opponents were unusually canny in appointing a Jewish advocate to defend them. But Kentridge, who had also taken on the Security Branch at the Biko inquest, was indestructible as he used the forensic detail embedded in Auret's memory.

Amid the ravages of his torture Auret had made note of much around him. He was able to name the anti-inflammatory pills the security police had given him when the beating he had taken from Prince's huge hands had made him swell so badly. His unexpected introduction of that fact became a crucial element of the case.

Ultimately, the precision of his account exposed his torturers, as they stumbled badly in their denials.

Justice T.H. van Reenan upheld Auret's charge of assault in detention, and granted him compensation. It would still take Auret van Heerden another twenty years to open up all the dark shutters he had sealed to protect himself. But, then, it was easy for him to show forgiveness and tolerance.

The security policemen accepted their defeat with equanimity. '*Ja*, Auret,' one of them said as they left court together for the last time, 'all's fair in love and war ...'

IT HAD BEEN THE MOST difficult year of my father's life. In the winter of 1983, as the worst drought in fifty years stretched across a barren country, dad's problems at home had to be pushed to one side. Rainfall had dipped alarmingly over the previous four years but the impact of the drought had since become severe. Dad might have felt he was losing the fight with me but he was about to try something much more dramatic, by reversing the flow of a mighty river.

Low voltage, load-shedding and blackouts had become increasingly common difficulties for dad . His long-term strategy, to use power generated by an 1800MW hydro-electric project from the Cahora Bassa Dam in northern Mozambique, had been affected by the ongoing civil war. The Renamo rebels, trying to overthrow the Frelimo government, had repeatedly sabotaged the high voltage line and planted landmines around the electricity pylons linking Cahora Bassa and South Africa. Dad had to cancel the contract, in which he had invested so much time, and also delay the commissioning of Koeberg's nuclear plant, following sabotage of the station.

Drought and war had reduced the output of Eskom's stations to just seventy-three per cent of their capacity. But dad's over-riding problem remained the increasingly low supply of water, which was vital to the cooling and maintenance of all South Africa's power stations. By May 1983, the Vaal Dam, providing water for much of the giant province of the Transvaal, was less than thirty per cent full. If the drought did not break, the most important dam in South Africa would be completely dry by October, 1984. Dad knew that, by then, he would almost certainly have lost me. But the thought of the country grinding to a halt, with the lack of water causing further loss of electricity, was even more concerning. It was already described as a drought that happened 'once in every 200 years'.

In my heavy-handed moments, and trying to prick his Christian conscience, I alluded to biblical droughts and famines. God might be sending white South Africa a dry reminder of his discontent.

Dad concentrated on more practical realities. He could not allow the Department of Water Affairs and his fellow executives at Eskom to simply assume that rain would eventually fall at some point in the next year. An emergency plan, to overturn the natural order, was concocted by dad and his senior engineers. Using 450 men, they would reverse the flow of the Vaal River over a distance of 200 kilometres, from the partially full Vaal Dam to the nearly empty Grootdraai Dam. It was a feat of engineering that required the construction of seven temporary earth and stone weirs in the river. This would raise the level of water by sixty-one metres. They also needed to build seventy-five kilometres of new power line to supply electric pumps in the weirs.

The first weir was completed on 20 June, 1983 and, in early September, a month ahead of schedule, eighty-four huge pumps reversed the flow of water and drove it back up the Vaal River. A man-made miracle had been achieved, at a cost of R35,000,000 [around £17.5m then]. The river's changed direction had an immediate impact and the output of power stations in the eastern Transvaal increased markedly.

My dad, as a man of faith, had prayed hard during that onerous process. It seemed as if some forgiveness had been granted to the arid country he loved. But the respite from drought was replaced by Cyclone Domoina, which tore through Mozambique and down the South African coast. Rain fell heavily for more than twenty-four hours. There was tangible relief only in later weeks when soaking rains, at last, ended the dry years.

Dad had reversed a river, and survived the terrible drought of 1982 and 1983, but still he felt powerless to stem the far more personal tide that would soon engulf his family and force us apart.

WE FINALLY BROKE on a cold Saturday night in the winter of 1983. It started out as just another argument, a routine shouting match over the ancient questions about my future. Dad was not about to relent. We needed to thrash it out once and for all.

I was twenty-two years old and we could not go on. I was ruining my life and, even worse, I was slowly killing my mother. I was breaking her heart, piece by piece. The sooner I gave in, and got the army out of the way, the sooner we could all move on as a family.

A kind of craziness took hold of me then. I moved up close to my father so that I could shout right in his face, rather than from across the study where most of our battles were waged.

Dad stood up to me. He was not about to let even unhinged melodrama deflect him. He matched me, word for word, shout for shout.

My mother could no longer stand it and she left the room, looking as bereft as if one of us had just died.

And so we were alone, dad and I, with my madness holding us in its grip. There was a moment when I thought dad might hit me, to pull me back to him, or maybe it was more that I felt ready to hit him. I was that lost and desperate. And so there we stood, nose to nose, glare to glare, and I gathered myself sufficiently to understand that talking softly was more powerful.

I told dad, with glazed eyes and muted words, what I had long known. I would do anything not to go into the army. I would leave the country or go to jail. In that moment, suddenly chilled by my own certainty, I finally meant what I said. I would go to jail.

I told dad then that my days in Soweto had changed me forever. I was no longer scared of the army. How could I be afraid of something I utterly rejected? I believed in a different country to the one he and mom had lived in for so much longer than me.

Hurt flared in dad's eyes. I turned away then. It was over. I was free. The army would never get me. I would go to jail, or to some lonely exile, and feel vindicated.

Yet there was little happiness inside me as I walked out into the night. I closed the front door gently, rather than slamming it, because I knew we had crossed a terrible line.

Slowly, in the dark, I headed down Whitfield Road. I didn't know where I would end up, but the walking and the silence helped. My mind turned blank and the world seemed small and empty.

I must have walked for fifteen minutes when, at home, mom persuaded dad that they needed to find me. The time had come to save me. She knew the state I was in, and it mattered more that they brought me back home, and stopped fighting with me. Something changed inside her, and dad too.

Dad backed his car down the long drive, with mom sitting calmly next to him. They did not know how long it would take to find me but they were ready to drive all night.

Eventually, they saw me wandering down the middle of Lake Road. Dad took his time as he drew level with me. He didn't want to scare me, and he didn't want to lose me.

After we spoke on that lonely suburban road, the houses around us lit by the blue blur of Saturday night television visible through so many curtains and windows, I climbed into the back seat.

I was crying as dad turned the car round and we headed back towards Cachet Road, and home.

'It's OK,' mom said softly, stretching out her hand to hold mine.

I glanced up at her then, and I saw dad turn to me as well. He could not take his eyes off the road for long but the way he looked at me, beneath the yellow street lamps, was enough.

'We know you have to leave,' he added.

I could not believe I had heard those words. But dad, having turned back to the road ahead as he drove, kept talking.

'We understand why you're going,' he said. 'And we love you. We're going to help you ...'

I FELL IN LOVE with Soweto. I worked every Monday to Friday at Bop High, alongside teachers like Josh and Stella and Baby and Shorty and Moses and Ken and others who became my friends. And I stood in front of crammed classes of kids, ranging in age from fourteen to twenty-one, and tried to teach English literature. After a life of suburban privilege, I could have found the township an ominous place. It was fringed by violence and poverty, but I was happier than I'd ever been.

On evenings and weekends I returned to normal white South African life. I went to gigs and clubs, I started another fanzine and went out with different girls. A few of my friends disappeared into an uneasy exile while many more succumbed to the army. Time was closing in on all of us but, for much of 1983, revitalized by my parents and Soweto, I felt unusually philosophical.

I could even shrug quietly to myself when, while playing league tennis every Sunday morning for Eskom, I heard some of my team-mates churn out the usual banter about 'kaffirs' and 'munts'. I no longer felt compelled to argue. It was a reaction I had learnt in Soweto when wise men like Josh Sepheto advised me on the simplest way to handle white South Africans: 'Say nothing ... but laugh a little on the inside.' Josh said he could laugh because he knew change was coming. He did not know how long it would take but its momentum would soon prove unstoppable.

'Just have a beer with them,' he always said, 'and a little laugh with yourself.'

I also came face-to-face with some township hardcases, the militant 'comrades' who had been through detention. They were the kids I'd been wary of meeting, wondering what they would make of a soft white teacher, not much older than them, from the suburbs of apartheid.

But they told me stories to which I could respond, despite our different pasts. They became ordinary kids who offered restorative proof in 1983 that, despite it being so divided, South Africa could still be a country like no other. It could be a fantastic amalgam of colour and emotion, of tumult and hope. My township believers helped lift me out of the slough of despond I had been in for so long.

In the beginning, I wondered if had succumbed too quickly to all the liberal clichés which insisted that black South Africans were dignified and proud and upbeat and, of course, even rhythmic. But I saw enough black groovers, reeling with drink or uncoordinated rhythm, to understand that not everyone in Soweto could conquer the dance floor. Some township hustlers danced as badly as me, and some Soweto men and women were equally shy or awkward.

I also did not see much dignity in the beatings some of my fellow teachers meted out to their pupils. In my first year at Bopasenatla High I had to decline an invitation, an initiation of sorts, to take a *sjambok* [the same kind of whip the security police had used on Auret van Heerden and Neil Aggett] and flog some wayward students. I was a white South African but, welcoming me into the community of male teachers at Bop High, one of my colleagues led me to a classroom where a small group of quaking teenagers stood. The *sjambok* was placed in my hand.

'We must make them respect their elders,' my fellow teacher said. 'They will be happy to be beaten by you. You must thrash them!'

He explained that he and a couple of older boys would hold down my victims while I flayed them. I had never felt more liberal than I did then as, with a hoity-toity touch, I said I did not believe in corporal punishment.

'This is not corporal punishment,' my pal said, with a trace of exasperation. 'It's just a thrashing, from a teacher to a student. I'll thrash them myself. But you must watch, *nê*?'

When I declined, my teaching comrade looked dejected and I found solace only in the expression of the boys waiting for their thrashing. They nodded to me, or smiled, as if they shared my philosophy, or perhaps just out of sympathy for my lily-livered excuses.

Later that day, when we had a drink after school, the thrashing-teacher and I found a corner in the shebeen. 'You know,' he said, 'if you were Afrikaans you would think like me. But don't worry about it. Let's have another nip.'

He plucked a cheap bottle of Martell from beneath the counter, slapping down enough money to keep the owner happy as he poured us each a large shot of brandy. 'And now, my *bra* [brother], let's find us some sisters to dance with us.'

The king of the *sjambok* was a masterful dancer and he soon enticed a couple of smiley Diepkloof girls to shimmy against us. There was much less spontaneous interaction in the white Germiston bars and Johannesburg clubs I frequented on the weekends. And so I loved Soweto for the way in which, however grim life seemed on the outside, we would have riotous celebrations inside those small and crowded township houses.

One day, at the end of another long Friday session in the she-been, Josh and I moved on. He took me all over Soweto, showing me more about township life than I'd ever dreamed of learning.

My mother woke at three o'clock the next morning to discover I had not returned home. Shaking my dad, she was convinced I lay dead in a township ditch. Dad was used to me stumbling in at all hours but he knew that a Friday night in Soweto was very different from hanging out at a dingy club in Johannesburg. He walked down to the garden gate, in his dressing gown, hoping to catch sight of my yellow Escort weaving slowly home. After he had stood forlornly there for five minutes he wandered back inside. It was 3:15 a.m.

'I'm calling the police,' mom said. A black constable at Soweto's police station heard that I had been in the township since eight o'clock the previous morning. My mother told him she was sure I'd been attacked, or worse. The black policeman assured her no report had been made in regard to any young white man in Soweto.

'My son is missing,' my mother shouted.

'Madam,' the black constable said patiently, 'maybe your boy is just having a good time.'

I WAS HAVING A GREAT TIME. My school-teacher friend, Baby, had invited me and the boys, Josh, Shorty and Moses, to a party at her house. It was one hell of a bash which had begun twelve hours earlier. Josh was always as thoughtful as he was exuberant. He had a habit of tapping me gently on the hand whenever he spoke about something he considered important. Josh was ten years older than me, with a wife and small children, and he lived in Sebokeng, near Sharpeville, a township bordering the Afrikaans town of Vanderbijlpark, seventy kilometres from Johannesburg. He had suffered from racism all his life, but Josh was the most hopeful man I had ever met.

'It's going to get better,' he would chortle. 'Much, much better ...'

Josh was convinced that life would become 'much, much better' for me once I had tasted the forbidden fruit of a beautiful black woman. We skirted over the fact that it was a jailable offence to have sex 'across the colour line'; but I was intrigued by the illicit idea of kissing a woman whose skin colour happened to be different from mine. Shuttling back and forth between suburbia and the townships, it was impossible not to see the difference while also wondering why a damaged country was so obsessed by the shade of our skin.

After nine months in Soweto I was relatively cured of the 'us' and 'them' mentality that hung over white South Africa. If anything, I had become one of 'them'.

But, when the drink flowed and black women got up to dance and sing, you could not help but notice. I didn't have a fetish for black girls, just like I did not have a fetish for red-headed or blonde or brunette girls. I just liked women. And if a woman got up to dance, to lose herself in a song while laughing and having a good time, I was happy to look at her. I didn't fall for every girl but some women were especially interesting to a boy like me. And those were the girls, those bright and mysterious girls, who invariably caught my eye. It happened often enough in Soweto, at occasional parties or shebeen sessions, when I made eye contact with a particular woman and she could tell I liked her. Yet I was still shy and never quite sure if she might be crazy enough to risk jail while breaking the law with me.

Twenty-one years before pure apartheid came into existence, with the unexpected election victory of the National Party, the Immorality Act of 1927 had banned sexual relations between white and black South Africans. The Nationalists invented apartheid, an

Afrikaans word literally meaning 'separateness', and introduced a draconian form of racism with their rise to power in 1948. Their Prohibition of Mixed Marriages Act (No 55) of 1949 made marriage between whites and members of all other racial groups illegal. A year later they carried out an even more widespread crackdown on inter-racial sex.

The 1950 Immorality Act extended to a total ban on sexual relations between whites and all non-whites. It became illegal for a white man or woman to have sex with people classified as 'Coloured' or 'Indian', while bolstering the law which already prevented sexual intimacy between white and black South Africans.

As an easily tempted twenty-two-year-old, I was amused by the curious law that I could not dance with a black, coloured or Indian woman, let alone kiss her, or go to bed with her. My more open-minded friends often joked about our compulsion to taste all three forbidden fruits before we escaped the country, went into the army or died on the border. So the Immorality Act concentrated our minds on inter-racial sex. What would it be like to kiss a black girl, or to have sex with her? Would it be that different? Could it be that deliciously subversive?

Josh believed in equal opportunities for all. He implied that, with his charm, he could arrange a suitable encounter for me with a township lovely, but he laughed when I said I'd prefer such an event to happen naturally without him acting as some kind of unpaid township pimp.

The months passed, and I was relaxed and happy. So much in Soweto seemed new and exciting to me that it hardly seemed to matter that I had not been seduced by a township woman.

But that night, at Baby's party in Rockville, Soweto, I met a black girl. We made a neat black-and-white match, I thought, because we were the exact same age. She was also studying English at university, at Vista, a Soweto college. Her name was Grace but everyone called her Honey. I knew I liked her because I stayed with her, in the opposite corner of the room to Josh, where all the laughter and hard drinking was happening, and spoke just to Honey. It felt exciting but, strangely, ordinary. She was just a girl, and I was just a boy. And I wasn't quite sure if she liked me as much as I liked her, or if she thought I could end up being as interesting as she was obviously fascinating to me.

I was at my attentive best, or worst, because she said: 'You're very serious, aren't you?'

This was my usual cue to pull out a show-stopping one-liner that would make her collapse with laughter and realize I was one hell of a bundle of fun, but, then, I just blushed. Honey, however, put her hand on my arm. 'I like it,' she said. 'It's kinda fresh.'

I looked down at her long slim fingers, with their lavishly painted nails, and felt the light pressure of her squeeze. She liked me, I guessed. And of course the more we drank the closer we moved together. It seemed easy after a while to ask her more personal questions, about boyfriends and the kind of men she fancied. Honey laughed then, and I said how much I would love to kiss her.

'You don't sound so serious now,' she said as she held my hand. And, then, she murmured a few loaded words: 'Should we be worried about getting into trouble?'

I shook my head.

'It is illegal,' she said.

'I know,' I said, suddenly feeling the enormity of the moment for us both.

'They put people into jail for this ...'

Honey did not have to say that, as a black woman, she would be punished far more stringently than me. If I was lucky I would probably get a suspended prison sentence if one of the fifty people in Baby's house turned out to be a police spy and he caught me and

Honey in bed. Honey would have no such luck. She would be locked up in jail for daring to have sex with a white man.

'The Immorality Act ... ' she said softly. Honey looked down at our entwined fingers and the contrasting colours. 'I guess you've broken it a few times ... ?'

'Not yet,' I said.

'Really?' she said in seeming surprise. 'Me neither ...'

And so, until then, we had been law-abiding South Africans, a privileged white boy from the suburbs and a black girl from the township, a young woman who was denied the vote, and most rights, and who could not sit on the same park bench or train as me, who could not eat in the same restaurant as me, or visit the same hotel as me, unless she was a cleaner or a maid.

But, sitting close together in Baby's house, I called her Grace, and told her how much I liked her. I was very serious. But I was also drunk and after a long pause as we looked at each other, she cuffed me on the arm and told me that she liked me calling her Honey, as long as I didn't say anything about her being 'as sweet as ...'

'OK,' I said.

'We've got a deal, mister,' she said, shaking me formally by the hand. I thought then if you were about to break your country's most grotesque and seemingly sacred law, you might as well do it in the company of someone beautiful and smart and funny. At two in the morning, I walked down a narrow corridor in Baby's house. Honey led the way, her hand holding mine, her bracelets and earrings jangling. Having got the wink from Baby, we headed for a spare room at the back.

It was only a small bed but we didn't care. And we no longer cared about the Immorality Act or security police spies. We were alone together. I didn't think once of apartheid or prison. I probably even forgot I was in Soweto because, having left our clothes on the floor in a flurry, it was consuming being with her, and inside her. I just thought of Honey, rather than our breaking any holy taboo of apartheid. It was some kind of bliss, between us, but an ordinary kind of bliss. It had been great with Sonja, an Afrikaans girl, and with Gillian, my English-speaking girlfriend, and then with Honey, my Soweto girl.

They were all amazing yet normal. The distinction stemmed from their individual characters rather than the colour of their skin, the texture of their hair or even the accent with which they spoke to me in English. Sonja, Gillian and Honey were just girls, young South African women that I was fortunate enough to know and fall a little in love with for a while.

Afterwards, Honey laughed as she pointed out how quiet the rest of the house had become since we disappeared into our back-room. 'The police cameras and recorders must have steamed up nicely,' she joked, as if it no longer mattered whether we were caught or not.

'We're the same, you and me,' I said, as I curled around her.

Honey turned and kissed me again. 'Of course,' she murmured. 'Under our skin, we're all the same . . .'

Don McRae and his Soweto friends, five days before he left
South Africa forever in August 1984

CHAPTER NINETEEN

THE BREAK-UP

ON A BEAUTIFUL DAY in Soweto, as my last South African summer slipped away at the end of April 1984, I stood in front of a class of township students and spoke about trench warfare. Just over three months from leaving the country, my mind felt shot to pieces. The previous night we had settled on the date of my departure. Friday 3 August. I had only fourteen weeks left in the country, and then I would be gone forever. My parents, especially my mother, seemed desolate. They would not only lose me. My sister and her husband would follow me to London at the end of the year. Our family, after splintering for years, was about to break apart.

In a slow limbo of waiting, with words of war and death suiting my mood, I lingered over the two Wilfred Owen poems I had to teach. My favourite class, the Standard Ten kids in their final year of school, seemed the right bunch to talk to about World War I poetry.

South Africa had often felt like a country at war. The pupils seated in neat rows of tightly-packed desks could tell me of the Soweto they remembered in June 1976, when many of them were not quite teenagers. Some had seen dead bodies in the street and heard the pop and fizz of bullets flying through air so dusty and thin that sometimes, they said, it felt painful to breathe if you were scared and running hard to get away. My best student, a Rastafarian called Michael, was a little older than me. His repeated political detention had affected his education, but it had also made him hungry and questing and determined to finish school. The most painful but uplifting moment of all in detention, Michael said, came one night when he heard the defiant singing of political prisoners who were waiting to be hanged, on charges of treason, the following morning.

And so, because of the South African experiences which had shaped them, Michael and many of my kids were moved when we read Owen's *Anthem for Doomed Youth* and *Dulce et Decorum Est*. They all knew someone who had died during the township's worst days. It also helped when I explained that my grandfather had fought in the trenches which Owen described.

Our classroom fell silent as they considered the various comparisons. None of my students had the option of flying overseas to start a new life. I asked Anastasia, a lovely young seventeen-year-old girl who always sat at the front and smiled sweetly at me, to read the last stanzas of *Dulce et Decorum Est*. As the words fell from her mouth, I was glad I would never become a soldier. But I also felt curiously sad, thinking of my family and George, and all they had endured:

> *Gas! Gas! Quick, boys! – An ecstasy of fumbling,*
> *Fitting the clumsy helmets just in time;*
> *But someone still was yelling out and stumbling,*
> *And flound'ring like a man in fire or lime...*

> *Dim, through the misty panes and thick green light,*
> *As under a green sea, I saw him drowning.*
>
> *... If you could hear, at every jolt, the blood*
> *Come gargling from the froth-corrupted lungs,*
> *Obscene as cancer, bitter as the cud*
> *Of vile, incurable sores on innocent tongues,*
> *My friend, you would not tell with such high zest*
> *To children ardent for some desperate glory,*
> *The old Lie: Dulce et decorum est*
> *Pro patria mori.*

As sunshine streamed through the cracked windows, and black boys and girls tried to grasp the seemingly overwrought language of a young English soldier, I asked if anyone could explain 'the old lie'.

Michael the Rasta, as usual, had done his research. His hand shot up first. But he looked shy when I nodded at him. 'It is Latin,' he said hesitantly.

'And what does it mean?'

'That it is sweet and right,' Michael said, piercingly, 'to die for your country.'

The way in which he said those words made me look down. I was not about to die but, soon, I would be without a country.

When it seemed as if the quietness would never end, Michael the Rasta cleared his throat. 'We are told it is sweet and right,' he said, 'but the men in this poem had a bad death.'

Those words, 'a bad death', sounded curiously poetic. I knew that young men like him, and probably most of the class in front of me, might be willing to die if it helped bring down apartheid. Their zeal and commitment would, in the end, overwhelm the white state. But, at the same time, they understood. Patriotism had meant little when soldiers, like the German and British men who had fought against and alongside Granddad George, 'die as cattle'.

After the lesson, once the class had emptied and I'd gathered up my books, Michael stepped back into the classroom. As if I was down to my last hours rather than weeks in Soweto, he stretched out his hand. I took it and he said: 'We know why you must go . . .'

Soldiers had already begun to enter townships around the country as the South African Defence Force moved to quell early signs of another student uprising. I did not have to tell Michael that I could not return to Soweto less than a year later in an army uniform, carrying a rifle, walking slowly towards the defiant students of Bop High. He understood.

'Anyway,' he said, his eyes crinkling with amusement, 'you would not be such a good soldier. You would be better in the shebeen . . . looking at the girls . . .'

O N AN OTHERWISE ORDINARY Thursday in the winter of 1984, at the crossroads with Baragwanath Hospital, I turned right and headed down the dip towards Bop High. And then, out of the gloom, a township coal-cart crossed over the dirt road in front of my Escort. Pulled by a big grey horse, covered in a light sheen of coal dust, the cart had just deposited the last of its early morning load.

The image seemed to belong to a different age, a Dickensian world of soot and hardship, and I knew I would labour the point when I saw dad that night. He might be the man responsible for electrifying white South Africa but, in a dingy corner of the township, there was little light and heat. Soweto was a dark world, only partly electrified, and it relied on the battered old cart-horses and their supply of coal on winter mornings.

My reverie was interrupted by the shocking sight of a white

soldier peering down at me. A rifle was slung across his back and he looked confused, staring at me, in his brown uniform. I turned away, not wishing any confrontation, and drove around the stationary coal-cart. The black driver had put down his whip and begun to untether the huge old horse. I watched them in my rear-view mirror. The soldier was talking animatedly to the man, pointing in the direction of my car.

It was a smoggy morning, for the biting cold meant even more coal fires had been lit long before dawn as black families awoke at the start of another June day. The pollution spread an eerie pall across the township, with the bright sunshine that lit up Johannesburg turned a ghostly grey in Soweto.

After I had parked in my usual prominent slot at school, because only a few of the teachers could afford a car, I grabbed a coffee and sauntered to my first classroom. It was a lesson with my Standard Tens and only a few students had arrived. I said my hellos, sat down at my desk and worked out my teaching plan in the five minutes left before school started.

And then, out of nowhere, the same soldier appeared. He sat on the grey horse, having left the cart behind with the coal man. His rifle was still strapped to his back. The sooty old horse stood, nostrils flaring, at the open door to my class. Steam curled from its ashen flanks, and uncertainty crossed the face of the soldier, as they stood there silently, man and horse.

I was not sure if they had come to arrest anyone, or shoot someone, and I felt paralyzed as the horse moved forward slowly. Its hooves echoed against the classroom floor. Eventually, the horse and the soldier were just a few feet from my desk. He was younger than me, the army boy, twenty-one at most, and he looked just as frightened as me.

For some reason he decided to inch the horse forward, moving towards the first narrow aisle of wooden desks. There was little space for the horse to turn. The tension in a near-empty classroom felt raw. I could not imagine what might happen next. And then, being smarter and wiser than any of us, Michael the Rasta began to read from the open book on his desk.

We were due to study *The Wild Swans at Coole* by Yeats and, typically, Michael had arrived early to prepare. The opening lines, read in his booming voice, echoed around that wintry classroom:

> *The trees are in their autumn beauty,*
> *The woodland paths are dry,*
> *Under the October twilight the water*
> *Mirrors a still sky;*
> *Upon the brimming water among the stones*
> *Are nine-and-fifty swans*

The Afrikaans soldier listened to the Irish poetry falling from the mouth of a Soweto dissident. And then, as if on cue, the big horse, less gracefully than any of Coole's fifty-nine wild swans, backed up the aisle as the reading continued of how 'those brilliant creatures' had not grown old despite the passing of the years.

Slowly, hesitantly, the soldier turned the horse around at the front of the class and click-clacked out of the room as Michael read on, wondering, in Yeats's voice, what he might feel:

> *. . . when I awake some day*
> *To find they have flown away?*

Responding to Michael the Rasta's nerveless reading, we brought our hands together in spontaneous applause. Then, I walked to the doorway and peered out. The soldier and the horse had already begun to disappear into the murk of another Soweto morning. He headed out of the school gates, presumably having satisfied himself that I really was just an English teacher rather than a political revolutionary. I hoped he would return the horse to its owner, even if the exhausted beast looked too weary to pull another load of coal.

A different student, Gibson, joined me at the door. He shook his head at all we had just seen.

'Trouble is coming,' he said softly, pointing towards the fading soldier. 'Big trouble ...'

O{N MY LAST SUNDAY} in South Africa, Joshua Sepheto arranged a farewell party for me. He held it at his house because none of us wanted to have a last day together in any of our old Soweto shebeens. We felt too sober, and in no mood for celebrating, when a small convoy headed out to Sebokeng, the township where Josh lived with his family.

It was a typical winter's afternoon on the Highveld, warm and sunny with a pale blue sky stretched out in a languid haze. Our chatter was muted because everyone knew how I felt with just five days left in the country.

But, once we had arrived, Josh and Shorty and Moses kept plying me with 'one more nip to keep us sweet'. Shorty laughed: 'Hell, my *bra*, we've had a hell of a time together.'

When I now see the photographs they took that day, it's possible to see that, on the inside, I was being wrenched open.

Another of my friends, Thandi, a young English teacher at Bop High, led me into a secluded alcove and, innocently, kissed me on the cheek. 'Honey asked me to say goodbye,' she murmured. 'Remember what she said?'

'Under our skin ...' I said as I kissed Thandi, and South Africa, goodbye.

'Yes, baby,' Thandi murmured, drawing me closer to her. 'We're all the same ...'

We GATHERED AROUND the dining-room table in our family home on the night before I flew away. This was the moment we had dreaded, the moment which my father, in a bitter argument, had once said would define our failure as a family and as South Africans. The idea that I would pack up and turn my back on the country and my parents had seemed like a betrayal of them. But mom and dad loved me, and had decided it was best to let me go.

My little mother might have felt like she was cracking apart, but on the surface she remained calm. She had packed my two suitcases methodically, having already taken me shopping the week before so that she could buy me a winter coat and boots to ward off the big freeze I would face in London later that year.

Mom and dad knew how much we would lose. They were already preparing to sell our old family home, and to move to a smaller townhouse. Heather and I would both be gone and we would never fill their home with children for weekend meals, during school holidays or at Easter and Christmas. The big house would always feel empty as my parents grew old on their own.

We did not speak of the unlikely prospect that I would ever return. Apartheid seemed so embedded that it would take decades before we were free from it, if ever. And so I knew they were much more courageous than me in choosing to remain in the country.

Looking into the unknown, and about to be separated from their children by six thousand miles, it was hard for them to imagine the best still lay ahead. They could not help but wonder, especially my mother, if the sweetest days for our family did not already belong to the past. I was young and reckless, and I thought mainly of myself rather than them, of the future rather than the past. But they knew that's how it should be when you're twenty-three, if not always.

'Granddad George was also twenty-three when he left Scotland for South Africa,' dad said.

George McRae had lied about his age when he'd snuck into the British army as a voluntary conscript on 5 August, 1914. Seventy years later, on 3 August, 1984, I would abandon South Africa to avoid military conscription. I did not feel brave, unlike the teenage Scot who eventually became my grandfather. In 1914, a sixteen-year-old boy from Aberdeen had confronted war with certainty. He had survived the countless trench battles and then left Britain for South Africa.

Dad, looking on the bright side as always, said I would complete the circle by reversing his father's journey.

The circle, however, felt broken.

I went to bed early, unable to stop myself thinking that this was the last time I would end a day in this house. I looked around my old room, stripped of my most important records and books. They had already been shipped to England. Everything was already changed, and I slipped into bed.

I lay awake in the dark, remembering my first night in this town, in this house, in this bed, listening to Samson's black gamblers in the dark until I got so scared I cried out to dad. The gambling ring had long since been shut down by the police and so the night was quiet and still. But I did not sleep much as I waited for the darkness to pass and the pale light of an African dawn to rise up over my old town.

Germiston, South Africa, 3 August, 1984

ON A LATE FRIDAY AFTERNOON, the sun sank low in the sky. I lingered a little longer. I could not bear the thought of my parents taking me to the airport and so Heather and Ross waited for me at the bottom of the driveway, in their blue VW Beetle.

I cuddled Ginny and George, the border collie and the black cocker spaniel we all loved, knowing I would never see them again. And then I turned to Wilson, our gardener, and Maria, our maid. An hour earlier they had welcomed Joshua Sepheto to our house. Josh had travelled from Soweto to say goodbye to me in Germiston. But, being kind and thoughtful, he said his farewell before it was time for me to leave my parents. I took Maria and Wilson by the hand and said goodbye. They retreated to her backroom, to the backroom where Maggie Thabang had once lived.

I looked at my parents. I held my mother, and then turned to my father, and put out my hand. He pulled me towards him. Dad kissed me on the cheek, which was something he had not done since I was a small boy.

'Look after yourself,' he said, before murmuring the same Zulu words he had used on the morning I started teaching in Soweto: *'Hambe kachle'* (Go well).

I turned away from them and the old house. My mother wrote to me later to say how she could hardly bear to see the way I bowed my head, as if broken, when I walked to the car.

But, reaching the door, I called out to them. My dad looked so tall and my mom so small, as they stood together at the garden gate. 'I'll write often,' I said. 'I promise.'

Dad lifted his hand as my mother's face crumpled. The Beetle's engine spluttered into life.

The car drove down the tree-lined length of Cachet Road, where I had lived most of my life. I did not lean out of the window to wave goodbye to my parents, or to anyone else. I looked down instead. Heather and Ross were also quiet, and I knew we felt the same.

At the T-junction, we turned right towards the airport. I gazed at the long line of black men and women walking towards the non-white bus stops and the train station as they headed home to the townships for the weekend. As the dented old Beetle picked up speed, the roadside figures became ghostly in the dusk, blurring as my eyes filled with the meaning of my leaving.

The army in Soweto in 1987, as Ian McRae prepares to enter
the township and become Mr Electricity

CHAPTER TWENTY

MR ELECTRICITY &
THE LITTLE GENERAL

O N A C O L D A N D R A I N Y Friday night in 1987 Ian McRae and
Moses Metsweni, his driver, descended into the depths of an
underground car park below the Johannesburg Sun Hotel. They
would meet their contact on the lowest level of the imposing concrete building and then travel into Soweto, because the man had
agreed to help them. The Reverend Peter Storey, however, was no
ordinary man. He helped families of detainees and all those who
came to him feeling lost in a country trapped in a State of
Emergency for two years.

Storey was a radical preacher of faith, delivering sermons of equality and justice from the pulpit at the Central Methodist Church, close
to where Ian and Moses waited in their darkened car. He had reiterated the risk they would face that night, especially if they were
caught in the midst of a clandestine township meeting with the
banned African National Congress. Nelson Mandela had been in jail

for twenty-three years and the ANC, whom he personified, were the most feared enemy of apartheid. Ian McRae, as the chief executive of Eskom, the state electricity supply company, could lose more than his job if the security police intercepted them.

There was as much uncertainty in trying to gauge the possible response of the militant black comrades of the struggle. How might they react when given the chance to be alone in Soweto with the white leader of a government-owned public utility? The ANC had, from its various bases in exile, called for the townships to be rendered 'ungovernable'. People's Courts had been set up, and retribution was meted out to black government employees or police informers. In extreme cases they were 'necklaced'. A human body being burned alive, by a dirty rubber tyre around the neck, was a savage reply to decades of white oppression.

The State of Emergency had come into force two winters before, on 20 July, 1985, when Prime Minister P.W. Botha resolved to crush resistance. Soldiers and armoured vehicles called Casspirs had invaded the townships, while the security police were given unprecedented powers. In the first eleven months of the State of Emergency, 2,436 people were detained without trial under the Internal Security Act.

On 12 June, 1986, four days before the tenth anniversary of the Soweto students uprising, the government extended the State of Emergency from its initial remit of thirty-six magisterial districts. The whole of South Africa, even the previously most peaceful corners of a vast and beautiful land, was in a permanent State of Emergency. Curfews could be implemented without any need to refer to the constitution or parliament. The police could also arrest anyone who called for strike action or tried to organize opposition to apartheid.

By the middle of 1987, over 25,000 people had been detained under emergency rule.

Resistance could still not be quelled. The most dynamic dissent was led by the United Democratic Front which, since its inception in 1983, had gathered together three million supporters. They formed the UDF's 'united front' of trade unions, churches, civic associations and student organizations to campaign against apartheid.

Peter Storey was close to both the UDF and ANC leadership. Ian McRae, however, was simply a man who believed in equality and the surging power of electricity.

By December 1984 Ian had lost both his children. His son had gone first, that August, and, four months later, his daughter and her husband also disappeared overseas. Heather and Ross left in the late afternoon of the same day in which Ian was asked to become the new chief executive of Eskom. The offer had come unexpectedly, and, being a religious man, he accepted it as a sign that a way had been found to fill the hole that had opened up inside him and his wife, Jess.

They had left the great old white house where the family had lived together in Germiston since 1967. Their new home, a small and functional townhouse in the suburb of Bedfordview, was just around the corner from where Auret van Heerden's parents lived. It often seemed unbearably quiet. In an attempt to get over their loss, which seemed akin to a death in the family, they worked even harder. Ian's new position consumed them both because the Chief Executive of Eskom was a role of national significance. It made him one of the most powerful men in the country, and he and Jess travelled extensively around South Africa and abroad.

Jess, remembering the old family joke, still called his briefcase 'Bertie'. When Ian brought Bertie back from the office, work transfixed him. It helped cover the ache of absence. But over dinner, with just Jess for company, or in bed at night when the lights were out and they wondered aloud how their son and daughter were coping so far from home, he was beset by difficult questions.

He felt troubled, at the age of fifty-eight, by the reasons for his children leaving South Africa, and anxious for the future. Ian thought often of the huge photograph spread across one wall of his plush office at Eskom's headquarters in the far north of Johannesburg. It had been given to him as a gift to honour the construction of a new power station. Against a canvas of blue sky, giant cooling towers and gleaming electrical plant shimmered in the distance. And yet, curiously, an African mud hut in the corner of the photograph always caught his eye. It was a black home without electricity, and its contrast with the lavish new power station haunted him.

Eskom supplied eighty per cent of the African continent's entire output of electricity, but just thirty per cent of the people in his own country had access to light and power. He had never forgotten the stories his son used to tell him of how Soweto, in the early mornings, resembled a Dickensian neighbourhood. Without electricity, people used coal fires for heat, and candles for light, so that the township was hidden by a dense pall. It was at its worst in the winter. In the freezing dawn Soweto seemed very dark. The sun eventually rose high in a cloudless sky to burn off the smog by noon, but those first few clogged hours every morning were a telling symbol of the differences between first world suburban comfort and powerless black South Africa.

At Eskom they called Jess 'The Little General'. When it came to rallying support for Ian's various causes, or setting up fund-raising or charity campaigns, she was a peerless organizer. And if she needed Eskom or some other corporate body to sponsor an orphanage or an old-age home, Jess kept at them until they relented. But, above all, The Little General had a heart.

Waiting underground with Moses, Ian remembered a different Friday night in their recent past. He had come home to find Jess fired up for change. She had been to the hairdresser's that morning, as she did every Friday, and a routine appointment to have her hair set in the usual style turned into a tangled, mind-changing hour. The black woman washing her hair had responded to an ordinary question about the upcoming weekend by revealing a sad story. She did not look forward to another two days in the Old Germiston Location. There was no running water, no electricity, no heating and no sanitation.

Normally, she smiled a lot at the sink and called every white lady 'madam' with apparent good cheer. But, that morning, the black woman looked weary and dispirited. Ian and Jess decided to drive into the township for the first time to see conditions for themselves.

The township occupied a filthy sprawl ten minutes from the centre of the white city where they had been born, educated, married and raised their children. Smooth tarred roads, linking the suburbs to the city, were replaced by a narrow maze of dirt streets littered with rocks and holes which made driving hazardous. Thousands of ramshackle tin huts were jammed against each other. Black children and adult squatters stared as the chief executive and his wife drove past in their gleaming white Mercedes.

The longer Ian looked the more he noticed the complete lack of street lighting and electricity cables. He could only imagine the darkness and danger at night. Ian could understand why the black woman washing his wife's hair had seemed so forlorn.

How much better might her life seem if she could turn on a light in the dark or plug a kettle into a socket? Those basic functions had become mindless in a white world. But they would appear magical in a place so devoid of light and power. Electricity could transform lives. And why should a code of colour be placed on its usage? Electricity was colourless.

Yet, even as the chief executive of a state utility, Ian McRae had no direct link to the people who needed electricity most. Eskom supplied electricity to the local councils who then distributed it to consumers of their choosing. Provincial politicians echoed the views Ian and Jess heard at dinner parties and business functions around the country. Whenever he had spoken of how he wished he could make electricity available to all, he had been greeted with derision. It was assumed that the black majority of South Africans didn't want electricity. Anyway, 'they' would never pay for their consumption of electricity. You couldn't trust 'them'.

When Ian and Jess left the Old Germiston Location it seemed plain you could only breed anger and revolt in such a world. Ian could not bring democracy, equality or peace to South Africa, but he was determined to offer electricity to everyone.

He moved quickly in the weeks that followed. Ian met first with Aggrey Klaaste, the new editor of *The Sowetan* newspaper. Klaaste had lived the typical life of a black South African under apartheid. One of eight children, whose father had worked at a gold mine in Johannesburg, his family had been forcibly removed from Sophiatown. Overflowing with gangsters and writers, musicians and activists, Sophiatown had occupied the black heart of white Johannesburg, and blurred the boundaries between racial groups. But, in 1955, the Klaaste family stood at the side of the road and watched their house being torn down before they were transported in government trucks, alongside thousands of others, to Soweto. In place of Sophiatown, which was flattened, a new white area was built. They called it Triomf, Afrikaans for Triumph.

Ian was struck by Klaaste's lack of bitterness and, instead, by his enthusiastic commitment to a new concept he called 'Nation Building'. Klaaste had not been deterred by his nine months in detention when, in 1977, he and Percy Qoboza, his fellow township editor of the influential *The World* newspaper, had been seized. He spoke more about the benefits of his education for he had been one of the last black students allowed to graduate at the University of the Witwatersrand, the same university which Ian and his children had attended. Such opportunities, Klaaste said, needed to be made available to all.

That heartfelt sentiment echoed Ian's commitment to Electricity for All. And so the editor and the engineer plotted an electrified future for black South Africa. It was essential, Klaaste stressed, that Ian met with the ANC to convey his vision that light and warmth should be brought to every township, rural *kraal* and shantytown.

Klaaste set up a meeting with an even more influential citizen of Soweto. Nthato Motlana was the most renowned black doctor in South Africa. A close friend of Mandela, Motlana had led the Soweto Council of Ten which took charge of the township after the 1976 student riots. Despite his temperate leadership, Motlana was detained for five months and the Committee of Ten became yet another banned organization under apartheid.

Motlana said of his own youth in the 1940s that: 'The attitude of whites was monstrous. They were boors, animals. We lived a life of subservience, obsequiousness and fear of the white man in a way nobody else can really understand. When you saw a white man, you saw God Almighty and you had to get out of his way. He could kick you, he could kill you and get away with it.'

In the 1940s, Ian McRae had lived a blissful life. He played soccer for Germiston Callies and sailed in a racing yacht at the local Victoria Lake Club. Ian loved going to dinner-dances at VLC and chatting up girls like his future wife, Jess, in the sunlit grounds of the lake. He did not really think much, then, about the fact that everything he loved was reserved for 'Whites Only'.

In the company of Klaaste and Motlana, in the dark and violent 1980s, Ian felt shamed by how much they had suffered. But there was no point feeling guilt-stricken. He had a chance to make a real difference to the lives of millions of black South Africans.

Dr Motlana was surprised. He had been convinced that Eskom was a government institution and it seemed strange that its chief executive should voice concern about a disadvantaged community's lack of electricity. But Ian's sincerity was plain and the doctor also advised him that he should obtain the ANC's backing for his radical proposals.

Ian knew that he would have to risk his career and, potentially, even his freedom and safety. Anyone caught collaborating with the ANC could expect to be detained. Ian was a measured yet compassionate man and he had not become a political agitator overnight. He was not seeking to overthrow the government but, rather, to find a way in which he could spread the light and power of electricity.

Treading across dangerous territory, Ian often felt uncertain. But the anguish he and Jess had been through steeled him. He could not turn back now because too much had happened, both personally and politically. And even if he and Jess had lost much, there was far more that they could still give.

Motlana could open the secret door to the ANC but, instinctively, Ian hoped for a discreet introduction. He was not sure how to proceed and so, for a brief time, he paused.

One Sunday night, in the winter of 1987, he and Jess went to a different church. They drove into central Johannesburg to listen to Peter Storey, the minister who was white South Africa's most public religious leader against apartheid. Storey was a powerful speaker, and his quiet certainty was persuasive. Listening to his sermon, hearing words of tolerance and compassion, Ian knew he had found his answer.

After the service, as they walked to the car, he put his hand on Jess's arm. She nodded when he said he felt compelled to turn back and speak to Storey. Jess waited alone in the car so that Ian and the minister might talk privately. It was better not to draw undue attention to themselves, especially as their home phone was already being bugged by the security police.

Peter Storey expressed his immediate support. But he reiterated the need for caution because there were police spies everywhere. Ian would also need to generate trust between him and a sceptical underground movement. Even with most of its leaders imprisoned on Robben Island, in exile or detained indefinitely without trial, the ANC remained a hierarchical organization. Ian would need to meet different strata of leaders before he finally spoke to those able to communicate personally with Mandela or Oliver Tambo. It would take months to build these bridges, with the threat of being caught escalating at every stage. Did he still want to proceed?

'Absolutely,' Ian said, speaking as one believer to another.

Storey said he would set up an initial meeting with the ANC. It would need to be at night, and deep in Soweto.

The two men shook hands and, a week later, the engineer waited for the minister in the appropriate setting of an underground car park.

Moses and Ian had arrived early, and they were comfortable in each other's company. After Jess, Moses had become Ian's closest confidant. Moses was always animated when he heard Ian talk about the way that electrifying black South Africa could reshape the country.

If he had been reluctant at first to accept Eskom's insistence that he should have a driver, he had come to value Moses in ways he would never have expected. Ian was so busy that the forty-minute journey to and from work became a time when he could work in the car or simply a chance for him to talk to an ordinary man. Moses was also invaluable when it came to describing the mood in the townships or amongst Eskom's black staff.

Their close relationship had been forged in the difficult days just before Moses's eldest son committed suicide, and the two fathers, together for so many hours, lamented their loss. Moses's son was dead, after he had failed to withstand the daily humiliations of life in black South Africa. Ian was luckier. His son was still alive, even if he lived six thousand miles away.

Ian remembered all the nights his son spent in the township, with friends, and how he had been transformed. His son was twenty-six and had been away from the country for three years. Ian looked at his watch. It was nearly 7 p.m. in Johannesburg, and almost six o'clock in London. On an English summer's evening, London would be light for a few more hours.

Soweto would be cast in deep darkness. Ian had never been into the township at night, and Moses's calm presence soothed him. He was about to enter a new world and he thought of his black secretary, a young woman from Soweto called Toy. Ian had never forgotten the Monday morning he had come into work and asked Toy if she'd had a good weekend.

'Oh, we had the most wonderful weekend,' Toy enthused. 'It was the best weekend in years.'

'Did you go partying?' Ian asked in amusement.

Toy looked at him wryly. 'No partying,' she said. 'It was wonderful because we did not hear one gun-shot. No-one got stabbed. We didn't see one police van. It was peaceful all weekend.'

Those were the moments which made Ian pause uneasily at the difference between black and white South Africa. But they also made him determined to push ahead with his radical plan.

Ian's reflections were interrupted when Moses spoke softly in the dark. 'He's here,' Moses said, pointing to the grey-haired figure of the Reverend Storey walking towards them.

'OK,' Ian said. 'We'll go nice and steady tonight, Moses, nice and steady . . .'

As Peter Storey slid into the back seat, smiling gently, murmuring his hellos, Moses turned the key in the ignition. He looked to the left and the right and then, satisfied they were not being watched, slid the automatic car into 'D' and, in a slow glide, aimed for the exit.

T HE THREE MEN – the executive, his driver and the minister – were dressed in black as the white car drove through the wet night towards Soweto. If they were stopped by a roadblock outside the township, Ian would talk to the officer in charge. He would know what to say when the moment came. The rain, however, had kept even the police off the road.

Their car swept deep into Soweto. As Peter Storey guided them through a muddied maze of dirt streets, they finally found the Soweto Methodist Church Hall where they were due to meet members of the ANC underground. Ian felt fraught with nerves but, also, curiously excited. He sensed that this could be a defining moment in his life.

There was always the danger that an informer would have tipped off the security police. The car was already surrounded, and Ian and Peter were hurried into the small hall.

Inside, the atmosphere was tense. The oppressive mood was accentuated by the fact that all the black men wore heavy overcoats. Looking like stone-faced hit-men in the candlelight, they silently watched Ian McRae get to his feet after a brief introduction from a local minister and then Reverend Storey, whom, at least, they trusted.

Ian suggested he might ask them a few informal questions first. This was his usual technique of breaking down the divide with his audience. He had done it often enough with his Afrikaans workers. But this was Soweto, and he was not in charge. A tall young black man in the front row raised his hand to stop the McRae flow. He had his own question to ask.

'What is your relationship with the government?' he asked of Eskom's chief executive.

Ian stressed he had come to Soweto as an individual, and not in his capacity as chief executive. No-one at Eskom, and certainly not in the government, even knew that he was in Soweto. Eskom was answerable to the state, but the government actually exerted little control over the utility.

The questioning comrade in the front row turned around, pointedly, to seek the reaction of an old man in a thick overcoat who stood at the back of the hall. Ian had noticed him as soon as they had arrived. He looked like a gangster. Ian learnt later that the man was Godfrey Moloi, the self-styled Godfather of Soweto who was famous for starting the first taxi firm in the township. Moloi was close to the ANC and he had been detained on numerous occasions. He liked to believe that he ran large sections of Soweto. Ian learnt later that the ANC had asked Moloi to decide whether or not the meeting should proceed on the basis of McRae's answer to that first loaded question.

As everyone stared at him, waiting for his reaction, The Godfather remained mute for a few moments.

And then Godfrey Moloi nodded with sombre emphasis. Permission was granted.

'This means a lot to me,' Ian said, 'and it will mean a lot to my family. We are not so different from you, except in some painful ways. We are privileged and have a plentiful supply of electricity, and you don't.'

A low murmur spread around the hall. Ian raised his hand and asked the men if an 'Electricity for All' programme might help bring about political change. Could a simple light switch and an electrical bulb transform black South Africa? Would people be willing to pay for such a small liberation, to have access to a kind of power white South Africa took for granted? Did they share his vision of Electricity for All?

The meeting was electrified as the same answer echoed again and again. 'Yes,' people said. 'Yes,' and, again, 'Yes.'

A pact was forged between the black underground and the white chief executive of Eskom to work together. All the men in that broken-down hall believed that, one day, apartheid would end. One day, even soon perhaps, they would all have light and power. One day they would all be free.

A N HOUR LATER the leaders took Peter Storey and Ian McRae to a private township house where, over a candlelit meal cooked on an open fire, they sat down together. The men told Ian of their fear that he might have been part of some sinister government plot.

'But then we saw you were different,' one of the men said. 'What changed you?'

Ian thought for a long while. He said that he had done nothing compared to men like Reverend Storey, who had fought on behalf of so many black and white detainees. It had taken him many more years to make this same journey into black South Africa.

'So, Mr Electricity,' another man persisted gently, 'why do you come now?'

'There are many reasons,' Ian said. 'But, you know, my son worked here, in Soweto, as a teacher. He told me what he had seen. He thought we were arguing but, in the end, we were simply agreeing. The country has to change. We all have to change. Tonight is just a first step ...'

Ian McRae told the men that electricity could transform the country. Most important of all, he said, he had listened to Reverend Storey. He knew they shared a faith. They both understood that people, whether they were black or white, were the same. And of course electricity, even under apartheid, was colourless.

The young man who had asked the first question of the night stretched out his black hand across the muted candle-light. And, when the chief executive of Eskom leaned over to clasp it with his own white hand, the black man smiled. His smile lit up an otherwise dark township room.

'Mr Electricity,' the black comrade said to Ian McRae, 'welcome to Soweto ...'

T HEY ARRANGED TO MEET AGAIN, a few weeks later, at the same Soweto Methodist Church Hall. But when Ian and John Bradbury, his trusted colleague in Eskom's distribution department, arrived at the hall with Moses they found only two ANC men. The Soweto comrades had received a tip-off that the security police planned to raid the area that night. Ian could imagine the following day's headlines if the chief executive of Eskom was caught in a meeting with the ANC. But, rather than abandon his journey entirely, he gave the men a brief update.

Ian stressed that he was determined to proceed with an Electricity for All campaign, despite any consequences he might face. The men appeared stunned by his confirmation, and suggested that he personally impart this information to the ANC's Soweto People's Delegation. Would he follow them to Frank Chikane's house?

Chikane, a high-profile spokesman against the government, had been detained and persecuted. But, entwined with the UDF, his opposition to apartheid remained.

'I'll be honoured to meet Reverend Chikane,' Ian said.

Chikane lived in one of the electrified areas of Soweto. But his neighbourhood was in total darkness when the small delegation from Eskom arrived. Once the reason for their visit had been established, Chikane laughed when asked how long his home had been without electricity.

'Three days,' the black minister said as he lit another candle.

Ian knew the outrage there would be if a black-out of a white suburb lasted three hours. Three days without electricity might be enough to start a white revolution.

'When do you expect your electricity supply to resume?' he asked Chikane.

The black minister smiled. He suggested that, in his position as chief executive, Ian might obtain an honest answer from the City Council, who distributed a small supply of electricity from Eskom to this corner of Soweto. Chikane was more positive in agreeing that the Soweto People's Delegation would meet Ian formally to plan a path to electrification. Another breakthrough had been made on a muddled night in the township.

The following morning Ian learnt that the security police and army had carried out separate raids in Soweto. But they had inadvertently run into each other and, in the confusion, shots had been fired.

A narrow escape concentrated Ian's mind. He eventually approached the Eskom board to explain his township venture. And yet, even when he received backing for his Electricity for All programme, he was still troubled by the prospect of being caught by the security police.

After another long night, punctuated with prayer, Ian rose at 5:30 the next day. He called General Joffel van der Westhuizen, a powerful figure in the security branch. Ian remembered that his own son, locked away in London, had written about the execution of the Craddock Four – Matthew Goniwe, Sparrow Mkhonto, Fort Calata and Sicelo Mhlauli – the brilliant quartet of UDF activists and teachers. They had been murdered, chillingly, in July 1985 on the Angolan border, on the express orders of van der Westhuizen, a good-looking Afrikaner and military leader.

Van der Westhuizen was notorious, but Ian McRae did not feel any need to vent ire or even pass judgement on the general. Ian believed he should talk to van der Westhuizen in the same direct and honest way he had spoken to Motlana and Chikane.

For a long time van der Westhuizen sat in his chair, looking squarely at Ian, as the impact of his work in the township echoed around the office.

Ian waited for the general's response. He felt extraordinarily calm.

'I should congratulate you,' van der Westhuizen finally said.

Ian trusted his judgement, and he believed the infamous general was being sincere.

'You are doing good work,' van der Westhuizen said. 'I think you should continue.'

That same afternoon, Ian telephoned Leon Wessels, the deputy minister of state security, to request an urgent meeting. Within ninety minutes, in a suite at Jan Smuts airport, a vision of Electricity for All was laid out to a politician charged with keeping South Africa in a seemingly permanent State of Emergency.

The man they now called Mr Electricity, in underground circles of Soweto, felt more surprise when Wessels said that the government would not oppose his work. The country, Wessels said, was about to enter a new phase and old certainties would have to change. Eskom could proceed without government or security police interference.

The two men, the Afrikaner and the English-speaking South African, shook hands. Despite his typical optimism, Ian McRae had been startled by the two Afrikaners he had met. He had always believed he would forge links in Soweto. But he had far less faith in the white men who had ruled the country for so long. He had assumed they would rise up and block him.

Ian felt strangely emotional as he left the airport late that afternoon. Electrifying work, at last, could really begin. A new country, ablaze with light and power, might yet emerge from the dark.

ALEXANDRA TOWNSHIP was even more dangerous and impoverished than Soweto. Its reputation, however, did not deter Jess McRae. She spent more and more time in Alex, driving in and out of the various township neighbourhoods, from 'Beirut' to the 'West Bank'. Those bullet-riddled nicknames had emerged in the wake of the 'Alex Six Days', when war gripped the township in February 1986.

Forty people had died as the comrades and the Alex Action Committee forced through People's Power and tried to wrest control from the old township council. Rent boycotts and mass funerals, necklacing and tear-gassing, spread among the 450,000 people crammed into eight square kilometres. The most vulnerable were the very young and the very old.

Jess McRae, in her late fifties, was still grieving the loss of her children. But, just like her husband was driven by a vision of electricity, Jess had become consumed by all that could be done in a township. She and her friend from Belgium, Elizabeth Lombarts, dared to believe they could build a modern care home for old people abandoned in Alex.

It was not easy. Even when they managed to form a small committee to raise the finances, none of the white men felt brave enough to enter Alex. And when Jess enticed overseas visitors to join her on a township tour, and to see the work being done on the home, her car was broken into and the army arrived. They insisted on using a dreaded yellow Casspir to escort her guests out of Alex. Jess had no choice and the giant armoured vehicle rumbled behind her. Afterwards, her relieved European visitors said they would dine out on their township story for years to come.

Jess became still more determined. Once the old age home had been built, and filled with people, she and Elizabeth established a nursery in Alex. It was possible to briefly forget all she had lost. But she was distressed by the death of black children around her, like a fourteen-year-old Alex girl cut down by the police as she stepped out of her family house. Jess could not imagine how she would have coped if she had lost one of her own children amid such carnage. And then, watching the parents stand by helplessly as the girl's funeral was turned into a political rally, she wondered how she would feel if her dead child became a symbol of the struggle.

She was struck by how little privacy Alex allowed its citizens in life and death. Jess saw how a large room had been divided by the police so that it housed ten families. A bare curtain separated one family from another. Children aged five or six simulated the sex they must have seen at night in a place devoid of personal boundaries.

Yet the old age home and the nursery were functioning, and Jess kept generating more income for both. Businessmen and financiers finally joined her in Alex. Jess and Elizabeth, and Father Cairns, whose church adjoined both home and nursery, would charm them with a tour and lunch in the township. It seemed surreal as Jess produced her immaculate 'finger lunches', offering decent wine as well, in a setting where the comrades and the army were at war a few blocks away. And when they needed to make an impression they would ensure that Ian appeared. He rarely failed to captivate people with the difference they could make in Alex.

Back in their townhouse in Bedfordview, there were still nights when Jess cried for what might have been. But she bristled whenever anyone criticised her son and daughter for leaving. It was more hurtful when some suggested their own children would never be so selfish. Her anger, then, choked off the threat of any more tears.

The letters from her son in London also helped. A couple arrived every week because the distance had, mysteriously, opened up a new intimacy between them. Her son seemed changed when he wrote to Ian and Jess. His letters were open and expressive in a way he had never allowed himself to be in his last years in South

Africa. Reading his letters about London, and a world of which they knew so little, they came to understand him more deeply.

They were also lucky that, owing to Ian's work, they travelled to London once a year, and so, usually in September, on days when the English sunshine was at its most beautiful, they saw each other again in person. It was hard to cram so much into a few days together, and the pain felt raw every time they said goodbye.

The letters kept coming, week after week, month after month, year after year, cataloguing so many little details that gave shape to life in a very different country. Their son wrote for the *NME*, the paper he had read ardently for years, and had begun to work on his first book. He had lost a girlfriend, found another, survived with barely any money, and learnt more in two years than he would have done in a decade at home. They wrote with similar intimacy but, for a long while, they had to keep secret the work that Ian did in Soweto. Even when he had been to see the security police and the government, and even when the State of Emergency finally ended and F.W. de Klerk replaced P.W. Botha as leader and began to discuss the release of Nelson Mandela, Ian remained cautious in letters which could be intercepted.

Ian McRae's son did not really know the impact of the work he had done in Soweto, and across the whole of the country, and up into southern and even east Africa. He met the leaders of Angola and Mozambique, Zimbabwe and Zambia, Zaire and Kenya to offer his vision of a high-voltage power grid that connected Eskom with the whole of the sub-continent. Mr Electricity had seen a way that light and power could spread from previously darkened townships like Soweto and Alexandra, in the dying days of apartheid, up into neighbouring countries. He even carried hopes of linking the entire African continent in a united electrical grid system and travelled to Egypt in the far north to discuss the possibilities.

It was only years later that Ian told his son and daughter the full story of everything that had happened, as he talked about electricity to men he did not always admire, like Robert Mugabe and Mobute Sese Seko, while doing his utmost to convey how their countries might still work together to develop an electrical grid and a spirit of co-operation. Eskom had the resources to set up an inter-connected power grid. Countries could tap into the supply to undertake extensive electrification programmes or to correct power and voltage loss in times of drought. Ian became exasperated only when some black leaders, echoing their despised white counter-parts who had upheld apartheid, replied that many of their people had no need or even desire for electricity.

He then always asked one question of the prime minister, pres-ident or dictator opposite him: 'What is the greatest threat to your country?'

Every time, except once, the answer was the same: 'Poverty.'

The exception was still linked to the same theme. President Daniel Arap Moi, who led Kenya from 1978 to 2002, told Ian that, 'the poverty of my neighbours is our greatest threat'.

Each time, as he wrote in his later years, Ian had a ready reply: 'I suggested that the President could go a long way to combating the threat if he embarked on an extensive programme of electrifi-cation, as an electric plug point and an electric power light bulb improved the quality of life of the most poor. It also created an energy base for economic growth. I then received an inevitable lec-ture on the evils of apartheid. I agreed with him. Apartheid had to go and, in fact, I already knew it would not last much longer. A new South Africa was imminent. Nelson Mandela would soon be free and he, of all men, would believe in Africans working together for a better future with no idea of profit or personal gain in mind. "Electricity for All" was no longer just applicable to South Africa. It was a vision that suited the whole of Africa.

'So I had not come to his Presidential palace to discuss politics –

but to present a vision for the region which had the potential to create economic growth through the provision of a reliable energy base. This plan would put his country in a position to buy and sell electricity and develop its resources and hydro-potential against the enduring threat of both drought and poverty.'

Ian McRae had grown from the white South African who used to call every black man he met 'John', because he thought it was more polite than just yelling 'boy'. He and his wife, Jess, were no longer quite the same people who had once insisted that the mugs and plates and knives and forks of their black servants, their maids and gardeners, should be kept separate.

Ordinary stories touched Ian the most. 'Elandskraal, an average black village in the Marble Hall area of Lebowa, has been electrified,' he wrote. 'One of the men who had lived in this village had worked in a bakery near Johannesburg for a time, and then he baked bread in Elandskraal over an open fire. But after electrification, when I visited Elandskraal some years later, he had borrowed money and installed two electric ovens in a brick building. He told me he was now baking bread twenty-four hours a day, seven days a week, except for when he shut down the ovens for cleaning. He employed six or seven people for deliveries. He was about to start making pies, cakes and other baked goods. A major door had opened and he was now running a successful business. He told me that electricity was the greatest gift he had ever received.'

Ian and Jess visited Orange Farm, an expanding black area which catered for the overflow of people from Soweto in the north to Sebokeng in the south. Even when there were a thousand houses in Orange Farm there was no electricity and no running water, apart from a lone stand-pipe in the street. Sanitation consisted of a sewage bucket system. A small building, which had once been a stable, was meant to be Orange Farm's school. But there were too many children and they had to be taught out in the open, on dirt tracks and under the shade of a few trees. Ian watched two pupils hold up a large piece of cardboard so that it could be used as a blackboard.

The Transvaal Provincial Association [TPA], which was responsible for Orange Farm, reacted negatively to his suggestion that the area should be electrified. 'They told me that people living at Orange Farm did not want electricity,' Ian wrote. 'It was not a priority for them and, in fact, they would not pay for it. This was the opposite of what I had heard in Orange Farm itself. All the community leaders and ordinary people I spoke to had given me the same answers I'd heard at my first meeting in Soweto. They wanted electricity, desperately, and they would pay if the service was good and prices were fair.'

Ian dragooned the TPA into touring the area with him, so that they could hear the views of the people themselves, and then he brought the white officials and black community leaders together. 'At the meeting,' he wrote later, 'I said that Eskom could initially electrify a portion of the township – say 500 houses – and we could reassess the situation afterwards and decide if we should complete the remainder of Orange Farm. I also said we would arrange to fit some windows in the "school" and install electric lighting. I secretly knew we would do much more, but I needed to secure agreement for this first step from TPA. After some discussion their representatives agreed to our proposal, while making it very clear that they would not be responsible for any costs of maintaining the reticulation.'

Within weeks electricity hummed and pulsed through Orange Farm, illuminating and galvanizing the area, even before Ian and Jess were asked to officiate at the formal 'switching-on' ceremony, which culminated in the symbolic lighting of a Christmas tree as they were surrounded and then almost swamped by singing and ululating black women.

One of the women drew them aside. She proudly led them to the new freezer she had somehow managed to find. Inside, it was stacked with ice lollies.

'It is a miracle,' she told Mr Electricity and The Little General. 'Before, I could never give my children an ice lolly. And now we have them. We have ice lollies ...'

She made it sound as if they had freedom, too, in the way she had already started a small business which sold ice lollies all over the hot and dusty streets of Orange Farm.

In that moment, each with a coloured ice lolly in their hands, Ian and Jess looked at each other, remembering their children and all those summer days of the past.

We had our memories, and proof of how they had shaped us, just like everything that seemed so magical or monstrous about South Africa had made us who we were, as the country prepared to celebrate the release of Nelson Mandela and tens of thousands of other political prisoners. Apartheid, finally, was almost at an end.

Licking their lollies in a sunlit corner of Orange Farm, my parents spoke of the letters they would write that evening to London. They would share that small moment with us, as a family divided and separated but, somehow, still together.

Ian McRae electrifies Orange Farm, 1996

PART V

AT LAST . . .

At last, in the second decade of a different century, with more than half my life spent in another country, it is easy to appreciate the work of Mr Electricity. The fact that he is my father once complicated that understanding, as did the memory that, for a long time, we had fought over the South African army. Having begun our lives together in white towns like Witbank and Germiston, I was often reluctant to see how much his work had transformed over the decades.

The secrecy around his electrification programme was finally peeled away and, eventually, his achievement seemed as radical as it was immense. I had spoken more than anyone in our family about hating apartheid but my parents, Ian and Jess, actually instigated some change in Soweto, Alexandra, Orange Farm and beyond. They made a difference to the lives of many.

There were numerous moments of surprise along the way. I remember my sister telling me how she had been called at work in London in 1987. A man with an undisguised South African accent spoke threateningly of how our family was being watched. Heather was told that the security police knew everything our father was doing in the townships. They also knew everything I had done in Soweto and were taking careful note of my writing about South Africa and interviewing members of the ANC in London. She was told we all needed to be very careful.

Even though this was a few months before our dad met the security police and the government to tell them about his plans to electrify black South Africa, he reacted calmly when we met in London. He knew his phone at home was tapped and he appeared unaffected by Heather's disconcerting call. But he did not to reveal to us everything that he still planned.

I only began to recognize the extent of his impact when, in February 1993, I read a story in the *Financial Mail* which speculated that, following his release, Nelson Mandela might ask Ian McRae to be his first Minister of Energy in a transitional cabinet to steer South Africa through its first post-apartheid years. Dad was amused because he was no politician, but he was far more thoughtful when detailing his private meetings with Mandela and Cyril Ramaphosa, who was then the leader of Cosatu [the Congress of South African Trade Unions]. He liked and admired both men and, for me, reading letters about dad's conversations with Mandela and Ramaphosa meant even more than the newspaper cutting I was sent soon afterwards.

Nine years since leaving South Africa, I sat in my girlfriend's flat in Southfields, less than a mile from the grass courts of Wimbledon. Alison was English and she had yet to visit South Africa. She did not really understand the significance when I read that cutting. It came from *The Star*, and confirmed that on 24 August, 1993, the Minister of Defence, Kobie Coetzee, announced the abolition of compulsory military conscription for white South African men. Seeing it in black and white, in the old familiar typeface of a Johannesburg newspaper, I paused for a long time.

It seemed as if my whole life had been shaped by the army. Even when I escaped South Africa it still lingered over me. Each summer in England I'd travelled to Lunar House, in Croydon, to the Department of Immigration, to hear whether or not a visa to extend my stay another year would be granted. In that Kafkaesque building, where immigrants like me queued before 5 a.m. so we would make it through the doors and be issued a small yellow or white ticket with a number on it, I thought repeatedly about the army and why I could not return to South Africa.

I always wrote detailed letters to the Home Office, and sometimes I had immigration lawyers check their validity because it was never easy to predict the reaction of an officer at Lunar House, in a country led by Margaret Thatcher and her Conservative government. Of course I was lucky every time. In a room packed with people from China and Africa, eastern Europe and the Indian subcontinent, I saw the relief on the faces of most immigration officers when my number was barked over a public address system. I was white. English was my first language. I even had a name which was undeniably Scottish. All four of my grandparents were Scots. My parents were both British passport-holders, as was my sister, and so I was granted another year every time. It never took the immigration men more than a few minutes to have a chat with me before they reached for the stamp and banged down a visa extension on a new page of my South African passport.

By 1993 I had only one more year to remain in the UK to gain a ten-year residency permit, and so all the tension had seeped away. And perhaps it was for that reason that I could look up calmly when Alison, whom I would marry eighteen months later, asked me how I felt after that last barrier to my returning home had been removed. She had always said that she would live with me in South Africa if the day came, but I knew something inside me had changed.

My first book had just been published in Britain. *Nothing Personal* was a book about prostitution in London, and a surreal kind of magic seeped from a grimy subject as it led my wife to me. As an architectural student, working on a post-graduate design based around the sex industry, Alison bought my book and tracked me down.

The chances of our otherwise meeting were minuscule but a book about the London sex industry brought a South African draft-dodger and a Home Counties girl together. Out of such strangeness, Alison and I soon knew we would marry each other and spend the rest of our lives together. I knew that, even when apartheid ended, I was never going to leave her for a country.

Alison eventually accepted an offer to expand her architectural brothel into a full-scale one-woman art installation at a Bloomsbury gallery, which had once been a horse hospital. The cobble-stone floors, iron hooks and a giant space devoted to the care of sick horses in the Victorian era allowed her to develop a site-specific art show. Eskom, and my parents, played a key role as Alison sub-verted the usual trick of London prostitutes who covered telephone booths with cards advertising their sexual services and telephone numbers.

Alison built a wall in her exhibition space devoted to a brightly coloured parody of both those telephone box ads and more tradi-tional businessmen's cards. They were easy to design, but to really make an impact she needed some photographs of middle-aged men.

Jess McRae, her future mother-in-law, came up with the answer. Ian might have just retired as chief executive and become the Regulator of the electricity industry in South Africa, but his influ-ence in Eskom was still plain. So Jess, The Little General, telephoned the head of personnel at Eskom in Johannesburg and asked if he could help supply a hundred-odd black-and-white pass-port photo images of the company's engineers and managers. She said, rather airily, that it was for an art project for her son's fiancée in London. Jess skirted the fact that the men's faces would cover an entire wall in an installation about prostitution.

I knew some of the men, for their names had echoed through-out my childhood as dad took urgent calls at home from Bruce

Crooks and Bussie Els, Paul Semark and Len TeGroen. And I helped write the logos printed in bold black typeface alongside their smiling South African faces.

'Oh look, here's Bruce Crooks,' my mother said later as she pointed to a senior Eskom executive who wore glasses and boasted a big white beard. She laughed when she saw the words written next to his beaming face: *'Moses' (50) Bible Salesman. Sinner Seeks Divine Retribution.*

'And there's Paul Semark,' dad murmured, seeing the familiar face of the man responsible for Koeberg, South Africa's nuclear power station. In Alison's world, he had been transformed by the words which now described him differently: *MILDRED: Mature Transvestite Offers Dungeon Cleaning Service.*

I had gained still more insight into my parents, and I was shocked they could be so helpfully deviant. 'But what if they find out?' I asked dad of the Eskom gallery of rogues.

'I've told Bruce and Paul that they're among the star attractions … ' my dad replied.

'Weren't they angry?'

'Of course not,' dad shrugged. 'They just laughed. They're very tolerant men …'

Dad, in his positive way, suggested that a new depth of tolerance had emerged in South Africa. After years of hatred and prejudice we were about to enter an era of hope in the Rainbow Nation.

Those words seem hopelessly romantic now. South Africa is, once more, a complicated and often fraught country, if fascinating and remarkable as well. But, then, in 1995, my dad seemed as right as he was sage.

Later that year, South Africa won the rugby World Cup and Nelson Mandela entranced the nation by wearing a Springbok shirt given to him by the team's Afrikaans captain, Francois Pienaar, in a saga Clint Eastwood eventually turned into a Hollywood film.

Alison and I had just got married as we watched the rugby in Southfields and danced around and got drunk and called my parents back in South Africa to celebrate the moment.

Later that year I took Alison to South Africa for the first time. She met all my friends, including the many who had fled the country to escape the army and, unlike me, had since returned to live in the new South Africa. There was violence and crime, but I was thrilled to be back. Alison also loved the country and, even when I had to return to London, she stayed on for a few days longer with my parents.

I was then deep into my second book which, still rolling around in the gutter, was about boxers I knew in America and Britain. My life, and my writing, had begun to find shape in a way that would not have unfolded quite so easily in Johannesburg.

Alison called me on the first night of my return to London and told me about the unforgettable afternoon she'd spent with my mother, driving into Alex to see the nursery they had built. She said she'd wanted to cry when the little black kids sang to her and Jess.

My new English wife, who had led such a different and more sheltered life, understood a little more clearly what had happened to me, my family and our country.

'It was painful,' Alison said of some of the sights she had seen in Alex, and of the contrast they presented to the high walls and verdant green gardens of white suburbia. 'But, as soon as your mother and these little children started to sing together, it was also very beautiful ...'

I FELT A SIMILAR RESONANCE when meeting Auret van Heerden and Liz Floyd. As I began writing this book, I emailed Auret, who had been tortured and detained in the cell opposite Neil Aggett during the last days before his death in February 1982. More than thirty years later, the memory of that time seems locked away in gritty black-and-white images. But, with Auret in London, hearing of his work with the Fair Labor organization around the world, as he strives to help workers in a way that Neil would have approved of, I felt I was back in South Africa in the 1980s. He spoke without sentimentality or anger as, in stark but moving language, he described everything that had happened to him and Neil. Auret explained his complicated relationship with his Afrikaans torturers and the impact his detention had had on him and his family.

We discovered how close our parents had lived to each other. And it helped to talk about why we had not returned to South Africa. Auret's wife was Croatian and they had met in 1991 when their countries were in the midst of deep transformation. 'We both understand conflict,' Auret smiled wryly, 'we both understand issues of ethnicity and race. But there seemed a lot less hate in South Africa than there was in Yugoslavia. We spoke about that a lot in the early days.'

It took Auret years to open up the emotional shutters he had sealed in detention, as a way of warding off vulnerability. Yet, in all our conversations and email exchanges, I'm always struck by his openness and generosity. When I emailed him one morning, after a long spell of writing, to tell him that I was nearing the end of this book, he answered me within minutes. Amid his typical enthusiasm and warmth he wrote, 'It must have been a really emotional journey . . .'

I smiled then, setting my little tale against his epic saga. My story is nothing compared to his, which is why I think now about people whose stories are far more significant than mine: Auret van Heerden, Liz Floyd, Neil Aggett, Barbara Hogan and, even, Ian and Jess McRae.

Auret had not seen Barbara Hogan since she had been detained with him in 1981, and imprisoned for treason early the following year. But they were in regular Facebook contact. He found that as amusing and heartening as the fact that, when Auret and I first met, Barbara had just become South Africa's Minister of Energy. She was soon addressing a conflict in Eskom, my dad's old company, which seemed in a state of perpetual crisis.

'Your story seems to have come full circle,' Auret said.

The circle felt complete when I spent a Saturday afternoon in Kensington, one of Johannesburg's prettier old neighbourhoods, with Liz Floyd. We sat in her kitchen, drinking mugs of tea, and I told her about this book and all she and Neil had meant to me. And she, in turn, told me about her life in post-apartheid South Africa. Liz, unlike me and Auret, had never left the country. She spoke with vivid authority about continuing problems that needed to be resolved. As the chief medical officer in the giant province of Gauteng, Liz had a demanding job. But she seemed to relish the battle. I was impressed by the way in which, unlike me, she had let the past slip away to immerse herself in the present.

Liz asked me about my dad and his work in South Africa. She made me believe it was worth writing about Mr Electricity because, after all, he was more than just my father.

I told Liz about the day when, soon after he became the Regulator, at the request of Nelson Mandela, dad's phone at home rang. A voiced boomed out: 'Hello, granddad . . .'

My dad had not become a grandfather yet, for the first of our three children, Bella, was only born in 1999. So he hesitated at the sound of a black voice calling him 'granddad . . .'

'It's Mr Khumalo,' the man at the other end of the phone eventually cackled. 'I want to invite you back to Orange Farm. I want you to come here to see the fruits of the seeds you and I planted years ago. You must come, granddad.'

Mr Khumalo was the principal of the school in Orange Farm where, before electrification, they taught their pupils outside and used cardboard boxes for blackboards. He had asked dad to help him convert some old chicken coops and stables into electrified classrooms which could accommodate a few hundred children.

Three new schools had eventually been established. 'But there is more, granddad, much more . . .' Mr Khumalo promised.

When my parents arrived in Orange Farm they found that Mr Khumalo and his community had built seven additional schools.

'You gave us the light bulb of the idea, granddad,' Mr Khumalo said.

'Orange Farm,' dad said later, 'epitomised Electricity for All.'

Mr Khumalo was killed the following year, just another victim of the violence and tragedy that continued long after apartheid ended.

But even now, in their early eighties, Ian and Jess McRae remain vibrant and hopeful about the future. They never doubt how right they were to stay in South Africa, just as they do not judge me or my sister for remaining on another continent, six thousand miles away.

Yet the pain we feel, every time we part, is still vivid. Whenever it happens I think of Moses Metsweni. The last time I visited South Africa on my own, Moses, my dad's old driver, came to see me. We sat in my parents' lounge, drinking coffee out of ordinary cups rather than the enamel type that would have once been reserved for the black men and women, the adult 'boys' and 'girls', who worked in our home.

Moses did not need to be polite. He could be direct because his own son had killed himself in the dark days of apartheid. 'When are you coming home?' Moses asked me bluntly that afternoon.

I launched into my usual explanation that my work was in London, and my wife and children were all English.

'You must bring them here,' Moses said quietly. 'You must come home to your parents.'

When I said I could not return, for too much had happened in my life away from South Africa, Moses nodded quietly. He did not offer me comfort. Instead, he spoke almost sternly.

'You must honour your parents,' he said. 'Your mother,' he reminded me, 'is a great lady. And your father, your dad, belongs to us. We call him *"Ubaba wethu futhi engiu baba wongezi iAfrika yonke..."'*

I waited for Moses, immaculate in his black suit, to translate his words into English. He paused, as if he wanted me to try and decipher the meaning for myself. And then, with a smile, as he stretched out his hands to clasp mine, he said: 'He is our father, our father of Africa...'

Moses held my hands fast. 'I am proud to call him my friend,' he said earnestly. 'You must be proud to call him your father...'

Ian McRae and Moses Metsweni, 2010

ACKNOWLEDGEMENTS

My parents, Ian and Jess McRae, and my sister, Heather Simpson, deserve my deepest thanks for the understanding way in which they allowed me to write about them when remembering some of the more difficult years we shared. It wasn't easy describing them, or showing them the first few drafts, but they always responded with typical generosity and patience.

I also owe my mother and father much for putting up with my delinquent years in South Africa – and, even though it caused us all pain, for helping me find another life in a different country. Hopefully the preceding pages help explain why they have been extraordinary parents – and people.

I used to call my sister 'Small' when we lived in South Africa but she has been a giant presence in my life – especially in the early 1980s when I always turned first to her and her husband, Ross. Heather also read these pages and helped clarify many of my memories.

I feel real gratitude and indebtedness whenever I think of Auret van Heerden and Elizabeth Floyd. Their detention, and the death of Neil Aggett, affected me profoundly. And so I will always value the warmth and openness Auret showed me when I first approached him. When we finally met in London the way in which he recounted some of the darkest moments in his life provided a humbling lesson in compassion and tolerance. Similarly, Liz was kind and thoughtful when I visited her at home in Johannesburg.

And I appreciated her allowing me to write about Neil and herself without ever trying to intervene in the way I described those last terrible days of his life. I never met Neil, but my admiration grew the more I learnt about him in the three years of researching and writing this book.

I would like to thank all the staff who assisted me at both the University of the Witwatersrand and the University of Cape Town. At Wits, my old university in Johannesburg, the Neil Aggett Collection was an invaluable aid. The massive archive devoted to the actual inquest into his detention and death contained so much information – some of it was misleading but the bulk of it shone a harsh light onto the methods used by the South African Security Police. The testimonies, affidavits, statements and personal accounts of a long list of contrasting figures created a compelling, if disturbing, account of the events that unfolded between September 1981 and February 1982. It might have produced a corrupt judgment, but the actual inquest into the death of Neil Aggett offers a shocking insight into life under apartheid.

At UCT, the Neil Aggett Papers evoked a more personal insight into his early life – as well as containing harrowing details of his detention and death. The collection, donated to the university by Neil's parents, is an essential supplement to the historical archive in Johannesburg. Thanks to my cousin Alan's daughter, Ceri Statham, for collecting and posting so much archive material.

I also found the testimony provided by Liz Floyd, and Paul Erasmus, to the Truth & Reconciliation Commission to be of great use – as were various newspaper archives. The interviews Joseph Lelyveld conducted with Liz Floyd in the *New York Times*, following her release from detention, helped depict the night of the arrest as well as her feelings in the aftermath of Neil's death.

The British Library's newspaper archive, an old haunt of mine, was again a place where I spent many detailed weeks of work as I trawled through, in particular, old copies of the *Rand Daily Mail* and *The Star*. Thanks to the staff in Colindale.

I owe a great deal to my oldest friend, Hilton Tanchum, who allowed me to write about his years in the army – and, also, who knows more about me and this book than anyone outside my family. He was an amazing source of encouragement both as I began writing and, afterwards, when he read an early draft. His comments and support meant much to me.

Similarly, our friend, Basil Lazarides, rekindled some rich and evocative memories for me – and one of my regrets is not being able to write about all that he witnessed on the border once I had left South Africa. But, at a difficult early moment in its writing, Basil's words gave me the impetus to keep working.

Dave Kaplan was terrific as he provided such a vivid account of his own traumatic departure from South Africa – and I was able to say some words to him that I had not managed when we were both so young.

I also valued the input of Mano Gougoumis – with whom I had also lost contact for over thirty years. His past in Germiston, and the recollections which he produced with striking clarity, supplemented my own. We shared some rollicking emails and telephone conversations after all those lost decades.

I would also like to thank my cousins, Brian Statham and Kevin Scott, for allowing me to include some of their army experiences in this book and for reading the relevant sections with real care and attention to detail. It meant a lot to be in contact with them again. My aunt and uncle, Laura and Frier Statham, added to my dad's memories of my grandfather, George McRae – and Brian did as well.

Staff at the Gordon Highlanders Museum in Aberdeen helped provide key details of my grandfather's World War I records – and pinpointed some exact dates to the stories passed through the family and in old newspaper cuttings.

I had some special moments when I went back to South Africa and sat down to talk to a few of the men who had worked so closely with my dad at Eskom. So thank you to Kevin Morgan, George Lindeque, Jacques Messerschmidt and a trusted old friend of my father and my family – Moses Metsweni.

Tim Musgrave, as always, read the proposal and a first draft. After his sister, my wife Alison, Tim has the task of being bombarded with my earliest ramblings.

Jonny Geller, my agent, was instrumental in encouraging me to write about my dad, and his work, and thanks to him for his continuing support. Melissa Pimentel, also of Curtis Brown, added some very useful suggestions – not least the decision to make 'The Detainees' a stand-alone section.

Karl French contributed a great deal with his close and incisive reading of the final draft – and thanks to him for suggesting that I add the prologue.

My editor Mike Jones gave me much guidance and assistance. He helped with structuring the book more coherently and paring down some of my more indulgent writing. Mike also showed considerable patience with my many delays and in our working together with the equally understanding Matt Johnson on the jacket. Thanks, too, must go to Rory Scarfe, Hannah Corbett and everyone else at Simon & Schuster.

Alison, my wife, remains my first reader, my greatest ally, my best pal and the person I spoke to most about this book. After eighteen years, this is our sixth book together and, having married into a wayward South African family, she still shows an extraordinary capacity to read yet more of my revised and rewritten pages. It must be love. A final and heartfelt thanks go to Alison and, of course, Bella, Jack and Emma.

Donald McRae is the award-winning author of six books. He is one of only two authors to have won the prestigious William Hill award twice, for *Dark Trade* and *In Black & White*. As a journalist he has twice won Sports Interviewer of the Year – as well as winning Sports Feature Writer of the Year. His latest book, *The Old Devil*, is also published by Simon & Schuster.